INFORMATION TECHNOLOGY IN 21ST CENTURY

INFORMATION TECHNOLOGY IN 21ST CENTURY
(In 9 Volumes)

ETHICAL AND SOCIETAL CHALLENGE OF CYBERSPACE
(Volume 7)

PROF. RAMESH CHANDRA

Vice-Chancellor, Bundelkhand University, Jhansi (U.P.)

Publication

KALPAZ PUBLICATIONS

DELHI–110052

INFORMATION TECHNOLOGY IN 21ST CENTURY
Ethical and Societal Challenge of Cyberspace
(Information Technolgy)

Rs. 8000 (Set)
Rs. 900 (each volume)

ISBN: 81-7835-158-7 (Set)
ISBN: 81-7835-165-X (Vol. 7)

Published in 2003 in India by
Kalpaz Publications
C-30, Satyawati Nagar
Delhi-110052
E-mail: kalpaz@hotmail.com

Laser Typesetting at: A.S. Printers
Printed at: Chawla Offset Printers, Delhi

Preface

The global internet network has tremendous potential to bring economic, social and cultural benefits to citizens all over the world. Because it will facilitate and expand the flow of communication between people and from place to place, internet can bring enhanced educational and employment opportunities, cheaper goods and greater choice of services.

The internet has revolutionised the manner in which we engage in commerce domestically and across international borders. E-commerce holds great promise for the future, and that the prospects for business growth are immense. However, unlike a traditional shopping experience, there is limited scope for internet shoppers to browse, or enjoy the time honoured practice of just looking and maintaining a degree of privacy in terms of not identifying themselves.

The internet is an environment that is challenging the jurisdictional boundaries of national consumer protection and privacy laws and the effectiveness of national enforcement agencies. Various 'click on' type contracts used in web pages today are often one-sided measures that unfairly limit consumer rights in a wide range of areas. These not only infringe on privacy but related areas such as the rights to benefit from exceptions and limitations of copyright, the right to criticise products, the right to offer competing products, the right to seek redress for defective products or service, and many other important consumer rights. Policy makers should be wary of measures that permit sellers to enforce unreasonable contract terms.

Privacy is a social good and society should avoid mechanisms that protect copyright at the expense of unreasonably intruding on personal privacy, particularly when less intrusive mechanisms are technologically feasible. There are conflicts between privacy and certain technologies that protect copyrighted materials by embedding a device in the material enabling a licensor to identify a user. Governments must conduct research now on the potential for abuse in the way internet transactions are carried out, to preserve the privacy rights that exist under current legislation. Without international cooperation, and coordinated global oversight, it will be hard for any individual or agencies to preserve consumer rights in their jurisdictions.

This book attempts to narrate the ethical and societal challenges of the cyberspace in a lucid style. It will serve as an informative reference tool for all netizens of the cyberspace.

Editor

Contents

1

The Cyber Community

In the past twenty years, many leading companies discovered that products could be developed rapidly by collocating all of the most important team members - R&D engineers, manufacturing representatives, marketing and other functions. As companies have gone horizontal, they no longer have the luxury of collocation. Today, most products are developed and manufactured across boundaries, time zones, cultures and enterprises.Geographically fragmented teams are a reality - making them work for the organization is the challenge. Smith is certainly correct in asserting that you will get poor results if you manage a virtual team the same as if it were a collocated team. New rules and disciplines must be adopted and learned along with the appropriate set of electronic communication tools for virtual collaboration. Companies and consortia that have mastered these rules and invested in the infrastructure are now developing product faster than they could have in a collocated environment. These companies are "co-wired".

The 80's was the decade of quality and productivity; companies invested in operational efficiency in manufacturing, but still designed in a serial fashion. Most companies were organized in functional silos. In the last decade, time to market became the most important success factor. Quality is now expected and organizations centered on cross-functional teams and concurrent engineering for speed. These teams were collocated whenever possible, and growth and market share became more important than margins. In the first decade of the new century, the trend is toward cross-enterprise virtual teams. Intellectual capital has become more important than physical assets. And these teams are busy inventing and growing new markets as much as they are trying to increase their stake in older ones.

Before the advent of the Internet, collocation was a key success factor for rapid product development. When key team members from the various functions sit next to each other all day, information transfer is frequent and rich - very "high bandwidth". Formal meetings keep the project on track and establish goals and commitments, while informal meetings around the coffee pot allow people to build trust and teamwork and to discuss ideas or get help with problems.

The informal information transfer of a collocated team has many benefits, including the development of a team culture. However, there are some downsides to collocation that can (and almost always do) slow down a project. The daily familiarity of the group can begin to distort the priorities and goals of the project.

Internal capacity is limited for many design services, and internal groups can be protective about going to outside services because of their own metrics.

Informal discussions lead to action items or contracts that are not written down or not taken seriously. The new ideas constantly emerging can cause feature creep - always adding one more attractive feature to the project and delaying milestones. Though physical presence is very important, as the bandwidth and communication methods of the Internet increase, the need for frequent physical meetings diminishes. Moreover, face-to-face interactions have drawbacks. For example, such meetings are often postponed due to schedule availability, delaying projects.

The Internet and teamware tools now allow remote, virtual collaboration in ways that were not possible just a few years ago. To use these tools successfully, product development teams must have a complementary IT infrastructure, matching tools, and the appropriate leadership, as well as the incentives and discipline to work together in a new way. These virtual teams - not "collocated" but "co-wired" - offer distinct advantages. For example:

In a "co-wired" environment, people can also communicate frequently, both formally and informally. Formal meetings should be held regularly to keep the project on track and coordinate actions. In addition, informal communication channels, such as chat windows, should be very easy to learn and to use. The CAD design tools must be compatible among all team members, so that communicating design ideas and innovations is seamless.

Most virtual collaboration software allows for automatic recording and tracking of the proceedings of meetings. Action items are written down and indexed. Repositories of knowledge are available that make the inventory of knowledge much more visible. Most virtual project teams have a knowledge manager position to care for this inventory. Collocated teams could take advantage of these same techniques, but few have the discipline to do so. For example, it is difficult to record and index coffeepot conversations.

Partners and suppliers may be in different regions and time zones. The project can carry on through non-real time threaded discussions and overlap meetings. Shopping the world for design expertise and manufacturing capacity allows you to concentrate your design capacity on the areas where you add the greatest value. Many of these outside designers are willing to share the risks and rewards of your product, giving them high incentives for successful delivery.

If managed correctly, this method of collaboration can significantly shorten time to market and time to volume manufacturing. Companies can gain a market advantage by improving their ability to do co-wired innovation faster than their competitors. The shift from a collocated to a co-wired environment requires a strategy for a Collaboration layer and a Control layer of infrastructure, the formation and training of distributed, collaborative teams, and the ability to change the way these teams are motivated and managed.

1. A strategy for a collaboration layer and a control layer of infrastructure

A co-wired product development team requires a communication infrastructure of two layers - a collaboration layer and a control layer. The collaboration environment includes areas for four levels of communication: project management, real-time design sharing, structured discussion and social and brainstorming spaces. The control layer builds and stores the knowledge inventory. The various design tools should smoothly connect these two layers.

2. The formation and training of distributed, collaborative teams

If they are properly organized and managed co-wired teams can develop products faster than collocated teams. Some types of communications, such as team building meetings, should be face-to-face or via video-conferencing, whereas other types such as technical exchanges can happen in real time or virtual time over the Internet, or by email. The meetings and communications should be "bandwidth-matched" to the needs at the time. Co-wired, virtual teams can take advantage of global expertise and diversity with very flexible capacity.

3. The ability to change the way distributed teams are motivated and managed

The infrastructure and leadership of co-wired teams must provide for fast acknowledgement of communications, mutual understanding of each communication and a path for commitment and actions. The leader of a virtual, collaborative team should invest significant time in achieving the trust and social inclusion of all team members. The leader's goal is to align goals, processes, skills and tools across the team. Remote team members should be treated with the same respect and given the same promotional opportunities as collocated team members.

Let's examine the following simple example of a service development team in the Solution Services

Division (SSV) of HP Test and Measurement (now Agilent Technologies). The people in this Division are scattered throughout the globe, but teams are still needed to develop common services. A collaborative environment was built based on the Agilent Intranet, to which all SSV employees have access. No specific technical tools were needed to develop these services, only common office software. The knowledge was stored on a shared server with rules set up for access and revision control. Real-time meetings were conducted by telephone and Microsoft NetMeeting, allowing efficient sharing of the office applications among groups of people.

For virtual-time and time-limited discussions, a discussion thread tool called Caucus was used. The Knowledge Manager led these discussions and extracted knowledge nuggets and decisions, placing them into a common file. Of course, much of the business and development took place over e-mail, the telephone and voicemail. The worldwide development group met face-to-face no more than once per year.

The major immediate benefit of this approach was a drastic reduction in the cost and stress of travel. New service products and deliverables (such as consulting processes and customer education courses) were rolled-out globally rather than locally. In addition, the duplication of effort was significantly reduced.

Another example of successful distributed teamwork is the development team for HP's DeskJet printers. These printers are designed by "co-wired" teams distributed over three continents; these products are introduced concurrently all over the world. HP Vancouver (Washington) takes the lead in developing the printers, but they are produced simultaneously in Singapore, Barcelona and San Diego. Over 150 suppliers and partners worldwide are involved in the design and production.

As the DeskJet became a global product, several challenges arose. Designers were making very frequent trips abroad - expensive, time consuming and stressful. Language and cultural differences made it difficult to collaborate over the phone. The lifecycles of these products is short and time to market is the whole game; project schedules are very aggressive. The suppliers for components were distributed globally as well - usually only one supplier of each critical part could participate in any single design team.

The HP team developed a co-wired environment based on OneSpace by CoCreate. Much of the real-time design collaboration is done with OneSpace. This application allows multiple remote users to see the same 3D mechanical model, which can be a file produced by any of a number of CAD programs. The designers can move and rotate the model, annotate it, and see how it fits with other models, which can be accessed from other CAD systems. OneSpace immediately improved the quality and quantity of design communications. During the first session, suppliers were asking relevant questions that never came up in the phone conversations. More people could afford to be involved in the design discussions, and travel decreased significantly.

These teams also use applications such as Microsoft NetMeeting over the HP Intranet for business meetings, or Webex when they need to go through the firewall.

For the control layer, HP developed a method for encrypting and sharing design files through the Internet, code named Gamma. The Gamma process allows partners, suppliers and customers to access design files that are approved by HP for sharing. The authorization and encryption code "tunnels" through the HP firewall to access a select set of files. The original files are controlled in the Product Data Management (PDM) vault and may only be changed by the responsible designers.

HP Vancouver now shares selected files with over 150 companies worldwide. All of these partners collaborate in the development of DeskJet printers for simultaneous global release. HP estimates a savings of more than US$6M just from initial inventory reductions, and much faster time to volume for each printer type. These examples demonstrate some of the ways that modern, high-tech communications technology can be used to expedite and enhance teamwork. collocation was an important and logical step in the direction of more efficient teams. It is now time for industry to consider the next step - accelerating the global reach of product/ service development through the deployment of distributed, "co-wired" teams. Increased globalization and industry consolidation, among other factors, render the use of distributed teams a necessary feature of the 'new economy.' Rather than evading the issues, it behooves product developers to look for ways of meeting this new opportunity by leveraging the skillful use of technology to produce sustainable competitive advantage.

Remote Collaborative Product Development

Remote Collaborative Product Development (rcPD) represents a new way of doing business that offers firms the opportunity to reduce time-to-profit and increase return on invesiment. However, remote collaboration is emerging as a business practice more rapidly than company cultures are assimilating the changes.

So says a recent study of twenty-three companies performed by Boston-based consultants Product Development Consulting, Inc. (PDC). PDC conducted structured interviews with such diverse firms as Boeing, Ford, Pitney-Bowes, Motorola and Sara Lee in order to understand strategies and practices firms use to collaborate remotely. PDC targeted Senior Managers or key players in firms with a strong extended enterprise presence, and which had completed product development projects involving remote collaboration. In addition to these interviews, PDC also administered a formal questionnaire with twenty-three questions covering such areas as collaborative strategies, success metrics and qualitative results.

PDC initiated the study in April 2001. After an approximately one-month effort to identify study participants, interviews were conducted over a six to seven week period. After gathering data from questionnaires and interviews, PDC used a language analysis method to organize diverse observations and qualitative information into useful conclusions. The firm released its findings in mid-August, 2001.

Remote Collaborative Product Development is not outsourcing, where products are divided into modules, and then a module is farmed out in total to another organization. Nor is it a joint venture, where two groups fund a third group to get a desired result. Remote Collaborative Product Development is performed either at multiple sites within an enterprise, or beyond the enterprise, where it involves more than one organization; it involves at least one representative from each site actually participating in the creation of a joint deliverable. The deliverable must contribute to the success of each party to the collaboration and yield a solution for an unmet need.

Experienced practitioners report undeniable benefits from remote collaboration. Participants in the PDC study reported that project return on investment can be increased, cycle time reduced, and innovative knowledge turned into customer solutions more quickly than with traditional forms of collaboration. This means greatly reduced time-to-profit.

The study also uncovered many of the reasons why firms choose remote collaboration. Sharing with other organizations with differing skill sets can increase the value of knowledge capital. Participants reported that project knowledge could be leveraged to other projects, reducing time-to-market by as much as twenty-five percent. Remote collaborators report that they can reduce project cost and minimize risk. It is also seen as a means of opening new markets or solidifying the product portfolio for a given market. In some cases, remote collaboration is simply necessary for accomplishing a strategic goal because the expertise does not exist in-house and it is either too expensive - or it will take too long - to develop internally.

The study suggests that realizing these benefits depends on firms focusing on the proper priorities. There is a tendency for collaborators to focus on the enabling technologies of rcPD, but it was participants' attention to structured and synchronized communications that fostered strong commitments and results downstream. In the early stages of collaboration, definitive commitments are less important than soft skill focus, PDC found.

But what best practices foster communications? PDC found that firms often begin with a single collocated meeting or set of meetings to kick off a new project. When asked what respondents found most facilitated effective remote collaboration, one participant told PDC, "Spend time together...to build trust during team formation." Another said, "kick things off in a personal fashion, and once you do that it is like night and day." According to Ron Lasser, Principal, PDC, such practices represent, "a striving to create a mutual identity in that gap between the enterprises. This creates an entity with its own governance, so new cultures are being created."

PDC also observed that successful collaborative projects have strong leadership from a project manager who can communicate and maintain a formal methodology. This includes guidelines and rules ensuring that the methods and processes are very clearly defined - and adhered to - in terms of both the interfaces and the actions. Study participants reported that they defined a formal methodology at the start and carefully managed communications through rules-based processes. They also managed projects to get the most out of time zone differences. For example, one participant reported that they identify a problem at the end of one team's day, then the next team works on it while the first one sleeps.

In addition to active management of knowledge interactions throughout the dispersed team, respondents also indicated that supplier integration was a key success factor. Participants reported that they carefully analyzed suppliers' processes, as well as their own, and arrived at a new process that was a blend of the best elements of both. Firms integrated even further with partners by formalizing around a common set of strategic suppliers.

Another emerging best practice is the use of ambassadors, an employee from a collaborating company who travels to remote sites to link cultures and to improve communications. Such ambassadors are dispatched when communications break down, or when there is an issue that needs personal interaction to solve it. Ambassadors can also provide a link to distant sites at the early stages of the project.

Web ools for remote collaborative product development are the following:

— Shared project management spaces can reduce project costs substantially

— Face-to-face travel is reduced by 40% in some cases

— Project knowledge can be leveraged to subsequent projects, reducing time-to-market by as much as 25%

— Projects can be monitored by executives using Internet browser software from any remote location to gain phase and release approval more quickly

— While web tools can offer continuous, daily monitoring of critical tasks and measures, development organizations do not have formal practices in place to capture required data

— It is the perception of developers that most web-tool product vendors are not selling solutions to the most critical problems

— Web tools are rarely utilized for social contact; interactions are more formal and business-oriented

The study also discovered that the current web-based tools are still first generation products, and that today's vendors are presupposing - rather than addressing - user needs. Says Lasser, "We heard from at least a third of the respondents that tools are not automating what needs to be automated; they are not solving problems that need to be solved."

Participants observed technological limitations in a number of spheres. They pointed to the lack of an effective replacement for kinesthetic contact, for example being able to read body language to understand if a statement was correctly interpreted. Another need was even more basic - the difficulty in tracking people down. The problem is the lack of a single, reliable means of getting a hold of people. Says Lasser, "Maybe I can find your pager, but you're pager is turned off. I've e-mailed; I've left a voice mail. What else can I do? In remote collaboration I don't have the visibility...to be able to go down the hall and ask: 'Have you seen so-and-so?'"

Many participants perceived limitations on the design side as well. For example, participants found that they needed to review a part in 3-D but only one person at a time could manipulate the model - not all participants could 'grab' the same part at the same time.

The research also found that some firms are using Microsoft Project as a raw database and then integrating other software as pipeline planning tools. Explains Lasser, "The problem is that this arrangement doesn't take into account getting the data in real time and updating it. The current tools are managing at the interfaces, but not managing toward the ability to update in real time. Often they do not address the need for synchronized communication." But the study also suggests a reason some firms might be avoiding comprehensive web-based spaces - the security of such tools is still insufficient. "There is no adequate security beyond the firewall," claims Lasser. "There's no way that the current technology allows firms to share in one remote connection that's secure. That's severely limiting."

The limitations of existing security technology includes:

- Existing security technology is largely inadequate for remote collaboration
- Inability to handle multiple supplier access to product data management system causes delays to deliverables; access privileges cannot be managed actively by developers
- Data shared on connected servers makes distributed information residences more vulnerable to attacks
- The highest security threat is losing an employee to a competitor
- Increased opportunity exists for former employees to work with a remote competitor
- Impact to company is greater than to the employee, as resource need not move family or change lifestyle
- Best-in-class suppliers working with competitors are potential security risks
- Possible inadvertent disclosure during competitor plant visits
- Proprietary methods/knowledge transferred to supplier may be utilized for competition, thus funding the competition

Despite the proven benefits, remote collaboration represents a new business paradigm that tends to encounter resistance. The lack of security, the limitations of current technologies and the inherent difficulty of merging the processes of different organizations present obvious challenges. Observing that a fundamental change has occurred in the closeness of customer/supplier relationships, PDC also found that organizations are not ready for the magnitude of the cultural shift required. This leaves them vulnerable to cost, schedule and legal issues.

Senior Managers, in particular, often find that this new way of doing business runs counter to the received wisdom, and are often perceived by others as impeding the success of rcPD. "Some upper level managers don't get it," declares Lasser. "They don't want to give up control or they're uncomfortable because they just can't see who's in control." As a result, the sharing of information between organizations is not seen as a core value or a core competency. Says Lasser, "If that's not a core value in a company and you don't have policies in place on how to share and with whom to share, you'll never realize the power of remote collaboration."

PDC's research describes "the power of remote collaboration" as an emerging way of doing business with clear benefits and a growing body of best practices. In the relatively immature state of rcPD, success depends on how senior managers, corporate cultures, technologies and formal methodologies continue to grow and adapt to new circumstances and to one another.

Firewall

If your company network is connected to the Internet, a firewall should be used to protect your data. However in today's marketplace, the presence of a firewall is currently (and most unwisely) not a certainty. In the last couple of years, the Internet has dominated technological news pages everywhere (this one being no exception). But when companies start adding ".com" to their names and finally join the e-commerce marketplace, their problems are only just beginning.

Many people don't realise that just linking two computers on a network, let alone setting up a website, causes a lot more difficulties than are immediately apparent. When one PC is connected to another to form a basic network, the security protecting the data on both machines is compromised. This means any sensitive information on one of the machines can be accessed by the user of the other.

Needless to say, this should be the exception rather than the rule when it comes to data protection. Users and data should be filtered so that one doesn't have all-access rights to the other. An internal network can be divided using as many firewalls as deemed necessary, so imposing a graduated form of access to highly secretive information. It may help to think of a computer network like your company building.

Every employee has access to the building itself (the network), but only certain employees have a key to your office. Even fewer co-workers can open the file cabinet next to your desk, and only you know the combination to the strongbox within the cabinet that contains your emergency Mars bar supply.

Here the Mars bars are the most protected data on the network (and quite rightly so). All of the files in the cabinet are slightly less protected, followed by the paperwork (and snacks) lying around the office. The least protected foodstuffs are the ones in the corridors and foyer of the building. However these still have access limitations, in that only employees of the firm are eligible to test their edibility.

Members of the public walking along the street outside the office building (non-users of your network) have no access to any of the data (or snackfoods) within it because the office doors keep them out. These doors are the firewall which protects your network from unknown and untrusted users outside the company. This perimeter firewall is needed if the network is connected to an external network, such as the Internet.

A firewall between the internal and external networks serves two purposes: it prevents any unauthorised communication from entering the internal network and stops any user of the internal network from accessing the external network without permission. This is, needless to say, extremely useful for scuppering company directors accessing unsuitable websites or spending their day surfing cyberspace. In the home environment, a firewall could act in loco parentis for children using their home PCs and block the viewing of certain pages on the Internet.

A firewall consists of two parts: the security policy and the physical implementation of that policy. The policy itself is the logical written statements allowing users their access rights to various facilities or parts of the network. It can conform to one of four general types.

As the name implies, the paranoid is the most protective version forbidding every connection or communication attempt - not exactly an ideal scheme for a network. A prudent policy refuses any communication as a rule and only permits those communications through the firewall which have an explicit clearance status.

The permissive type of network security is slightly more easy-going, having a default setting of accepting everything sent to it, unless the communication has been unequivocally forbidden and the final, promiscuous, kind allows every communication or connection request to enter.

In the main the ideal security policy would be a combination of the prudent and permissive types, as the other two options would inhibit (completely) the performance of the network (paranoid) or endanger the security and integrity of the data stored on the network (promiscuous).

For the physical implementation of the firewall there are yet more choices depending on the security measures to be implemented. The oldest and most insecure form of firewall is a packet filter.

This type of firewall checks the destination and source addresses of the communication packet (the data) requesting access to the protected network and decides, after consulting a set of rules, whether to permit the communication to enter the network.

The primary disadvantage of this system, is that it can only distinguish the machine the request came from and not which user used that machine to send the packet, so connections can only be permitted or denied based on the locations sending and receiving the data.

Circuit level firewalls are a step up from packet filters in that they can distinguish between a connection request and a packet containing data. Only data packets relating to an existing, valid connection are allowed through the firewall. Any connection request must follow a handshake procedure to establish communication between two machines in order to pass through the firewall.

Both machines must also be approved for communication with each other according a specified set of rules listed in the firewall's memory. A major disadvantage of this type of firewall is that the only communication protocol which follows the handshaking procedure is TCP/IP (Transport Control Protocol/ Internet Protocol) the most common - but not the only - Internet communication protocol.

A yet more advanced form of security is the application layer firewall. Many examples of this type of firewall use proxy servers and clients to interact with the external network on the user's behalf. This means that the machine into which the user enters his commands never actually connects with the desired network directly; every request is filtered through another machine - the proxy - which processes and examines the packets sent. The proxy also checks whether the requests it sends and receives are permitted by the policy rules relating to the proxy.

The proxy server, protocol analysis and proxy client are the three invisible parts which together form the proxy service. A well set up proxy service will be transparent to the user and make him think he is interacting with the real machine partner. The only occasion when the user should be aware of the proxy is if the requests made are not permissable, and he is alerted to the fact.

These three types of firewalls all have their advantages and problems. Although the proxy, application level firewall is generally considered the best protection, it requires twice as much processing time to complete the clearance checks on each data packet passed between machines.

The circuit level firewall is quicker than the application level security checks, but only works with the TCP/IP protocol and testing the 'accept' and 'deny' rules is difficult. The fastest protection is provided by the packet filter type of firewall, but this only performs a cursory check on any communication packet and offers minimal security.

Cybersquatting

Cybersquatting, the practice of registering an Internet domain name with the hopes of profiting due to its association with a trademark owned by someone else, can be punished by fines of up to US$100,000 under a law recently signed by President Clinton. With domain names selling for millions of dollars, an intense battle over their regulation has begun and the battles are expected to grow more intense. The number of registered domains increased by more than 100 percent from 1997 to 1999.

The Anticybersquatting Consumer Protection Act seeks to stop people from registering Internet names that they will never use but hope to resell at inflated prices. The new law also imposes fines on those who register other people's personal names with the intent of profiting from them. Courts can also order the cancellation of Internet names that were registered in bad faith.

According to Stuart S Malawer, director of the Oxford Trade Program at St Peter's College, Oxford University the statute passed due to lobbying by many "Old Economy firms that failed to register their desired domain names early on and were only able to play catch up by congressional intervention." Critics of the legislation claim the First Amendment right of free speech is being violated.

Businesses who want to expand their operations internationally often reorganize to confront foreign competition. As such, the fight over domain names is becoming international. Companies from Germany, India and Japan are battling over the rights to domain names.

Complaints, fueled by an objection from Japan, are starting to be heard around the world about the influence of the US government in setting the rules concerning domain name disputes.

The US legislation does not help foreign companies that claim rights to domain names held by US firms. The US law also does not protect US firms from lawsuits filed abroad. The law does protect US trademarks, but not foreign trademarks.

As such, foreign firms may find themselves at a huge disadvantage. And, without a global consensus, US firms may find themselves dragged into foreign courts to defend their rights to domain names.

There are 249 different domain designations used in the US and other countries. It is no longer enough to register yourcompanyname.com in the US and not register yourcompanyname.co.uk in the UK. Other nations are developing their own rules for domain names. Mr Malawer says the United Kingdom and Germany already apply tough remedies that would very likely conflict with US decisions such as a trademark dispute involving an American subsidiary of a foreign firm.

Companies like Morgan Stanley Dean Witter and Microsoft as well as organisations such as WWF and the

NFL have launched suits against alleged cybersquatters. In the first big shakeup for 10 years, the private corporation ICANN (Internet Corporation for Assigned Names and Numbers) which has overseen changes in internet naming since 1998 has approved the creation of a slew of new "top-level domains", the suffixes attached to internet addresses. They will be created early next year, with details hammered out before the end of December.

Next year you may have to decide whether a.shop is a real shop, whether .web is a web-only business and whether any of them is different from what went before. The move, likely to create at least six top-level domains, is a reaction to what is perceived as too much jostling for space among companies and individuals trying to stake valuable claims in cyberspace.

The Crest of the Internet Wave

"The next crest of the Internet wave will come from markets that are already well along the way—particularly in Western Europe—with the most capacity for upside surprises, since their social structures and communications infrastructures offer few barriers", Cruikshank says. He continues, "In these countries, it's simply a matter of time before more people go online—we have already started to see Europeans representing a larger proportion of the global Internet population."

Rhere are more adults with intentions of going online than there are adults with Internet access. These countries include South Korea and urban markets in Malaysia, India, Mexico, and South Africa.

"Far from being dead, the Internet has a large growth potential everywhere, but progress is destined to be slower than its most enthusiastic advocates might have envisioned a few years ago", concludes Cruikshank. To expand the reach of the Web in developing countries, he says, public venues—libraries, schools, offices and Internet cafés—will have to play a more crucial role.

Still, widespread availability is a long way off in the most populated areas of the world. Overall, Ipsos-Reid found that 98% of respondents own a television, 51% own a cell phone, 48% own a home computer—but only 36% have home Internet access.

These international survey research data were collected via Ipsos-Reid's Global Express, a quarterly international omnibus survey. Fieldwork was conducted in November and December 2000. Data are based on individual surveys taken with a random sampling of adults (18+) across 35 national markets.

The target sample size in each country was 500, except for the United States and Germany, where 1,000 interviews were conducted, India, where 1,700 interviews were conducted, and Turkey, where 1,200 interviews were conducted.

Within each country, the survey results can be said to be within at least ± 4.5 percentage points of what they would have been had the entire adult population been surveyed (± 3.1 percentage points in the United States, ± 2.9 percentage points in Turkey, and ± 2.4 percentage points in India).

In 20 of these 35 surveyed countries, the samples provide full national coverage; in these countries the data were collected via randomized telephone interviewing, with the exception of Poland, where in-person door-to-door interviewing was conducted.

Table 1
Internet Usage Rates by Country

	Past-30 Day Internet Usage		
	1999 %	2000 %	Difference %
Rank 1: Leading Edge			
Sweden	53	65	12
Canada	56	60	4
U.S.	59	59	0
Netherlands	40	57	17
Switzerland	45	51	6
Australia	48	54	6
Finland	44	53	9
Singapore	33	46	13
South Korea	31	45	14
U.K.	33	35	2
Germany	29	37	8
Rank 2: Advancing			
Belgium	28	36	8
Urban Mexico	27	33	6
Hong Kong	35	34	-1
Taiwan	29	35	6
France	22	30	8
Japan	33	33	0
Urban Malaysia*	23	26	3
Italy	16	28	12
Rank: 3 Emergent			
Urban Brazil	21	22	1
Urban Colombia	14	17	3
Spain	18	22	4
Urban Egypt	8	17	9
Urban China	12	21	9
Urban South Africa	9	6	-3
Urban Argentina*	13	20	7
Poland	11	19	8
Rank 4: Nascent			
Urban India***	5	9	4
Turkey**	14	13	-1
Urban Russia	5	6	1

* Mainly urban samples, not exclusively.
** Quasi-national samples.
*** Middle, upper sec's.

Door-to-door interviewing was also used in the non-national samples, whether quasi-national in representation (Malaysia, Egypt, Argentina, Turkey, and Philippines) or urban only (Mexico, Brazil, Colombia, China, South Africa, India, Russia, Peru, Saudi Arabia, Chile, and Thailand) where the sample coverage was limited to large cities.

Ipsos-Reid has been tracking public opinion around the world for more than 20 years and has become a leading provider of global public opinion and market research to private, public and not for profit organizations in over 50 countries. With more than 1,300 staff in 11 cities, Ipsos-Reid offers clients a full line of custom, syndicated, omnibus and online research products and services.

It is best known for its line of Global Express opinion polls, the World Monitor market trend quarterly, and The Face of the Web, the most comprehensive study of global Internet usage and trends. It is a member of Paris-based Ipsos Group, ranked among the Top 10 research groups in the world.

Netiquette

There are distinct advantages to E-mail and the phenomenon of electronic communication. A large amount of paper is saved on a global scale, with reduced amounts of paperwork flying between businesses and internal departments. Speed of delivery is an undisputed plus, as your message can be delivered in minutes to anywhere around the world.

It can be easier to get to 'the top', as E-mail addresses of those executives friendly enough to open their Inboxes to the masses are often available. In addition, E-mail is perceived by many to be less intrusive than a phone call, as it offers the luxury of being dealt with whenever the recipient has the time, although that obviously favours the person being contacted, and not anyone who needs an immediate response.

A diverse group of people learning how to browse the Internet . However, as use of this medium increases, with a diverse group of people of various religions, nationalities, genders, age groups and experiences learning how to browse the Internet, the question of netiquette arises.

A quick guide to some of the do's and don'ts of online communication

— When it comes to E-mails, it is a good idea to know your mailbox's limit. You should even choose them according to their capacity if you think you will be getting big files that could clog up your Inbox. Rinaldi suggests that you check E-mail daily, delete unwanted or used messages immediately, keep stored messages to a minimum, and remember that you can download or copy text to a word processing package, or even to a floppy disk, for storage there. This will reduce the pressure on your account's storage space, and generally make your Inbox easier to use.

— Form a habit of frequently virus-checking your system, especially after a bout of downloading from other systems or over the Internet.

– Do remember that your files may be accessible to others, so refrain from maintaining anything personal on your hard disk.

— An argumentative or belligerent E-mail message is called a 'flame', and the general rule is that you should not send any, even if you receive one yourself. Should this happen, go make a coffee and calm down before replying.

— Be professional and careful what you say about other people. E-mail is easily forwarded without your knowledge.

— Today, it is easy to copy, or 'cc', practically anyone on your mail. And we sometimes find ourselves copying people almost out of habit. In general, this is rude. People have less time than ever today, precisely because they have so much information to absorb. Before you copy people on your messages, ask yourself whether they really need to know. If the answer is no, don't waste their time.

— Consider the difference in time zones. If you require an immediate response, remember that the person you are writing to might be asleep while you're just finishing your lunch, so be patient and log onto a time zone Web site.

— Ensure your E-mail messages are succinct. Because E-mail is so easy to use, everybody's using it, and your message will certainly be one of many that day. When replying to previous correspondence, include relevant information from the original text but no more. Do not return the whole message back to its creator, simply select the appropriate parts in order to clarify the emphasis of your response.

— Your mail should have a concise subject title that reflects the content, that way the user can locate the message quickly and easily. However, look out for the tricks that Spammers use, as they will often put subject titles such as 'The Information You Requested' or 'My Reply' to engage your curiosity.

— Smileys :) and emoticons @—;—, so long as you're on relaxed terms with the recipient, can add a little personality to your words.

— Asterisks surrounding a word denote *emphasis* and underscores should be used for underlining, when referring to _Book Titles_, for example.

— If you TYPE AN ENTIRE SENTENCE IN ALL CAPITAL LETTERS, you are 'SHOUTING!' It is not proper netiquette to SHOUT, in fact, it's utterly annoying. Capitalize words only when it is necessary to highlight an important point.

— A signature is a good idea, as it renders you credible and accessible. Around four lines is a reasonable length. Your signature footer should include your name, position, affiliation and Internet address.

— Should you receive an important E-mail that warrants a considered response, send a short reply to indicate that you have received the message and will reply shortly. This is professional and most useful to the individual biting their nails at the other end.

There are a plethora of do's and don'ts to consider when writing and managing e-mails, but the important thing to remember is that none of this is enforceable, merely desirable. Arlene Rinaldi writes that "netiquette is just a set of guidelines," to be ignored or followed as people see fit. Following the guidelines, however, can prevent you from annoying people and raise your profile with associates across the world with whom the only contact you might ever have is an E-mail. At the very least, following netiquette can make your messages be welcomed, treated with a higher priority and above all, more enjoyable to read.

Each organization on the Internet should provide and inform its users on expected standards of conduct when using its network and when accessing other networks while using Internet resources. The punitive measures for not adhering to the organizations policies should also be provided.

Technology is supposed to be our friend: it is meant to improve our lives, make things easier for us and assist us in doing many complicated things quicker and all at once. "How did we ever do 'this' before our ever-helpful technological device was invented?" is what we supposedly all ask ourselves whilst shaking our heads in wonderment. However, according to new research there is a fine line between using PCs and software devices that is often slipped off to violent effect. A recent survey conducted by Massachusetts-based Concord Communications showed that 83 percent of 150 respondents from the US have witnessed physical attacks upon computer equipment as a result of a growing trend.

Another investigation by Symantec Corp., which worked with the UK's National Opinion Poll organisation, discovered that over 40% of British PC users have sworn at, kicked and physically abused their computer equipment. The London-based international research company MORI completed a survey, aptly named Rage Against The Machine, which showed how 40% of 1,250 UK workers surveyed have witnessed colleagues abusing their computer machinery both physically and verbally. The same results also indicate that almost half of all those who work with computers suffer from frustration or stress because of IT difficulties. According to the MORI poll it's not just the machine itself that causes such an extreme reaction, as aggravation can also be aroused by the time taken to fix a problem and the jargon sometimes used by the support personnel. Crashing software and un-cooperative mice are also triggers for bouts of computer rage. Pulling cables out to cause the system to crash is apparently a popular method for taking revenge upon a troublesome machine.

The costs of machine or software failure are expensive to say the least. The Confederation of British Industry claims that £25,000 per person per year is the price of one hour lost everyday at work. But when it comes to having these problems fixed, a massive 75% of those questioned said their IT support staff were unable to fix the problem.

Over a fifth experience the same problem again as the symptom was dealt with, but not the root cause. According to MORI's statistics, one in eight people have seen staff from the IT department being bullied by office workers after their technology crashes.

The real issue here, of course, is stress caused as a result of technological failure. MORI's poll claims that almost one in five people within the manufacturing industry say they feel stupid as a result of their computer problems. A third of people who suffer regular computer crashes have to work late or take work home as a result, which will probably lead to higher stress levels and is not healthy for the individual's morale.

PC manufacturer Compaq says that many IT problems are easy to fix. Around half of all calls to its help line, for example, are from individuals who have forgotten their password and are locked out of their machines. As well as choosing a more memorable password, using good quality reliable equipment, insisting upon a high standard of cabling for your office network, using reliable methods of backing up data, deleting unused files to keep your system clear and keeping your virus checking software up-to-date will all help to minimize computer failures and keep your staff happier.

Full and proper PC training is another simple premise that is very often overlooked by companies, but one that can de-mystify and simplify the whole computing process and maintain harmony in the long run.

Within the next 15 years, the steady progress in producing faster, cheaper, and more powerful computer chips will be unavoidably impeded by the laws of physics. It all started 37 years ago.

"Integrated circuits will lead to such wonders as home computers, "wrote Gordon Moore, a young researcher at Shockley Semiconducter,"...automatic controls for automobiles, and personal portable communications equipment." The year was 1965, three years before he would co-found the largest silicon chip manufacturer now in existence.

Gordon Moore inadvertently set a precedent with his paper, which Electronics magazine asked him to write for their 35th anniversary edition. His submission entitled,"Cramming more components onto integrated circuits" presented the idea---a new idea at the time---that the development of smaller transistors at lower unit production costs would translate into exponential progress in silicon chip complexity at minimum cost. In other words, performance would double each year.

In 1965, chips could hold 60 transistors. Moore predicted that by 1975 as many as 65,000 transistors could be crammed onto a single chip. In perspective, Intel's Pentium 4 chips now hold over 42 million transistors. The ability to fit more transistors on a silicon chip simply means that information can be processed faster.

The press dubbed the observation"Moore's Law", and it has become a widely accepted and universally acknowledged precept that has come to account for not only chip complexity but also faster performance, translating into computer performance that doubles every 18 to 24 months.

In an interview with Dori Jones Yang in 2000, Moore admitted he used to cringe every time someone used the term, and stated about his original ten year prediction that,"Really, that's as far ahead as I've ever been able to see."

Moore's predicted rate of progress has been embraced by the industry, becoming somewhat of a self-fulfilling prophecy. If a company progresses faster, fabrication and development costs become prohibitive. If it progresses slower, components may be less expensive but the company falls behind the competition.

In the late 90's, the digital world started becoming increasingly anxious about the supposedly inevitable demise of Moore's Law. Chip manufacturers had two major problems: physical barriers blocking the continued diminution of transistor size, and financial barriers in fabrication costs.

While computing power was doubling every two years, fabrication costs were doubling every three years.

This situation would inevitably lead to the slowing or stop of chip manufacturer's progress.

If Moore's Law holds true, manufacturers will need to individually place atoms to manufacture silicon chips throughout the 2010's. At the 0.10-micron stage (each transistor would be composed of less than 100 atoms), small silicon chips containing millions or billions of transistors would no longer be able to control the flow of electrons.

With each generation of increased performance, the size of computer-based products becomes smaller. If manufacturers simply made larger chips to fit more transistors on them, the products would also have to become larger to accommodate them, or our smallest electronic products and applications would not be able to be improved upon.

What do we want when we buy a new computer or other electronic gadget? We want it to be fast, reasonably priced, and as small as possible. This has been the trend maintained by the progress of companies such as Intel and AMD, making the new products we see on the shelves of electronics stores available and affordable.

Moore's Law is why our computers become obsolete so quickly. By the time Intel or another chip manufacturer can work out the kinks of doubling performance, again, the cycle of Moore's Law has taken us through another two years or so, and current products are half as powerful as the next generation of technology.

Technological progression itself demands faster performance. Philip Wong of IBM said,"...There are many things we could do with increased computing that people want to do today. For example, on-the-fly language translation and instant communication in a small form factor..."

Business advancement necessitates better, faster computational power. As our computers become faster and more powerful, software companies step in and develop more powerful and robust applications and software. In our personal lives, increased computational speed means faster Internet access, better entertainment, smaller and more powerful cell phones, and better performing and safer cars.

Learning to be a Citizen of Cyberspace

Most researchers agree that the growth of a knowledge-based society will bring about fundamental changes in the production, distribution and exchange of information and that most every social and cultural institution will be changed in some way, but none more than education. This is because, more than any other social institution, education is fundamentally about knowledge, information, and communication. Although it certainly makes use of material tools and sometimes results in the production of material goods, these are ancillary to the fundamental process of education: people use knowledge to create more knowledgable people.

It is therefore not surprising to find considerable support for transforming education so that it is as fully independent as possible from geographic location and physical space. If education does not require a specific spatial location or a building then it can be delivered from anywhere to anywhere. This will, some argue, transform the fundamental infrastructure of education at every level, starting particularly at the post-secondary level, and will fundamentally erode local community, or even national control over education. The development of on-line courses, libraries and other information resources, and the marketing of distant or on-line education by businesses and schools eager to profit from opportunities to expand their horizons, are the beginning of what some see as a revolution in learning.

In addition to overcoming geographical constraints on the delivery of education, new technologies promise to expand the basic nature of education. In quantitative terms, computer communication is opening up vast new sources of information and learning by enabling on-line access that frees schools from complete dependence on paper delivery. Associated with this is the ability to link written with audio and visual material that can enrich the full range of the learner's senses.

The technology also creates a qualitative expansion in the means of education by taking a process rooted in the one-way delivery of knowledge and making it more participatory and reciprocal. Education moves from an emphasis on transmitting information to the active creation of knowledge.

Moreover, according to this view, computer communication takes a system of learning based in narrow linear, narrative forms, and opens it up to a wide range of non-linear, exploratory processes that allow the learner to make full use of his or her own multiple cognitive maps. As a result students mutually constitute their learning environments, all of which grow in the learning process.

But researchers are increasingly acknowledging that the promise of computer mediated education is sadly falling far short of the reality. As one generally supportive OECD report concluded:"... the classroom revolution foretold decades ago has failed to materialise. Overall, the school system has not kept pace with the rest of society in terms of IT use... ." Indeed, some argue that the promises themselves have been clouding our ability to see the reality and especially to see that, in our rush to realize the dreams of its leading advocates, we have neglected important values, particularly the values of citizenship, that have historically grounded traditional education.

There are several tendencies in computer-mediated education that raise important questions about these conclusions. First, almost all of it takes place in the developed world or in those pockets of the less developed world that are urban and rich. This is largely because, in spite of much talk and some action to provide vital network infrastructure, the vast majority of the world's peoples are without the means to learn in cyberspace.

According to the International Telecommunication Union (ITU), only 34 per cent of the world's households have telephone service and most of this is concentrated in the developed world. At the beginning of 1997, 62% of all main telephone lines were installed in just 23 developed countries (i.e. Australia, Canada, the European Union, Iceland, New Zealand, Norway, Switzerland, and the United States).

Africa, including South Africa, contains 2 phone lines per 100 population while it is 65 and 35 lines per 100 in the U.S. and Europe respectively. Fully 97% of all Internet hosts are found in developed countries. Regarding the gap between the level of service provided in the richest and poorest countries, progress has been made, though there is still a considerable way to go before equality will be reached. For example, it is remarkable to note that there are more Internet hosts in Estonia than in Sub-Saharan Africa (excluding South Africa). In 1993, the U.S., Western Europe and Japan accounted for about 71 per cent of all computers shipped; in 1996 it was 73 per cent. In that time the developing world has gone from 19 per cent to 14 per cent of all shipments.

One might argue that we are in the early stages of computer development and that we are likely to see the gap narrowed as costs decline. Yet, the consistent failure to overcome substantial historic inequities in telephone penetration does not inspire optimism about expanding equity in cyberspace. Moreover, there are also significant gaps within the developed world with the U.S. and UK enjoying about nine students per computer and Japan and Portugal averaging about 50 students per computer.

In addition to the concern about the quantitative gap in access, there is also cause for reflection on the type of training that is taking place in cyberspace and in the type of content that is most heavily emphasized. Specifically, although there are exceptions, much of the learning in cyberspace is technical training that reflects the one-way, linear, and passive approaches that have characterized traditional education.

According to one multi-million dollar U.S. study, schools use networks for teaching and learning in, what the researchers concluded, were the most obvious and pedestrian ways. Experts in instructional design worry that educators are seduced by the sheer amount of information available on the Internet and administrators, attracted by the potential to save on instructor costs, conclude that it is only necessary to point students to the data and learning will follow. Instructional design expert M. David Merrill demurs:" We need to wake up and recognize that information is not instruction. There is this belief that all you need for learning is information and collaboration: Put enough people and enough information on the Web, and learning will happen.... There isn't enough guidance and structure there [on the Internet] for someone to learn a systematic body of knowledge."

A Harvard professor of education agrees, noting that"the most mindless use of computers is at the elementary level." Relatedly, there is significant concern that we are moving ahead with computer applications in schools, without conducting serious research on their impacts.

The Dean of the Faculty of Education at Queen's University in Canada provides a sobering summary of what we do know about the impact of information and communication technology on education in comments on a multi-million dollar study funded by three U.S. government departments:" The overarching conclusions were that school districts had not evaluated the impact of computer networks on student achievement with scant attention being paid to their effectiveness.

The critical question remaining was stated as such: 'Do computer networks improve student education'? -- ironically the very question the study sought to answer. But what is startling--inconceivable, in fact--is that the researchers nevertheless recommended that government policies, supported by the private sector, should be established to ensure stable and long-term funding for computer networks, so that school district networks might become more widely accessible to teachers, students, parents, school staff, and computer members at large."

It is unfortunately easy for this form of logic to win out, however, because another form of logic, the logic of the marketplace has made the business of education and its cost-effective delivery by technological means a very attractive option for firms like Microsoft, which is now one of the major forces in what is increasingly called the education industry.

As a result, there is a growing concern that cyberspace is evolving into a largely commercial space, an electronic mall whose main activity is electronic or e-commerce rather than public debate and education. By 1997, one-fourth of all Internet sites were fully commercial and many of the rest were partially commercial sites that used national or other domain names.

Although information retrieval and electronic mail helped the Internet to a remarkable beginning, the fastest growing uses of the net are now electronic commerce and advertising. Anyone contemplating the use of cyberspace for genuine education must confront an increasingly commercial environment whose goal is to teach new generations of consumers how to shop electronically.

Notwithstanding the value of technical and consumer skills, it is important is to make learning how to become a citizen of cyberspace an ethical imperative of on-line education. Indeed, citizenship education is a necessary grounding for learning how to fully use the Internet and the Internet itself can be an important tool for developing effective citizenship. It is absolutely essential to invoke citizenship today because citizenship elevates human activity beyond the commonly accepted view that the best way, indeed, for some, the only way, to define human activity is by its marketplace value, its worth as a consuming or labouring commodity.

The widely accepted view of citizenship is that elevation has also been accompanied by extension. Here it is common to invoke the work of T.H Marshall (1964) who charted the progress of citizenship in modern Western society starting with the legal sense of basic rights and protections, for example, habeas corpus, due process, the presumption of innocence and the right of trial by a jury of ones peers. From here, citizenship was extended to encompass political rights, particularly the right to vote and public assembly. Finally, social citizenship stretches the notion to include the right to employment, housing, health care, and other social welfare benefits.

Citizenship in the new electronic age means treating cyberspace as a public space or"new commons" to which all people have rights of access and participation, reasonable expectations of privacy and security, and, along with these rights, civic responsibilities of active involvement in this new commons and mutual respect for fellow cyber-citizens. Genuine education for an information society starts by teaching these principles and uses the Net as one among the many means to implement them.

We are beginning to accumulate a body of exemplars which provide important guidance for developing the practice of citizenship in cyberspace. One of the most important is the establishment of community nets or freenets which bring together people in a city, town or neighbourhood, providing essential information about public services, in addition to all of the material normally found on the Internet. Freenets provide two essential elements missing in most of the commercial networks. First, because they make use of servers provided by educational, non-profit or other donor organizations, freenets offer low cost access for users.

This is particularly important for low income people who, even in the most developed societies, have little chance of making use of the net. Secondly, they locate terminals in public places like post offices, libraries, schools, and markets, enabling people to make use of the net without having to purchase a computer.

With regard specifically to education, several countries have initiated programs to provide hardware, develop content, establish public networks, provide teacher training, initiate research on educational innovation, and promote distant and adult education. For example, the Canadian government has established the Computers for Schools program that channels surplus computer equipment and software from public and private sector partners to needy schools. Its joint federal and provincial School-Net programme connects libraries and schools to the World Wide Web.

The Ministry of Human Resources Development conducts research and supports demonstration projects across Canada on learning applications in schools and in employment training. The federal and provincial governments have also pioneered in delivering distant education to the scattered populations of the Canadian North. Canada provides just one among several other national examples of a commitment to the principles of citizenship in cyberspace. Nevertheless, as with other nations, Canada's commitment is under constant challenge, particularly from those interested in making cyberspace a private space, largely oriented to commercial activity, and open only to those who can pay for access and security.

In conclusion, there is considerable potential in the educational uses of cyberspace, but there are also many challenges and dangers. Computers can provide the means to explore new forms of learning that break out of the traditional hierarchies of educational bureaucracy and develop genuine alternatives to rigid, passive approaches to learning.

But they can also reify those hierarchies if they are applied without a commitment to the principles of equality, participation, privacy, mutual respect, and responsibility, that historically provided the foundation for many of our systems of public education. New technologies can also entice us into thinking that the technology alone will overcome problems of equity and excessive commercialization.

Experience suggests that this is not the case and calls for a commitment to the principles of citizenship, including strong support from the agencies of civil society and the public sphere, in order to make cyberspace a rich community itself and an instrument to enrich our existing communities.

2

Ethics of Digital Information

The evolution of the legal framework of digital information in India and the associated ethical framework are traced with specific reference to land records and land use information: case law, archiving, privacy and freedom of information, considerations of competitive situations, etc. The case of legal information of NICNET and the ethical aspects of government digital information are described in order to clarify what could be the desirable guidelines for the future development of ethical and legal aspects of informatics in India. Issues linked to the co-development of the Internet and Intranet for scientific, educational and cultural information management are also presented.

Protection of Computer Software Rights

Computer programs are created by highly qualified specialists using intricate procedures which are time consuming and therefore, represent a high manpower cost of development. Piracy is meant to avoid this investment and the copier profits from the work of the creator of the programme. If piracy is rampant, new investment in the creation of new programmes will get discouraged and the software industry will suffer in consequence. The need for protection of computer software and databases from piracy arises from this enlightened self-interest of the industry itself apart from the ethical and moral considerations of protection of property.

Protection by patents in the past has been found to be broadly infeasible as a computer programme does not always constitute an invention. It is for this reason that a number of countries have excluded computer software from patent protection. However, the software can be an integral part of a process in physics, chemistry of biology, e.g., the distributed digital control of chemical manufacturing processes. If it can be proved that the software forms an integral part of the process, patent laws permit implementable protection as long as other requisites like novelty are fulfilled.

Majority of citizens all over the world are law abiding. When it comes to copyrights the same majority of citizens are not serious. Before violating the copyright law of the land concerned, most of them take it easy. This may be due to:

— Law is not stringent

— Non-Existence of proper enforcement authority

— Ignorance, greed, desperation

The prevailing copyright laws in most of the countries needs to be looked into to match with Technological evolution. Certainly the laws meant for print media are inadequate to effectively deal with the emerging Technology trends. The ability to transmit voice, image, sound and data leads to highly technical operations than those occupying on the traditional networks. No serious attention has been paid to many legal issues related to these developments. Unless there are sufficient legal guarantees, the impressive technological developments may not be acceptable to the society. The consumers will be interested to use these, new developments if they can offer a degree of legal security as provided to them by the traditional operations. The law needs to be more stringent because the revenues from copyright theft is hundreds of thousands of dollars in every country. The laws which were made for print media could have never foreseen such a vast financial involvement.

Several countries have copyright laws in their constitution. The violators of copyright can not always be punished because the native country's laws are not equal with the laws of source country. Due to this reason an increasing number of crackers are operating on INTERNET'.

In India, the copyright laws are broadly framed and generally effective. The laws are bound to be amended as the technological developments takes place. Many of legal, social, political and ethical issues which have guided the society in the past, may not stand very well in the age of Information Technology.

Protection of computer software by copyright is prevalent in most countries. Some countries question whether software is protectable "works" in the sense of copyright laws. The traditional list of categories of protected works do not directly or indirectly include computer software, nor do they come under the category of "scientific work", "book", or"writings". It is for this reason that some countries like USA, France, Germany and India have specifically stipulated that computer programmes be included in copyright laws as "protected works".

Under the copyright laws, works are protected against making copies and public performance, but there is no mention of using the work for private use. For this, the mechanism of copying itself has been subjected to intricate scrutiny and the fact that computer programmes have to be copied in some computer or the other, before it can be used on another computer, have been taken as reasons for defining even private use as copying.

Arguments have been advanced that in a computer network mode, a person sitting at a terminal in one node of the network can use the software situated in another location without having to make an explicit and full copy of the programme. The counter argument advocated is that such a use still copies instructions in a programme statement by statement into the memory of the user computer and hence comes within the laws of infringement.

Countries which have protection against the violation of trade secrets are in a better position to protect computer software rights. However, this applies only to software which is communicated with stipulations of confidentiality or non-disclosure agreement.

The New Threats

A number of issues of computer software rights protection have been reasonably well settled. Regardless of whether the copied software is object code or source code or micro code, whether it is systems software or application software or whether it is fixed in hard copy or magnetic form, copyright has proved its ability to protect the computer software. Protection also extends beyond the literal code to broader aspects of software. In the famous case of Whelan Associates, Inc. Versus jaslow Dental Laboratory, Inc., the court held that the structure, sequence and organisation of a computer programme are protected by copyright. If one copies a copyrighted program by writing a programe in a different language that copied the structure, sequence and organisation, even though the actual original code was not copied, it has been held as infringement. However, it is not established as yet, how far beyond the code copyright extends, with due regard for the idea/expression dichotomy which states "In no case does copyright protection for an original work of authorship extend to any idea, procedure, process, system, method of operation, concept, principle or discovery, regardless of the form in which it is described, explained, illustrated or embodied in such work".

As between the programme code and ideas, several stages of abstraction are present, it is observed that there is a point in the series of abstractions where they are no longer protected since otherwise the author could prevent the use of his ideas to which, apart from their expression, his property is never extended.

The new innovations in software system engineering, especially in the use of CASE tools, the possibility of using these innovations for reverse engineering of a software package frequently arises. The legal question asked is whether reverse engineering of computer programme is itself a copyright infringement.

Going from the object code to the source code form, if it becomes necessary to copy it on to any medium like paper or RAM within the computer to enable viewing on the computer screen, implicit copying steps are involved. If the motive of copying is reverse engineering of the programme instead of the use of a programme, the legal excuses available for copying may not hold. However, the reverse engineering may be done so intelligently that it may come within the purview of "far use' of the copyrighted work. Such a fair use clause should satisfy one or more of the following factors:

i) Use for non-commercial or non-profit educational purposes.

ii) Substantiality of the portion used in relation to the copyright work as a whole

iii) The impact of infringement on the potential market of the copyrighted work

The use of CASE tools of SEEM, with the increasing sophistication in which they are being put into the market, makes reverse engineering more and more intractable and less and less amendable to comparison with the original software codes. It is a basic technical fact that ideas, procedures and methods of operation embodied in the object code cannot come within the comprehension of human beings except through reverse engineering of that code so as to obtain a source code like representation. It is argued that unless reverse engineering of object code is permitted, copyright in fact, will be protecting ideas and not be expression, thereby violating a fundamental principle of copyright laws.

It is clear from the above that new innovations have created a conundrum which has to be resolved soon by legislation if the progressive erosion of effectiveness of copyright protection for software has to be checked before it is too late.

The increasing number of new innovations coming up in the wake of growing multi-billion dollar database industry are creating special problems for copyright protection of databases. Not much thought has been given in this direction so far by legal experts. This is increasing the difficulty experienced in protecting databases because of the steadily increasing number of innovations which are throwing up more and more problems. An important example of this is copyright protection laws relating to remote network access of databases, query response system using expert systems and artificial intelligence methodologies etc. Regarding the protection of databases, while many of the conventional protection clauses apply to the contents of the databases which are like pages in a book or literary work, some vexed problems still remain to be tackled.

It is normally believed that the structure and organization of computer programmes including the screens, menus, file structures and languages embodied in these products can be protected under copyright laws. However, it is not clear as of date whether syntax and commands of a language can be unambiguously protected by copyright. Solutions may have to be found by the analogy of copyrightability of systems of telegraphic and short-hand codes and works describing such systems. Many legal decisions have been given that the component elements of a particular system of telegraphic codes like Morse Code or Stenography are not subjected to copyright though aggregates of these give a written expression describing that the system can be copyrighted. These situations are very similar to cases involving software copyright decisions in which various courts noted that one can rightfully use the same words, phrases and arrangement of these words which were protected by copyright. Therefore, individual components of a computer language may not be protectable by copyright and anyone may use them to independently develop computer programmes. This will give rise to difficult problems in protecting some of the operating systems and basic packages like Dbase from being used for creating unlicenced programmes.

Reconsideration of Patentability

Though copyright afforded a reasonably good protection for software during the eighties, new innovations like the ones described above, are steadily determining its effectiveness. It is, therefore, necessary to revisit the patentability premises so as to find new approaches to legal protection.

In 1981, The Supreme Court of the United States held that a patent claim is not unpatentable merely because it includes steps or elements directed to a law of nature, mathematical algorithms, formulae or computer programme so long as the claim as a whole is drawn to subject matter otherwise statutory. If a computer programme invention is only based on a mathematical algorithm, it is not patentable, because mathematics parse is not patentable. If however, a patent claim contains algorithms or mathematical ideas which are of one consequence to the claims made for patentability of a computer programme which otherwise passes the tests of patentability, they may be treated as any other invention.

A more tractable protection is by making a computer programme subject of a trade secret intrinsically. This would require an unambiguous corpus of law supporting trade secret laws in the country in which the software is marketed. Also the number of licensees should be limited. Unfortunately, this very same clause which qualifies for consideration under a trade secret, prevents wider sale of other software. A via-media perhaps lies in devising innovative approaches for contract protection.

The structure of licensing agreements has to be devised imaginatively. For example, licences may be given a right to reproduce computer software; secondary adaption of a licenses software into another licensed software should be permitted; and it may also provide for translation of a software from one computer language to another.

The Scenario in India

National Informatics Centre (NIC) created by the Government of India is promoting informatics culture in the Government at all levels of its hierarchy such as Central Government, State Governments and District Administrations.

Thus NIC has become a nodal agency to implement Information Technology in the country. Associated with this responsibility, NIC has emphasized Ethical & Legal aspects of Digital Information in implementation of various application on its computer communication network NICNET'. Because of its nodal role the copyright theft within the Govt. Hierarchy is under its control, to a great extent. As it is common practice, if the control is centralized, the evils associated with the system would be under control. The same has been witnessed in all Government Departments in India. The NIC's share of IT in India accounts to about 40%. At least with a degree of confidence, it can be said that this much share of IT is free from copyright theft. Several steps have been taken to remove piracy and violation of copyrights. . NIC after having hard negotiation with several software vendors has taken site licences which has resulted in the lowest possible price. Because of its structure and size, NIC needs thousands of copies of each software product to implement them across the country. Because of its volume, most of the vendors have been more than willing to bring down the prices of software product well below the listed prices. This has encouraged NIC to strictly stick to the law of copyrights as applicable in the country. Because of the easy availability of software products to all one thousand and odd units of NIC across the country, and strict enforcement of the policy NIC, could ethically stick to the law of the land.

For the Software and Database products developed and implemented by NIC, several steps have been taken to prevent copyright abuse by individuals and organisations. NIC has produced several CD-ROMs related India's Caselaw, India Code, Land Records, etc. It also has several on-line databases on its network such as: COURTNIC, the Supreme Court of India's pending cases Information System, JUDIS Judgement Information System of Supreme Court of India , INDIA CODE, the Enactments of Indian Parliament, etc. Following are some of the technical solutions considered by NIC.

Bootable CDS: In order to prevent copyri ght theft an attempt has been made to produce Bootable CD ROMs. Bootable DOS CD-ROM is created by loading first the command interpreter, COMMAND -COM and the device Driver for the CD-ROM, then MSCD X.EXE can be started for accessing files on the CD-ROM. The process of creation of bootable CD-ROM is tedious. Phoenix Technologies and IBM have jointly released the EL torito'Bootable CD-ROM Format specifications which designs how a boot image or ima es should be placed physically on the CD-ROM.

Once CD is accessed, the control would be passed on to the system and it will not be possible to down load the data illegally.

Even for accessing CD the system has to be rebooted all over. Effectively system control is passed to the application Software residing on CD. As the user can not use any commands other than the application software, he is effectively prevented in down loading huge amount of data. However, if a multimedia producer decides to violate copyrights, he can down load everything.

Copy Prevention Technique: Here the software is made available in a format which is not recognizable by the operating system of the computer. With the result it can not down load the software and run it from the computer system. This method has posed the following difficulties to the user:

- The user can not make back-up copies of the software
- By using always the original Software, there is a risk of loss or damage to the original software.
- Bit Copier' technique can bypass copy prevention

Copy protection: It can be made by makin g use of dongles which are attached to a port of the hardware before the software is accessed. The dongles, a serial no., which is matched with the one that is in the software. If both are matched t e software starts functioning. If the serial nos. are not matched the machine, does not function.

The disadvantage with dongles is that it occupies an important communication port, which is difficult to accept. Some Hardware vendors have come out with an extra communication port on the dongle itself.

Time Locks: Another technique to prevent copyright theft is to provide time locks into the software. That means the software is operational only during certain time frame. Once the stipulated time duration in the software is over, the user is prompted to contact the software supplier. However, during the time frame one can violate copyright with case. This is not an effective one.

The British Technology Group tried to prevent copyright theft by storing proprietary software in a mix of clear and encrypted text. The clear text is then run on the systems CPU but is dependent for its authorization on the scrambled data which is run on a separate CPU and associated RAM operating in temper proof mode.

In function the secondary CPU and RAM are under the control of the main OS, but only as far as determining when it is to run. The BTG system is believed to have a high level of security in LAN and WAN situations.

Digital as Media

Copyright laws are universally medium specific. By treating Digital as a medium for all electronic items, most of the existing copyright laws will be still valid and enforceable. This is because the new technology has brought Music, pictures, sound, texts and movies together on digital platform. This may help us in generalizing all classifications of copyright laws thus eliminating all media-specific copyright laws. This will bring simplicity to copyright laws.

On the other hand, treating Digital as a medium will lead to other complications. For example: A literary work or a graph recorded in a digital form, can be viewed as a musical notes by writing another software routine giving another interpretation. Can it be a violation of copyright law?

The developer of musical notes has not copied anything from the existing work. But he has utilised the existing work to produce altogether a different kind of work. Can the author of the literary work sue the programmer who developed musical notes? There may be may such questions to be answered.

It is now abundantly clear that there is a lot of room for the improvement of Ethical and legal issues related to copyrights of Digital Information. At the same time while tightening the grip on the laws, it should be seen that there should be exceptions for fair use user groups such as researchers, libraries, teachers, journalists, etc., from whom the society at large is going to be benefitted.

Information Industry growth depends on how society changes the copyright laws. The society should not over do of cracking. Because it leads to witch hunt and becomes hurdle to the development of skills of Information Industry workforce. It also propagates negativism to Information Technology.

It is worth considering to protect privacy, making it illegal to intentionally use a computer to knew confidential information about another person without specific authorization as Missouri passed a law on this.

3

Intellectual Property Rights

Among the challenges that information technology is posing to universities, none is more contentious than the issues it raises for intellectual property. The controversy pits administration against faculty, scientists against humanists, and academic values against financial interests.

Some administrators seek control of the products of information technology in order to use the potential profit for the benefit of all members of the university rather than for the gain of individual faculty members. Some scientists see an opportunity at last to make sure that humanists' books are treated in the same way as the products of scientific research (either by giving the university control of both, or of neither). And both administrators and faculty face temptations to compromise academic purposes for financial gain. The battleground is intellectual property policy, and the hope is that victory, or at least a peace treaty here, will finally resolve the dispute.

Much of this controversy, Information technology raises important new problems, some of which should be addressed by changes in university policy on intellectual property. But the changes should not deal only with the products of information technology, and some of the problems that may seem to be about ownership go beyond the province of intellectual property.

Beyond Information Technology

"Is a CD-ROM more like a textbook, or more like an invention?" The first meeting of our Intellectual Property Committee had hardly begun when the members found themselves engaged in a spirited argument about the true essence of the products of information technology. The stakes seemed high. If we concluded that CD-ROMs should be treated like textbooks, the faculty who created them would own them, but if we decided that they were inventions, the university could claim them. Like that of most universities, our intellectual property policy grants faculty ownership of copyrightable work, but gives the university the option of taking title to most patentable products.

The rationale for the different treatment is not entirely clear, but it appears to rest on several considerations. Inventions are less likely to be developed if they are not patented, and patents are relatively difficult to secure; inventions usually involve substantial use of university resources allocated exclusively to the inventor. Copyright is less necessary to promote the dissemination of ideas (though it may be necessary to encourage their production), and is easy to secure. Copyrightable works are generally assumed to draw less on substantial university resources assigned exclusively to their creators.

The committee quickly recognized that the sensible answer to the question with which we began is that CD-ROMs and almost all products of information technology are like textbooks in some respects, and like inventions in others. While this answer is unobjectionable, the implication that is too easily drawn from it is not. By focusing on the distinctive features of information technology, the answer fosters the temptation to create a new category, a special set of rules just for "encoded" or "digital"works. Some universities have followed this approach, but their policies seemed to us to reproduce the problem that prompted the revision in the first place. Under these policies, the university sometimes claims ownership of information technology products (for example, if the expected profits of a piece of software are high), and sometimes does not (for example, if a chemistry professor produces a jazz video). The bases for the distinctions may or may not be arbitrary, but they have little to do with the nature of the product itself -- its status as information technology.

The fundamental problem is that what makes the products of information technology distinctive (to the extent that they are distinctive) does not correspond to what usually justifies a property claim. An interactive Web page may be easier to produce, and its contents more readily reproducible and accessible, than traditional forms of scholarly and pedagogical communication. But none of these factors in itself offers a reasonable basis for determining who should own it or profit from it.

The question of whether information technology products are more like books or more like inventions is therefore precisely the wrong one to ask. It focuses attention on the nature of the product instead of the way it is created. A simple shift of perspective — from the attributes of the product itself to the circumstances of its creation—is an essential step in developing a coherent policy for information technology products. Once that shift is made, it becomes clear that the policy must reach beyond information technology. The policy can then be based on general principles that appeal to the core interests of the university and therefore apply to all kinds of products produced by faculty, staff and students.

If the university contributes substantially and specifically to the making of a product, the university should share in its profits and have some control over its uses. This principle in some form is widely accepted, and indeed is at least implicit in many existing university policies. The principle states sufficient though probably not necessary conditions for a university claim. There may be other factors, such as effects on the university's reputation, which could justify some control in the absence of a specific contribution. Even using the principle as statement of sufficient conditions, we still have to decide what contributions should count as substantial and specific in particular cases. But discussions about these questions are more likely to be fruitful when they take place against a background of agreement on this general principle.

The university may contribute to the creation of a product by providing any or all of three kinds of support: financial, intellectual and reputational. In return, the university and its members have a legitimate claim on some of the profits of the product, some access to it for using in teaching and research in the institution, and some control over any effects it might have on the university's own reputation. This reciprocal relationship is a matter of fairness. It should not be thought of as a relationship only between two parties—an individual faculty member and the university — but rather as one that exists among faculty and other members of the university, both present and future students and colleagues. That important point can be further reinforced if the university's proceeds from intellectual property are not consigned to general funds, but are directly and visibly allocated to promoting further research and teaching.

Each of these three kinds of support provides a basis for some claim by the university on an intellectual product, but the claim does not apply only to information technology products, and it is not necessarily one of ownership. Even if the university has a legitimate claim, its interests may be satisfied by retaining control of the product for certain purposes, such as for use by the library, students and other scholars.

1 Financial. Why should the university not treat products created by faculty members in the same way it treats products created by staff members — as "work for hire," which belongs entirely to the university? The answer is not so obvious as many faculty would like to think. Tradition exempts teachers from the "work for hire" provisions of the copyright law. But the literal language of the statute does not support the exemption for faculty, which exists mainly because judges have declined to overturn the tradition. The only strong justification for the tradition is the protection of academic freedom, but that would not require that faculty receive all or even any of the profits derived from their work. (It does require giving faculty some control over the content and use of their work, even when they do not own it.)

If we were creating a university system ab initio, we might well decide that educational goals could be better served by allocating all profits to the university to promote the overall educational mission of the institution, while giving faculty sufficient control over the content and uses of their products to protect academic freedom. But in practice we begin with an existing system, with a complex set of benefits and burdens already in place, and we need to justify any departures that significantly shift the balance in favor of the university (or the faculty). A fair reform would require changing far more than the package of intellectual property rights. Changes in levels of compensation and patterns of work would also need to be considered—and not only in one university but (to avoid the problem of competitive disadvantage) in all comparable universities.

A more constructive approach would rely on principles already embodied in current practice, and seek to generalize them to new situations and new kinds of products. The most promising basis for such an approach is the principle already cited — that the university has a legitimate claim if it provides substantial and specific support. The principle is implicit in current practice, and can be independently justified on grounds of reciprocity, as suggested earlier.

Reciprocity might of course also justify the university's sharing the proceeds of products created with collective resources that are not specifically dedicated to an individual faculty member (such as the library). But determining how much or even whether such a resource was used in the creation of the product would be difficult if not impossible in practice. In addition, such a policy would be vulnerable to the general objection, mentioned above, that changing one part of a system of benefits and burdens without making compensating adjustments in other parts would be unfair.

What should count as a substantial and specific contribution may be contestable in particular cases, but the general distinction it implies is clear enough. On the one side, the ordinary benefits of employment (such as salary, office and usual library usage) should not count. On the other side, some facilities assigned to an individual faculty member (such as a laboratory) should count. The reason is not simply that not all faculty members receive the contribution, but that it is relatively large and relatively exclusive. Unlike the salary of an individual faculty member, the marginal cost is high enough that the expenditure represents an allocation that could have supported some other major priority. Unlike a contribution to a collective good such as the library, the expenditure supports a resource that is not accessible to other faculty and students. When the university decides at the margin to expend funds to provide a faculty member with an exclusive resource instead of allocating the same funds to a collective resource, it has a legitimate claim on the products created using the exclusive resource.

A principle that grants the university a claim if its support is substantial and specific would in many cases yield the same result as the current practice of treating copyrightable and patentable products differently. Most textbooks, software and CD-ROMs are produced using ordinary facilities, and most patentable inventions come out of large research labs. But the principle cuts across the distinction between patent and copyright, and provides a broad standard that can apply to all kinds of intellectual property, not only information technology products. When the creation of copyrightable materials draws on substantial and specific university resources, the university would be justified in making a claim. The proceeds of a multimedia encyclopedia that employs extra university staff and occupies exclusive space, for example, should not belong only to its faculty producers.

"Substantial" cannot be specifically defined in advance for all cases, but its indefiniteness is actually an advantage, as it permits variations in the sharing of resources depending on the extent of university contribution.

The best approach may be to adopt a general template for dividing royalties and fees (such as many universities already have in their patent policy), and negotiate departures from it. The important point is that the negotiations focus on the nature of the university's contribution, not the character of the product.

The university's financial contribution may be sufficient to support a claim to intellectual products, but it is not necessary. Some patentable works that do not consume substantial or specific university resources may still be subject to university ownership. Universities generally have the right to acquire the title to products of sponsored research supported by the federal government.

In this respect, the university acts as an agent of the government, which sets the terms of the contract to ensure that the university adequately oversees the research. Furthermore, there is a public interest, shared by universities, in encouraging the commercial development of scientific knowledge. As noted above, most scientific discoveries, unlike most copyrightable work, are not likely to be turned into useable technology unless they are patented.

2. ***Intellectual.*** The disputes about intellectual property tend to neglect the most important kind of support that faculty members enjoy in a university -- the intellectual resources provided by a professor's students, colleagues, and the shared activities of university life such as performances, conferences and museum exhibitions. To some extent the neglect is understandable. This kind of support is part of the background culture to which faculty themselves contribute. No policy could possibly capture the value of such a diffuse contribution.

Nevertheless, some kinds of support are specifically linked to a particular work -- support without which it could not have been produced at all. When a faculty member publishes a catalogue of a special collection in a university museum, posts the proceedings of a university conference on the Internet, or produces a video of a concert by the university orchestra, the university has a legitimate claim. This is so even if the main value of the work is due to the creative contribution of the faculty member.

Where students play a significant role in the production of a work, the university has a special responsibility for regulating both the creation and the subsequent use of the product. The university's interest is not simply in ensuring that the students and the institution receive fair compensation if the work turns out to have commercial value. The more important concern should be that the role of the students and the use of the product is consistent with the educational mission of the university. The students' contribution should also be acknowledged in any publication or dissemination of the work, but because that does not require that the university own or control the product, it should be dealt with by policies other than those of intellectual property.

In other instances, the students' contribution may not be very creative, but their role is still sufficient to give rise to a university interest in the product. If a faculty member uses students to test course materials in ways that go beyond ordinary classroom practice and then distributes the materials for commercial gain, the faculty member cannot reasonably complain that academic freedom is jeopardized if the university asks whether the students consent to being used in this way, and whether the students and the institution are receiving a fair share of any profits resulting from the sale of the materials.

3. ***Reputational.*** Paul Samuelson's name may bring more value to a textbook than the name of any institution, be it MIT or Harvard. But in the case of most faculty members the value of the name of the institution is at least as great as their own. Publishers, producers and Web page system operators seek to identify the author's institution, sometimes to increase profits or at least audiences, sometimes just to enhance the authority of the content.

The main concern should not be the commercial value of the name, or even the extent of its recognition, but rather the effect of the use of the name on the university as an institution and its members. The reputation of any university is a collective good, easily damaged by the actions of individual members, to the detriment of the other members, present and future. By attaching the university's name to a product, a faculty member makes use of that collective good, for better or for ill.

The rationale here is based not on the nature of the university's contribution (whether it is substantial or specific, for example), but on the effects of the individual's use of a collective good. The university, on behalf of the other members of the university, takes a legitimate interest in the use of its name. It has a responsibility to ensure that the use of the name (and phrases and symbols that carry the same implications) meets at least three standards that express core values for any educational institution.

(a) Accuracy. Attaching the university's name to an event, project or publication implies a close connection, usually sponsorship or endorsement. That means that phrases like the "Princeton Primer on Basketball Defense" or the "Yale Guide to God and Country" should be used only when they refer to activities for which the institution or one of its officers is accountable. Participation by individual students or faculty should not, by itself, be enough to attach the institutional name. Rather, the activity should be one for which the university takes institutional responsibility.

(b) Appropriateness. The university also needs to make sure that even if the connection with the university is accurately represented, the activity is consistent with the educational mission of the university. The UCLA Association .for the Promotion of Tattooing may be objectionable quite apart from whether it is a recognized university organization. Even some activities that meet relevant standards of quality and serve educational goals may still not be appropriate (for example, partisan political activities or certain outside commercial ventures carried on by individual faculty or students). In the case of most academic activities, the normal processes of review should be sufficient to maintain standards of appropriateness. But for other activities some special procedures may be necessary. In general, groups and organizations should be encouraged to use the more precise name: Harvard Divinity School Students for Peace and Quiet, or Cornell Hotel School's Guide to Careers in Wine Tasting.

*(c) **Fairness.*** The university has a responsibility to protect its assets by seeking a fair share of the commercial value that the use of its name produces. Any commercial fruits of its reputation are largely attributable to the contributions of many generations of faculty, students and staff, and therefore should be allocated for the benefit of the university as a whole, and its individual members present and future.

Beyond Intellectual Property

To deal with the emerging problems generated by information technology, intellectual property policy, should embody principles that apply beyond information technology. The extension no doubt complicates the task of revising the policy, but it offers the advantage of a more coherent and equitable set of principles and practices than found in current policies. The other side of the relationship, and show why policies dealing with information technology should go beyond intellectual property. Information technology raises questions that are not best addressed by policies that speak mainly the language of ownership and control.

Consider first the critical problem that university libraries are now confronting -- the increasing costs of serials and other forms of scholarly publications. Faculty members sign over their rights to their articles to journal publishers, who then require university libraries to pay high prices for the hard copies they would rather not have in order to gain access to the digital versions they prefer. Many academic publishers reap large profits while university libraries struggle to cover their increasing costs. Faculty in their role as producers benefit little, and faculty in their role as consumers suffer much, along with their colleagues, students and their institutions.

As important as this problem is, attempts to solve it by changes in intellectual property policy are not likely to succeed. If the university were to hold the copyright on all articles, it would of course enjoy a stronger bargaining position in negotiations with publishers. But such a change would be difficult to implement and in any case would not address the root of the difficulty. The problem calls for a collective response by all universities and the scholarly community to reduce dominance of traditional journals in academic advancement. One of the more promising approaches is the effort to establish an alternative medium for dissemination of research on the Internet, which would include the equivalent of refereed processes. If such a medium becomes an affordable and widely accepted method for communicating and assessing the results of scholarship, the question of who actually owns the copyright to most scholarly work of this kind will become less important.

Another set of issues that go beyond what universities should attempt to resolve in their internal policies on intellectual property concerns international agreements to protect the copyright of digital work. The U.S. government has been a leader in seeking such protections, but many of the proposals do not necessarily serve the interests of universities, their faculty or their students. Faculty are not only producers but also consumers of intellectual property, and they care at least as much about having access to others' scholarly work for the use of their students and their own research as keeping control of and profiting from their own work.

Broad license for "fair use" is therefore more important than strict guarantee of fair profits. Universities should certainly take an active role in these discussions, but the action that counts is that which shapes legislation, treaties and trade agreements in national and international forums, not the university's own policies and procedures.

A third group of issues that go beyond intellectual property more directly raises questions for a university's own internal policies. As advances in information technology encourage the expansion of distance learning, some educators are promoting a grand vision of a virtual university, in which faculty's lectures are digitized and distributed to students scattered throughout the country and the world, connected only through their PCs.

More than lectures in a classroom, these cyber-encounters will encourage students to interact, if not with virtual professors themselves, at least with the sequence of questions and responses they have programmed.

The fears that the virtual university may replace the real university are surely exaggerated. More likely for most universities, distance learning will supplement their regular offerings by reaching mature students and alumni who might otherwise rarely return to the classroom. Distance learning may simply expand the market for higher education, attracting new students without displacing the traditional ones.

But one fear is not so easily discounted: Distance learning vastly increases the opportunities for faculty to distribute their own course materials, and in effect to offer on the Internet what may appear to be the equivalent of the courses they teach at their own university. These opportunities, though not entirely new, pose some potentially new problems because of the scale and flexibility of the new technology. This is what may be called the courseware problem -- the control of lectures, syllabi, study questions, exercises, case studies and exams prepared by faculty for their own courses, but offered in various forms, virtual and otherwise, to students at home or at other institutions. The problem is important in itself, but it also serves to illustrate why information technology challenges are not best handled by changes in intellectual property policy.

Some changes in intellectual property policy can help with some aspects of the courseware problem, specifically those that raise the same concerns as with other kinds of products. But for at least three reasons it is mistake to go further and assert a university claim to own Internet courseware produced by faculty.

First of all, it is difficult to justify any principled distinction between courseware presented on the Internet and courseware distributed in more traditional forms. The audience may be greater, and therefore all the potential effects, including financial gain, are likely to be greater. But it does not follow that the university is entitled to ownership.

Even if we accept the optimistic assumptions about the commercial future of Internet courseware, we should doubt whether any of these potential effects in themselves justify separate treatment on the basis of the medium. If the large profits are the concern, then we should have a policy setting a limit on outside income from courseware in whatever form. If the concern is possible distraction of faculty or lack of availability of materials, the effects may go in the opposite direction. It is easier for faculty to distribute and for students to retrieve material on the Internet. As for the university's reputation, it is at stake no less when courseware is distributed in traditional media, perhaps even more so when its professors give lectures in person at other institutions.

Second, in the absence of any principled distinction, problems of equity arise. Faculty members who distribute their courseware on the Internet will legitimately feel unfairly treated compared to those who do not, if the university claims ownership in the former case but not the latter.

Third, treating Internet material differently may create an incentive to distribute it by other means, and thereby discourage the use of the Internet for purposes we should seek to encourage. The university itself could and should find ways to encourage Internet education in the right ways, and should provide assistance for doing so. But these efforts do not require university ownership of courseware, and are likely to be more effective without it.

A more sensible approach is to define the courseware problem not in terms of the faculty members' rights to own their creative products but rather in terms of their responsibilities to the institution, specifically to their students, colleagues and the institution. The general policies regulating outside activities, especially those dealing with conflict of interest and conflict of commitment, thus become the more appropriate instrument for dealing with the problem.

Following that approach, these are the key considerations on which we should focus, and some ways in which we could begin to deal with them:

1. Financial. The chief concern here is that the distribution of Internet courses might deny the university a fair share of the commercial proceeds. Intellectual property policy could certainly address part of this concern. A policy that grants the university some claim to profits when the institution provides substantial and specific support for developing courseware would take care of the financial interest in those cases where the university's claim is strongest. Going further would run into the problem of distinguishing Internet courseware from more traditional teaching materials.

2. Intellectual. The concerns relevant to the intellectual life of the university are the most important. Two kinds deserve special attention: those involving the commitment of the faculty, and those affecting availability of materials for students and colleagues.

The worry about faculty commitment refers to the danger of creating a conflict or competition between what the faculty members offer their own students and what they offer elsewhere. Even in the absence of economic competition, there is the possibility that some faculty members could be distracted from giving due attention to their own courses and students, or could shape their courses more in response to market imperatives than to educational goals.

Most universities have rules governing the outside activities of their faculty. To deal with the problem of faculty commitment posed by courseware, they could amplify these rules to make clear that the objection to teaching at other institutions is not simply the absence from campus. Universities also have a legitimate interest in avoiding self-generated competition and in preventing divided loyalties such as those that could distract, or appear to distract, faculty from giving full attention to teaching at their own institution.

Specifically, we could include a provision describing a limiting case that would be clearly prohibited — such as a faculty member's offering an Internet course for which another institution gives credit — and indicate that the closer any arrangement comes to that case, the more it is subject to university oversight.

The risk that the content of the faculty's own courses might be excessively shaped by market forces probably cannot be prevented by any direct regulations, but could be adequately handled by the normal procedures of review and the informal culture of collegial opinion.

No less important is the need to make sure that any outside arrangements faculty members make to distribute courseware do not affect its availability to students at their home university. To deal with this problem, faculty could be required to make available at cost, at least to their own students and to the university library, any courseware distributed on the Internet.

3. ***Reputational.*** Courses presented by a faculty member on the Internet pose a danger of conveying the impression that the material is being offered as the equivalent of a course taught at the home university, or is otherwise endorsed by the university and subject to normal collegial accountability.

An intellectual property policy that controls the use of the university's name (and other language or symbols that imply institutional sponsorship) is probably sufficient to deal with most of the reputational problems that courseware creates. Phrases such as "the same course that Professor Smith teaches at Cal Tech" or "just like being in a class at Duke" run against the spirit of any adequate name policy. They could be specifically prohibited unless the faculty member entered into partnership with the university to produce the courseware (as in a licensing arrangement).

Making such partnerships more attractive is a desirable part of any intellectual property policy for more general reasons. They can help bring distribution and advertising more under the control of the university, thereby providing better protection for all of its interests, whether reputational, intellectual or financial.

And they can help make available to many more people the benefits of high quality teaching and research, which is an increasingly important part of the educational mission of many universities. An enterprising office that is prepared to assist faculty in converting their creations, whether inventions or CD-ROMs, into marketable products is an essential part of an effective intellectual property policy.

Universities—and their faculty, students and staff—have a great deal at stake in the efforts to meet the challenges posed by developments in information technology. The problems the new technology presents, as well as the opportunities it offers, implicate some of the central values of the university. Teaching and research, in their individual as well as their institutional modes, take on new forms that are forcing changes in traditional practices and established procedures throughout the university.

The question of who controls the products created by and for this new technology naturally comes to the fore, and quite properly prompts reviews of internal policies on intellectual property. But the framework of intellectual property does not adequately capture many of the serious concerns we should have about the products of information technology, and those that it does capture are more general than the preoccupation with information technology suggests.

We should keep our attention on the significant financial, intellectual and reputational interests of the university as they affect its central educational mission. If we do, we will see that changes in intellectual property policy should follow principles that go beyond information technology, and we will recognize that problems of information technology call for policies that go beyond intellectual property.

4

Privacy in Cyberspace

Much of the discussion of the information technology and e-commerce assumes near universal connectivity to telecommu-nications networks. This is true for developed market economies but is generally not true for countries of the South. As a result, firms and individuals from the developed market economies will populate much of the virtual spaces within which electronic commerce and other cyberspace interactions will take place. In addition, these actors have had decades of experience with technologically mediated non-proximate communication and have relatively well developed legal and ethical frameworks that can serve as foundations for dealing with cyberspace issues. Actors based in countries of the South do not have this base. In most cases, they are experiencing very rapid growth in basic telephony and the introduction of multiple new communication technologies such as mobile telephony and the Internet simultaneously. The combination of these factors makes the task of influencing the development of ethical and legal frameworks for cyberspace a challenge for actors based in the South.

Over the past few years, the cyberspace discussion has been reframed in terms of electronic commerce signifying the importance of transactions (defined as interactions that involve exchanges of value) and relationships (defined as iterated interactions or transactions between the same parties). Electronic commerce throws into sharp focus problems of trust and privacy. If a secure environment characterized by trust can be established for the conduct of transactions, one may assume that interactions and relationships will be looked after as well. This presentation focuses on electronic commerce for this reason.

Electronic commerce, and the wider concept of cyberspace, do not map one-on-one with the geographical spaces of countries or regions, such as Sri Lanka. A Sri Lankan may conduct electronic commerce with another Sri Lankan in Sri Lanka. But this would be the exception. In most cases, the transactions will occur between Sri Lankans and those located outside that national territory. The question of which cultural mores and ethical and legal frameworks apply to these transactions does not have a clear-cut answer.

A preliminary definition of the key concepts of trust and privacy is necessary. Trust is defined, following Giddens, as "confidence in the reliability of a person or a system, regarding a given set of outcomes or events, where that confidence expresses faith in the probity or love of another, or in the correctness of abstract principles (technical knowledge)." The primary condition that creates a need for trust is lack of full information, generally associated with a person who is separated in time and space or a system whose workings are not fully known. Lacking complete information about a system, a user has to develop a trust-related attitude toward it. This can range from complete trust through mistrust to angst. Dealing with any commercial organization necessarily requires a trust-related attitude. When transactions with such complex systems are mediated by a technological system such as an electronic commerce platform, the importance of trust is heightened. Trust is dynamically generated and has to be worked on. In interpersonal relationships, one party's actions, particularly self-disclosure or lack thereof, can reinforce, diminish, or destroy the other party's trust. With care, this claim can be extended to commercial relationships. Trust building behavior on the part of a commercial organization would include absence of coercion in making and receiving disclosures and a degree of self-disclosure.

The above understanding of trust overlaps with a definition of privacy derived from research on everyday social practice'"the capability to explicitly or implicitly negotiate the boundary conditions of social relations." The definition includes control of outflow of information that may be of strategic or aesthetic value to the person and control of inflow of information, including initiation of contact. Privacy is a precondition for trust. Trust affects privacy. A user's trust in the information practices of a system is likely to make possible consensual surveillance, which can enhance trust. The resultant spiral will lead to stable and productive customer relationships. Where low trust leads to coercive surveillance, the opposite spiral leading to mistrust and angst is likely to result.

The above definitions of trust and privacy are abstract. They take different forms in different situations including cultures. As Fukuyama has discussed in a broader context, trust varies across situations and cultures. What this short comment seeks to do is to identify the key factors that must be taken into account in developing ethical and legal frameworks for effective electronic commerce outside the developed market economies, drawing primarily on the case of Sri Lanka.

In most countries of the South, basic telecommunication connectivity is still a distant goal, leave alone the advanced Internet infrastructure that provides the basis for electronic commerce. Electronic transactions between companies and organizations, particularly those involved in worldwide commercial relationships, do take place within the context of Electronic Data Interchange (EDI).

However, these closed user systems do not fall within the commonly understood meaning of electronic commerce that involves transactions with consumers in an open system such as the Internet. The availability of telecommunication connectivity from home, office, or personal device is the precondition for electronic commerce. In addition, a computer and modem (or equivalent) plus a subscription to a service provider are required. These preconditions do not exist for all but a small number of individuals and organizations. The situation in Sri Lanka is illustrative.

In Sri Lanka, less than 10% of households are equipped with telephones and teledensity (calculated only for fixed-access lines) has just gone over 2 in the past year. Even with the current extraordinary growth rates for fixed-access telephones that were over 30% last year and may be as high as 40% for the current year, it is unlikely that universal connectivity in the form of telecommunications access from every home will be achieved in the near future. Domestic tariffs being driven up by the loss of international subsidies are likely to stall network expansion unless the country experiences sharply improved economic growth, most likely associated with the end of the war with the LTTE terror organization.

In the near-term, electronic commerce in countries such as Sri Lanka will take two forms: elite individuals and firms with the wherewithal for electronic commerce will purchase goods and services through electronic commerce, primarily from off-shore suppliers; vendors in Sri Lanka who establish electronic commerce sites will engage in transactions with off-shore individuals and firms. This will be in addition to the closed electronic commerce systems that will involve local firms participating in multinational production and trading relationships. Given the asymmetry between the Sri Lankan and off-shore participants (e.g., a Sri Lankan reader buying books from Amazon.Com; a Sri Lankan Bed & Breakfast operator accepting reservations from European tourists), it is unlikely that there will be a specific Sri Lankan component in the design of the commerce sites or the practices that will be developed around them. The book purchaser will follow the general practices of Amazon.Com; the B&B operator will adapt to the needs of her clients. In the same way that many American cultural practices form the basis of the current Internet culture simply because a majority of the early Internet users were Americans, it is likely that the mores and frameworks of the developed countries will pervade the emerging virtual marketplace.

Individuals and organizations in developed market economies have had decades to get accustomed to interactions in the "virtual space" of the public telephone network. The basic ethical and legal frameworks have been established for telephone-based interactions; though some of the newer uses of the network such as credit card based purchases, audiotex, and the use of calling-line identification have required attention. The remedies to the problems posed by these new applications draw on the frameworks developed for basic services over the past decades. In the same way, the more complex challenges posed by Internet based applications draw on past experience.

In common with most less-developed countries, Sri Lanka has relatively short experience with widespread everyday use of technologies for non-proximate communication. The telephone was introduced to Sri Lanka in the late Nineteenth Century, within a few years of its invention, but it took 106 years to connect the first 100,000 telephone lines, in contrast with the third and fourth 100,000 lines that were connected in months.

The slow growth in the early years and the explosive growth in recent years mean that most telecommunication users are "newbies." Users have little experience with interaction in the virtual spaces created by the different telecommunication networks.

The overall environment of a society has an impact on how its members approach electronic commerce. Fukuyama talks of high and low-trust societies and generally correlates low-trust societies will low-growth societies. While there are problems with parts of his analysis, in general it is correct to state that commercial transactions in relatively poor countries such as Sri Lanka are not marked by high degrees of trust. While trust exists in family and similar settings, it is low in organizational and commercial settings.

Trust allows transactions to take place with lower transaction costs because the parties allow consensual surveillance or proceed with less information. When the starting point is low trust, there is a much greater likelihood that the technological system through which the transactions occur will be designed to coercively extract information, which if known to the other party, leads to mistrust, which in turn could lead to greater reliance on actions hostile to trust-building in countries such as Sri Lanka.

This vicious downward spiral is not counteracted by the experience of users in effectively functioning in virtual environments such as telephone networks.

Trust in the system provider could facilitate the friction-laden relations between consumers and vendors. Usually, a telecommunication provider such an Internet service provider or a telecommunication operator, broadly defined, provides the platform for electronic commerce. In the US, studies have shown that telephone companies are among the most trusted institutions in society (this trust has been rapidly declining in the past two decades).

But telecommunications providers in most of Asia that were until recently or are still unregulated, inefficient, government-owned monopolies are unlikely to have that legacy. Because of poor service, corruption and related factors, they may be among the least trusted institutions in these societies. Whether the many new entrants to the telecommunications field will be capable of building up trust is to be seen.

It is not commonly accepted what measurable privacy attitudes are. However, attitudes to a key item of access information, the home telephone number, may be used as a proxy for the present purposes. The attitude to disclosure of home telephone numbers in the US has changed over the years. Despite it being common practice to penalize those who wish to keep their names and numbers off directories by charging extra fees, as much as 50% of subscribers in states such as California and Nevada have unlisted numbers. In all parts of the US the proportion of unlisted numbers is increasing. This is perhaps driven by the use of the telephone for direct marketing, polling, and similar activities that disrupt home life.

In Sri Lanka, and perhaps in other Asian countries of similar status, the attitude toward disclosure of telephone numbers is quite different from contemporary US attitudes. Perhaps as a result of thinking of the telephone as a status symbol (which was justified at a time when one had to wait 10 years and/or exercise much political or other influence to get a phone), it is common to include home telephone numbers in business cards and even under the business entries in the telephone directory. The absence of direct marketers and polling firms may also contribute to this attitude.

It is possible tnat this tendency to disclose personal information is not a characteristic of a particular culture, but is a feature of a network in the early stages of formation. As connectivity increases, the members of the network may understand the value of controlling access. As long as the network is relatively isolated, as was the case with national telecommunication networks until recently because of high international calling charges, this "natural" evolution has an element of symmetry built into it. But in the present situation where "between-network" communication is increasing very rapidly, the members from the low-penetration networks may tend to exercise less control over their personal information while those from the mature networks will guard their privacy. This asymmetry may have to be addressed in designing ethical and legal frameworks.

There is one qualification to the above argument. It is possible that economic factors can powerfully override the above-discussed forces shaping privacy attitudes. In Sri Lanka, cellular operators charge most customers for incoming calls. As a result, the attitude toward disclosure of cellular numbers is diametrically opposed to the attitude regarding fixed-access numbers.

Generally, these numbers are not given out freely and there is no demand for a cellular telephone directory even though a significant number of subscribers are using the cellular phone as a substitute and not as a complement to fixed-access service. It may be worthwhile to consider economic incentives in designing ethical and legal frameworks for electronic commerce.

An Asian or Sri Lankan perspective on cyberspace developments is inherently contradictory because cyberspace does not map with geographical spaces.

However, it is true that human beings and organizations that interact in cyberspace are still located in physical spaces, still have a majority of interactions in, and are subject to the laws and culture of, those spaces. Hopefully, the above exploration of the contradiction yielded some new insights.

The cultural mores and ethical and legal frameworks emerging in cyberspace will be disproportionately influenced by actors based in the developed market economies, though not necessarily by national cultures. Language and other factors that may function as cultural screens need further examination. Actors based in the rich countries will also bring with them a heritage of experience of interacting in non-proximate settings unlike those from the South who have gained access to telecommunication networks only recently. In the end, the key difference will be between those who are wired into the networks and those who are not, whatever be their geographical location.

Privacy has become one of the most important human rights issues of the modern age. At a time when computer based technology gives government and private sector organisations the ability to conduct mass surveillance of populations, privacy has become a crucial safeguard for individual rights.

According to opinion polls, concern over privacy violation is now greater than at any time in recent history. Uniformally, populations throughout the world report their distress about encroachment on privacy, prompting an unprecedented number of nations to pass laws which specifically protect the privacy of their citizens.

The basis for this legal activity rests on a growing understanding that privacy is a fundamental right. Privacy is a concept which underpins human dignity and other key values such as freedom of association and freedom of speech. These rights are established squarely in international covenents, and are protected specifically in the constitutions of many nations. Moreover, the increasing sophication of information technology, with its capacity to collect, analyse and disseminate information on individuals, has introduced a sense of urgency to the demand for legislation.

New developments in medical research and care, advanced transportation systems and financial transfers have dramatically increased the level of information generated by each individual.

Computers linked together by high speed networks with advanced processing systems can create comprehensive dossiers on any person without the need for a single central computer system. More important, surveillance has become a fixed design component in virtually all information technology.

Rapid advances in the development of powerful technology, in conjunction with the demand for greater bureaucratic efficiency, are promoting a seamless web of surveillance from cradle to grave, from bankbook to bedroom. New technologies developed by the defence industry are spreading into law enforcement, civilian agencies, and private companies. At the same time, outdated laws and regulations are failing to check an expanding pattern of abuses.

Human rights groups are concerned that much of this technology is being exported to developing countries which lack adequate protections. Currently, there are few barriers to the trade in surveillance technologies.

Government and citizen alike could potentially benefit from some of the IT schemes being implemented in the private and public sectors. New "smart card" projects in which client information is placed on a chip in a card may streamline complex transactions. The internet will revolutionise access to basic information on government services. Encryption can provide security and privacy for all parties. However, the successful implementation of these initiatives require a bold, forward looking legislative framework. Whether governments can deliver this framework will depend on their willingness to listen to the pulse of the emerging global digital economy. It will also depend on industry recognising the need for strong protection of privacy.

Privacy is seldom recognised outise Europe, either by government or the private sector. Industry continues to pursue models of self regulation that are, at best, lowest common denominator protection for consumers. Ever since personal information became a "value added" component of business, few companies have been willing to relinquish the opportunity to amass and process all manner of data.

In 1994, conscious both of the shortcomings of law, and the many differences in the level of protection in each of its States, the European Parliament passed a Europe-wide directive which will provide citizens with a wider range of protections over abuses of their data. The Data Protection Directive sets a benchmark for national law. Each EU State must pass complementary legislation by October 1998.

The Directive also imposes an obligation on member States to ensure that the personal information relating to European citizens is covered by law when it is exported to, and processed in,countries outside Europe.

This requirement has resulted in a growing pressure outside Europe for the passage of privacy law. Those countries which refuse to adopt meaningful privacy law may find themselves unable to conduct business with Europe.

The passage of the Directive highlights an interesting irony. While it is clear that privacy invasion is recognised more than ever before, it is equally true that privacy invasion has never been so substantial. And while Europe sets out to pioneer a global privacy regime, it is also setting out to create the foundations for a global surveillance society.

Earlier this year, a report commissioned by the European Parliament confiormed the existence of a network of supercomputers operated by the secretive US National Security Agency (NSA), an agency responsible for intercepting communications across the world for the benefit of American business and government.

The report "Assessing the Technologies of Political Control" commissioned by the European Parliament's Civil Liberties Committee stated "Within Europe, all email, telephone and fax communications are routinely intercepted by the United States National Security Agency, transferring all target information from the European mainland via the strategic hub of London then by satellite to Fort Meade in Maryland via the crucial hub at Menwith Hill, Yorkshire".

The report added that the NSA, in collaboration with Germany and the UK, indiscriminately intercepts electronic communications to extract valuable information using artificial intelligence systems to identify key words.

At the same time, the UK civil rights organisation Statewatch uncovered the existence of a document "Memorandum of understanding on the lawful interception of communications", signed jointly by European nations and the US, creating a global communications intercept arrangement that appears to have been agreed outside the purview of national parliaments..

The revelations have sparked activity amongst civil rights and direct action groups in some countries. The European Parliament is set to take the unprecedented step of debating the issue in plenary session on September 16.

Until recently, these and other surveillance schemes went largely unnoticed. In the past two years however, dozens of activist groups have formed loose alliances to - as one campaigner described it - "put the pieces together".

At a more mundane level, domestic surveillance and privacy invasion as falling prey to an increasingly educated public and media, who are less willing to accept "public interest" arguments in support of surveillance.

Laws for Privacy Preservation

The right of privacy is well established in international law. The core privacy principle in modern law may be found in the Universal Declaration of Human Rights. Article 12 of the UDHR states "No one shall be subjected to arbitrary interference with his privacy, family, home or correspondence, nor to attacks upon his honour and reputation. Everyone has the right to the protection of the law against such interference or attacks."

The UN Guidelines for the Regulation of Computerized Personal Data Files set out Fair Information Practices and recommend the adoption of national guidelines to protect personal privacy. Appropriately, the UN Guidelines note that a derogation from these principles may be specifically provided for when the purpose of the file is the protection of human rights and fundamental freedoms of the individual concerned or humanitarian assistance.

More generally, the protection of privacy is considered a fundamental human right, indispensable to the protection of liberty and democratic institutions. William Pfaff made this point well when he wrote recently, The defining characteristic of totalitarianism is its assault on privacy. The individual in a totalitarian state is deprived of privacy in order to destroy his or her liberty."

We are asked at the UNESCO forum to explore the ethical and legal dimension of cyberspace and to identify a set of core principles to promote democracy and empower citizens. This effort could lead to specific recommendations for UNESCO. Our specific task is to consider protection of privacy and human rights in the Digital Age. To address this challenge, it is necessary to review what we know about the protection of privacy, what we know about threats to privacy, and what we do not know about the future of privacy protection. Then we should consider the competing views of government, the private sector and citizen organizations as to how we should proceed. Finally, we must review our fundamental concerns as citizens and representatives of organizations involved with matters of human rights and outline a plan for future action. The protection of privacy is not a new subject. It has multiple dimensions and a well established history. Among its key characteristics is the recognition that privacy is a fundamental human right, that it is firmly established in law, and that Fair Information Practices provided a useful articulation of privacy principles in the information world.

Privacy as a fundamental right

Philosophers and ethicists have described privacy as indispensable characteristic of personal freedom. Privacy is associated with autonomy, dignity, spirituality, trust, and liberty. References to the value of private life may be found in the bible, the history of Periclean Athens, as well as the history and culture of many people around the world.

The American jurist Louis Brandeis described privacy as the right to be let alone and as the most fundamental of all rights cherished by a free people in a famous article on the Right to Privacy (1890). Brandeis noted that French law provided relief for invasions of private life and urged the adoption of a similar legal right in the common law countries. The right was first recognized in the United States in a 1902 case in the state of Georgia. Since that time courts in the United States and around the world have often allowed individual plaintiffs to seek legal remedies for invasions of private life.

In the realm of information technology, the right of privacy has focused on the ability of individuals to control the collection and use of personal information held by others. A German court has described this as the right of informational self-determination. This right is often articulated as fair information practices and codified in civil law.

The right of privacy is established in law

The right of privacy is well established in international and national law. Following the adoption of the

Universal Declaration of Human Rights in 1948 and article 12 which speaks directly to the issue of privacy, similar provisions were adopted in the International Covenant on Civil and Political Rights, the European Convention on Human Rights, and other regional conventions and agreements.

At the national level, most governments have a general right of privacy set out in their Constitutions. Privacy rights have also been established by means of case law and enactments of legislatures. Such laws typically seek to protect privacy in a particular context, such as laws that protect the privacy of communication by limiting the circumstances in which police may undertake wiretapping or when a merchant may sell personal data.

Interestingly, the integration of the European countries and the creation of the European Union have underscored the clear establishment of privacy as legal claim. The European Union Data Directive resulted from the need to carry forward certain legal rights even as the legal and economic arrangement among the European governments was undergoing a substantial transformation. The effort in Europe to extend legal frameworks for privacy protection has encouraged similar efforts in East Asia, North America, and Latin America. That privacy protection remains a central concern for governments on the eve of the twenty-first century is a significant indication of the importance of this fundamental human right.

Fair Information Practices

Privacy principles are often articulated as Fair

Information Practices. Fair Information Practices set out the rights of those who provide their own personally identifiable information and the responsibilities of those who collect this information.

Although there is not fixed agreement on what specific principles constitute Fair Information Practices, there is general agreement about the types of principles that are likely to be included in a set of Fair Information Practices.

These include the right of an individual to limit the collection and use of personal information, to obtain access to the information when it is collected, to inspect it and to correct it if necessary, transparency, and to have some means of accountability or enforcement to ensure that the practices will be enforced.

The responsibilities of data collectors include the obligation o maintain security of the information, to ensure that the data is accurate, complete and reliable so that inappropriate determinations about an individual are not made. Some commentators have recently proposed that Fair Information Practices also include such principles as the right to anonymity and minimization of data collection.

Fair Information Practices provide the basic structure of most privacy laws and polices found around the world. They can be seen in such general agreements as the OECD Privacy Guidelines of 1980 as well as more detailed legal code as the Subscriber Privacy provision contained in the US Cable Act of 1984. Current efforts to establish privacy protection for the Internet typically focus on the application of Fair Information Practices to Internet-based transactions.

Threats to Privacy

The threats to privacy came from multiple sources. They can be broadly classified as technologic threats, threats from actions of government, and threats from the private sector and commercial services.

Technology Threatens Privacy

In the modern era, technology has long been viewed as the source of many privacy concerns. But the relationship between technology and surveillance is not a simple one. Technology takes on certain forms and may lead to the adoption of new systems for surveillance by a process that might almost be understood as a dialectic between the purposeful creation of particular system for surveillance, the subsequent development of a means for surveillance not previously considered, and then the resulting creation of a new purposeful system for surveillance. It would be tempting to view this process as almost autonomous, but human accountability should not be ignored in any system of surveillance.

Among the key characteristics of technology in the surveillance realm are amplification, routininazation, and sublimation. Amplification refers to the ability of technology to extend the ability to gather information and intrude into private life. Examples of amplification are linked directly to the sensory abilities. A zoom lens on a camera allows a reporter to see further and record events that might not otherwise be observed.

A listening device permits a police agent to intercept and overhear a private communication. New techniques for the detection of heat behind walls make it possible for police to determine whether grow lamps are in use inside a home, possibly indicating the presence of marijuana.

Techniques for amplification invariably also capture information even beyond that the may be justified by the initial inquiry. A papparazzi's lens turned on a celebrity may capture a private or personal moment. A listening device installed by a police officer to monitor the activities of criminals may also record the conversations of innocents. The device to detect heat behind walls may detect two people making love upstairs as well as the marijuana grow lamps located downstairs

There is considerable debate about whether it is appropriate to regulate techniques of amplification. While it is true that some of these methods intrude into private life, it is also clearly the case that such technologies have beneficial applications. Regulating the technique rather than the activity inevitably raises the danger of criminalizing behavior that might otherwise be considered permissible. Thus one of the first lessons of legislating to protect privacy is the need to focus on the underlying activity and not the technology itself.

Routinization is the process of making intrusion into private life an ongoing process Here technology is used to establish a pattern or practice of surveillance. Again it is possible to conceive of both appropriate an inappropriate forms of routinized surveillance. A camera turned of a bank cashier's desk is probably an appropriate use of surveillance technology as it provides protection to both the bank and the customer in the case of a robbery or simple dispute. However, a camera placed in the changing room of a department store would be more problematic. While it could be argued that the purpose of the camera is to deter shoplifting and lessen the unnecessary costs to the merchants, customers are likely to find a camera in a changing room is simply too intrusive.

Techniques for routinization are increasingly joined with methods for recording so that a camera trained on a street corner now routinely records all activities that are viewed and a phone line for a service representative routinely records all conversations with customers. We are still in the early stages of incorporating new techniques in the realm of routinized surveillance, but it should be anticipated that the next stage in theses systems will be the adoption of methods for processing information so that it would be possible for the camera in a airport to view the facial profiles of passengers in a terminal, compare these images with a massive database of facial profiles, and determine in virtually real-time the actual identity of individuals in the terminal.

Sublimation is the means by which a technique for privacy invasion becomes increasingly difficult to detect. Hidden cameras, listening devices and similar data gathering techniques are particularly problematic because there is little opportunity for the data subject to escape detection and frequently little opportunity in the political realm to challenge the desirability of such techniques. Illegal wire surveillance by law enforcement agencies is a long-standing privacy concern in part because it is so difficult to detect, to assess, and to challenge. One legislative approach that has been adopted to address this problem

While technology is not required for an invasion of privacy, the ability of techniques to amplify, routinize and sublimate surveillance has traditionally raised some of the greatest privacy concerns.

Governments Threaten Privacy

Many of the most serious threats to privacy come from government. In the most extreme form, when a government arrests and imprisons a person it has denied the individual the dignity of privacy almost absolutely. Government can also diminish privacy through schemes for compelled identification, drug testing, physical searches of one's home or person, database profiling, genetic testing, and polygraph examinations to name just a few.

Government threats to privacy are particularly problematic because once established, citizens have little choice but to comply. There are no alternatives to a requirement for national identity, or drug testing as a condition for public employment.

Those actions by government that have provoked the most outrage oftentimes involve proposals for national identity, census enumeration, and recently proposals to regulate the use of privacy enhancing techniques such as encryption.

Transparency, which is a laudable goal for the functioning of democratic society, takes on a different meaning in the context of government surveillance. Governments often seek a transparent citizenry, a populis whose actions are readily identifiable and easily monitored.

Corporations Threaten Privacy

Corporations threaten privacy in a variety of means. In the workplace, corporations seek to exert greater control over workers through a variety of monitoring and surveillance practices. Such practices include the monitoring of telephone calls and computer use, the video surveillance of change rooms and bathrooms, drug testing, and polygraphs.

More generally, corporations threaten privacy in the marketplace through the extraction of commercial value from consumers in their personally identified transactions. It is no longer sufficient for customers to offer payment for goods and services.

They must now also provide personal details that can then be used by companies for subsequent purposes. Some requests are necessary and appropriate for a particular transaction. For example, a person who wishes an item to be shipped to his or her home should expect to provide a home mailing address. In many more data collections are unrelated to a particular purpose.

This process of extracting commercial value in the marketplace might be called the "commodification of identity." Efforts to limit this process focus on either regulatory restrictions on the collection of information or technical means to promote commercial transactions that do not require the disclosure of personally identifiable information.

In summary, the danger with corporation is the emergent of the "transparent worker" or the "transparent consumer," individuals who because of their economic relations with private corporations are compelled to disclose aspects of their personal lives they might otherwise choose to keep private. Transparency in this relation, as in the relation with government in the context of surveillance, is one-sided. It is not the transparency of a window, but that of a one-way mirror.

There is certainly a strong case that the Internet will usher a new era of massive, routinized surveillance. It is possible with the current protocols for Internet communication to record virtually every activity of an Internet user, the information he receives, the people he communicates with, his preferences and his predilections. Such extensive data collection is far more instrusive than was possible in the previous era of broadcast communication or in typical commercial relations. In the broadcast era, recipients of information were largely anonymous. In typical commercial relations, information is typically obtained only once a purchase occurs.

There are also strong commercial incentives on the Internet to reduce privacy. Many of the current business models are based on concept of "personalization" and "one-to-one marketing" that require far more knowledge about individual preferences and buying habits than was previously available in a mass market commercial environment. Many web sites today offer to "personalize" their display for users or ask extensive questions about a users interest before any commercial relationship has been established.

The technical methods of Internet come together with the personalization marketing goals in the implementation of such protocols as "cookies," which allow the tracking of users across various web sites and the targeting of commercial advertising. Elaborate "ad servers" crate customized advertising on a web site for a particular user based on what is known about the user from other web sites he or she has visited. These techniques threaten to make real that what is viewed on a computer screen in one's home could be known to almost anyone around the world.

Still, it can not be ignored that the Internet provides a platform for new forms of communication and interaction that can literally builds in privacy safeguards. The use of encryption techniques in browser software, for example, permits the transfer of credit card numbers and other personally identifiable information in a secure manner. Anonymous payment techniques would allow commerce without the disclosure of personally identifiable information. Anonymous remailers make possible the sending of messages without requiring the disclosure of the sender's identity.

Whether these new techniques for privacy will get the upper hand in the on-line world remains to be seen. There are government objections to these techniques as well as strong commercial incentives to minimize anonymous activity. But for the first time it is possible to conceive of a technological environment that properly designed could provide new levels of privacy protection

One of the great challenges to privacy protection is only partially technical in nature. The growth of the Internet has coincided with the increased globalization of world trade, the rise of the European Union, the diminished ability of central banks to control currency markets, and even the question of whether individual nation states can effectively exercise their sovereign authority.

In this environment, it has become a commonplace to simply assert that national governments will be unable to exercise any legal control over the Internet and also that current law is unlikely to have much of an impact in this digital world. But this view is wrong in at least two respects. First, governments do in fact exercise a great deal of control regardless of what the "cyber-intelligentsia" claim. Internet disputes are resolved in real courts and computer criminals are thrown in real jails.

Second, as the Internet has become more commercial and more mainstream, the reliance on traditional legal institutions has increased not diminished. There are no formal methods for adjudication in cyberspace and thus governments and private parties have turned naturally to traditional means for dispute resolution and the prosecution of harmful acts.

Third, and perhaps most significantly, governments have found that where there are interests that should be protected, collective action can be taken at the supranational level to protect these interests. Thus, for example, national governments particularly the United States, have moved aggressively to establish international agreement to protect copyright in the digital environment.

The World Intellectual Property Organization, the World Trade Organization, the Berne Convention all reflect the ability of national governments to act collectively to protect interests that may be impaired by the emergence of digital networks or the increase in global trade.

In many respects, privacy protection anticipates the problem of protection across national borders. Indeed, the OECD Privacy Guidelines were a direct response to questions about privacy and transborder dataflows. Further, the Data Directive of the European Union is a clear attempt to harmonize protection across national borders. While it is not clear if national legal norms will survive this process of globalization, it is clear that a good foundation has already been put in place.

For much of the history of privacy law, the relationship between law and technology was understood as a simple equation: technology creates the risk to privacy, it is the role of law to protect privacy against this incursion of technology. Thus privacy law has been established to control the use of personal information collected by means of computerized databases, private conversations overhead though telephone networks.

Although it has sometimes been said that technology outpaces the law, raising the question of whether law can operate effectively in a technological environment, it should be noted that legal standards based on fair information practices, rather than the regulation of particular technique, have actually withstood the test of time fairly well. Thus the US Privacy Act of 1974 is still operational a quarter of a century later and he OECD Guidelines of 1980 continue to exert enormous influence on the shaping of privacy practices almost two decades after their adoption. Thus the current discussion regarding concerning the OECD Guidelines is not about updating or revising the principles, but rather applying the principles in the new information environment.

Still, given the opportunity that the Internet provides for new technical solutions for privacy protections, it is worth considering how such methods might be developed and adopted.

The limitations of law have renewed the focus on technical methods to protect privacy. But it remains unclear whether technology to provide a comprehensive solution. It is necessary in the first instance to distinguish between genuine technical means to protect privacy and those technical means that in fact promote collection of personally identifiable information. Privacy Enhancing

Technologies (PET) are generally understood as those that limit or eliminate the collection of personally identifiable information.

Such methods include techniques for anonymous and pseudo-anonymous payment, communication, and web access. By limiting the collection of personal information, these approaches enable transactions avoid the creation of personal information. By analogy to the environmental context, this would be much like the design of an engine that generated no pollutants

Privacy Extracting Techniques (~PET) typically create a technological framework that facilitates the disclosure of personal information, often without any assurance of protection or legal safeguards. These techniques which are often confused with true PETs are put forward by commercial firms and others as a "technical solution" to privacy when in fact they are designed to make it easier to obtain personal data.

Whether new technology can protect privacy will thus depend on several factors, including the progress in the development of these techniques, their acceptance by consumers and others, and the ability to discern actual methods for privacy protection from those that are likely to further erode privacy protection. A variety of arguments are put forward about how to address these new privacy challenges.

The private sector argues that market systems and new technology provide new opportunities to protect privacy that do not require regulation or the rule of law. They believe that it is possible to use contract-based interactions to negotiate privacy preferences. These preferences, they believe, will vary from individual to individual and circumstance to circumstance.

Techniques to implement this approach include P3P, the Platform for Privacy Preferences. P3P is a technical standard that allows a web client or user to articulate a privacy preference and a web server to specify the level of privacy that will be respected. When a client contact a servers a negotiation takes place between the two rule sets. If the clients privacy preferences will be accommodates by the server, then the session will begin. If the client's privacy preferences will not be accommodated by the server, then the client can decide whether to continue.

A related approach is trust labels, which provide a visible image on a web page that is linked to a privacy policy. There is no assurance with the seal that any particular privacy policy will be implemented, but the seal does provide a readily identifiable link to a company's privacy policy. An example of this program is Truste. There is also an effort underway among the Better Business Bureau in the USA, the European Commission, and the Japanese government to develop new privacy labels for the Internet.

There are many problems with the so-called "self-regulatory " approach to privacy protection. Fundamentally the initiatives eliminate any baseline requirement for privacy protection and eviscerate currently establish privacy rights and norms. One of the consequences of the contract approach is to exclude from certain activities individuals who express high or even moderate privacy preferences. Thus the problem of discrimination against those who wish to exercise a privacy right emerges. Privacy laws, which generally recognize a principle of fair or lawful obtaining of personal information, would generally not permit such an open-ended negotiation.

There is also the interesting question of whether negotiating privacy relations is actually efficient as the economic argument presumes. Consider the application of a negotiated privacy protection to the current regime of telephone communication. Such an approach would require individuals to consider at the time of each call how much privacy they desire and then determine whether the recipient of the communication, or for that matter, the communication carrier, will respect the individual's privacy preference. On first pass, a call to a doctor may require a high privacy preference. A conversation with a friend may require a moderate privacy, while a call to a merchant may be only a low privacy need. What if the call to the doctor is only to confirm the time of a previously schedule appointment, while the call to a merchant is to purchase a surprised gift for a family member.

Such a negotiation over privacy preferences in routine telephone communications would certainly introduce new transaction costs. Moreover, it would tend to squeeze out the high level of protection that all telephone users currently enjoy for telephone calls of all purposes. Serious doubts remain about the Private Sector claim that privacy can be adequately protected by self-regulatory means. Moreover, the self-regulatory approach is likely to result in a substantial reduction in the protection of privacy.

The government often emphasizes the benefits of new technology to protect public safety and to promote efficient administration. One of the most problematic recent debates concerns the use of CCTV. The government argument is that these cameras placed on street corners reduce the incidence of crime by subjecting individuals to ongoing surveillance. Governments have also proposed means of national identity to promote the efficient administration of services

In the development of these new means for monitoring the activity of citizens, government might acknowledge a privacy concern but are unlikely to allow a privacy to substantially change or preempt the development of such systems. Privacy is sometimes accommodated so as to legitimate a new system for social surveillance.

Citizen groups argue that our primary concern should be to extend fundamental legal norms to the new digital world. The Global Internet Liberty Campaign, a coalition of more than 50 NGOS in 20 countries, took action on the question of the citizens right to use cryptography and other technical methods to protect personal privacy when the subect was under consideration by the Organization for Economic Cooperation and Development in 1996.

The matter of government efforts to regulate the use of encryption was already a controversial matter, particularly among users of the Internet. A noted cryptographer Phil Zimmerman faced prosecution in the United States for the alleged distribution of cryptographic techniques, that were then considered by US export regulation to be a munition requiring license. Internet organizations had organized campaigns against the prosecution of Zimmerman and the restrictions on the use of encryption. These campaigns invariably emphasized the excesses of government control in this area. But it was the GILC that first clearly articulated the basis for this claim as a matter of international legal norms. The organization issued a Resolution in Support of the Freedom to Use Cryptography in Paris that stated at the outset that "the use of cryptography implicates human rights and matters of personal liberty that affect individuals around the world," and further that "the privacy of communication is explicitly protected by Article 12 of the Universal Declaration of Human Rights, Article 17 of the International Covenant on Civil and Political Rights, and national law." On the basis of these norms, the GILC urged the Organization for Economic Cooperation and Development base its cryptography policies on the fundamental right of citizens to engage in private communication

The Cryptography Guidelines of the OECD included a principle on Protection of Privacy and Personal Data that stated "The fundamental rights of individual to privacy, including secrecy of communications and protection of personal data, should be respected in national cryptography policies and the implementation and use of cryptographic methods."

Faced with theses new challenges to privacy, and these competing views of how best to protect privacy, how should we proceed? If we were primarily concerned with the economic benefits of our actions, we might ask which course would provide the most short-term commercial gain. But as our focus is principles of human rights and the realization of the citizen in the Information Society as full participant with meaningful claims in the political world, we should take a different approach.

First, we should accept the premise that law has a fundamental role in the protection of human rights and democratic institutions. While is an imperfect instrument, it also establishes the principle that all people in all countries of the world, regardless of wealth or social status, are entitled to certain essential freedoms and one of these freedoms is the protection of private life. Law not only imbues citizens with the rights that are necessary for self-governance it also provides the legitimacy that allow others to rely on a legal system for redress.

Second, we should not adopt a view of technology that it is autonomous or stands apart from the actions of specific individuals or institutions. As Thomas Edison said, "What man creates with his hand, he should control with his head." We should call for accountability for those who develop systems of surveillance while at the same exercising our own responsibility to engage the political process to seek technical methods that advance the aims of privacy protection.

In the end, we must side with the interests of the citizen. Neither governments nor corporations are in much need of political assistance these days. Both can take care of their interests with great efficiency. But citizens and citizen organization must continue to engage the political process if the rights of the individual are to be preserved in the online world.

We have learned in recent years that privacy is more than a subject for debate among academics. It is a matter of personal concern that has often resulted in direct political action. Citizens in Australia have taken to the streets to protest a national identity card. In Germany, the population objected to a national census. In the United States, users of the Internet expressed their opposition to efforts by the government to limit the availability of strong techniques to protect personal privacy. Currently, the members of the Global Internet Liberty Campaign are organizing in more than thirty countries to end the treatment of encryption as a munition so that it could be more widely available to protect the privacy of citizens. The protection of privacy is increasingly a call for political action.

There is a tendency in all discussions of cyberspace to imagine that our society has gone directly from the era of the horse-drawn cart to the age of space exploration with hardly a step in between. But of course, the history of communications technology is filled with many stages at which time issues such as technological change, internationalization, the role of law and technical standards are considered. The protection of privacy is one of the issues that has been previously considered in the development of new technology, and it would be wise to recognize and understand the previous efforts to address this issue.

Article 12 of the Universal Declaration of Human Rights, the OECD Guidelines, the UN Convention, and other similar documents are all still relevant to the current effort to preserve privacy in the information society. Indeed, these documents may provide the best, most well informed consideration to date of how best to protect this fundamental human right in light of technological change. Thus the starting point for an international effort to protect privacy in our new online world should be to reaffirm support for international instruments on privacy protection.

A second effort to be to assert the applicability of legal norms across national borders. Although it may be fashionable to speak about the Internet as a "regulation-free zone," in fact there is plenty of regulation for the Internet, except not enough to protect the privacy of its inhabitants. Users of the Internet have at least as much right to claim a legal right to protect their personality as authors and holders of copyright have to claim a legal right in their artistic works. The creation of the borderless cyberspace has not slowed the call for the adoption of new laws to protect digital works; it should not slow the effort to adopt new safeguards for the digital persona.

The protection of privacy across national borders benefits in particular from the establishment of international legal norms, such as Article 12 of the Universal Declaration of Human Rights, as well as previous efforts to promote the transborder flow of information while respecting the privacy of the individual as was the aim of the OECD Guidelines of 1980. It would be a grave mistake for UNESCO and the human rights community generally to turn its back on these well established legal norms and leave the protection of privacy to the cold logic of the marketplace and the technical methods that are intended to promote the disclosure of greater amounts of personal data.

While we should not lessen our efforts to ensure the effective application of privacy rights across national borders, we should also not ignore the possibility that technology may provide some solutions to the protection of privacy. But here we should be careful to distinguish between means that in fact protect privacy and those that merely appear to.

In the first instance, the best form of privacy protection by technological means is that which ensures anonymous transactions. Anonymity is the ideal privacy technology because it avoids the creation and collection of personally identifiable information. Anonymity exists by custom and practice in many contexts today. Travel, communication, commerce, as well as the receipt of information typically occur with a high degree of anonymity, at least to the extent to the actual identify is rarely known for the person on the sidewalk, the fellow at the payphone, the woman who purchases lunch, the reader of a magazine or the viewer of a television program.

Techniques for anonymity should be robust, trustworthy, and simple to implement in routine commercial transactions. All reasonable efforts should be made to promote the development and adoption of techniques for anonymity and related approaches for the protection of actual identity. This defense of anonymity is not intended to promote the life of the hermit or to discourage social relations. Quite the opposite. A strong right of anonymity gives individuals the opportunity to freely choose with whom to share aspects of personality and to form bonds of trust.

Anonymity is not a description of a static state. It is a rather the starting point for a dynamic, evolving series of social relations that derive their authenticity and value from the opportunity for each individual to choose his or her friends, colleagues, neighbors and lovers.

In the second instance, the next best form of privacy protection by technological means is that which ensures the application and enforcement of Fair Information Practices. For example, techniques that allow individuals to limit the use of data, to gain access to their own data, and to make corrections where appropriate should be encouraged as they seek to establish by technical means those rights and responsibilities that would otherwise be accomplished in law.

The least desirable means to protect privacy by technology are those proposals that encourage individuals to enter into negotiation with the purpose of obtaining consent for the collection and use of personal data. Such techniques have no independent privacy component and simply offer a framework for market-based transaction over privacy claims. Such techniques may be appropriate for the purchase of soap or shoes but they are hardly compatible with the protection of fundamental human rights that are well established in law.

It important to emphasize the procedural consideration that should guide the development of all law and policy concerning the development of the Information Society and that is the active and meaningful participation of citizens in the decision-making process. Such interests are invariably underrepresented in decisions taken by national and international governing borders. No group has a greater stake in the protection of privacy than the new inhabitants of cyberspace. Let us enjoy the benefits of the future while preserving the freedoms of our past.

5

Protecting Information Privacy

The ongoing worldwide revolution in communications technology is fundamentally changing the way people conduct their business and private lives. These changes are producing challenges for both privacy and law enforcement interests, stretching the limits of existing legal rules. Striking the proper balance between privacy and law enforcement in the electronic realm has always been a complex endeavor. Changes in communications technology have required periodic reexamination of privacy protections and law enforcement capabilities. It is time again for such a review.

There are broad grounds for concern that modern systems of communication are not private. Despite the convenience and the widespread popularity of cellular and other wireless telephones, they are notoriously insecure. The open, networked nature of the Internet, while the source of its power as a medium, also makes it uniquely vulnerable. Electronic communications systems generate vast quantities of transactional data that can be readily collected and analyzed. The globalization of communications infrastructures threatens to turn the Bill of Rights into a local ordinance.

Meanwhile, law enforcement agencies, particularly at the federal level, are putting increasing emphasis on electronic surveillance. The use of year-long wiretaps on multiple individuals in the "Pizza Connection" drug trafficking case, the "Ill Wind" defense procurement fraud investigation, and the "Operation Polar Cap" money laundering investigation is seen as representing the future of law enforcement. Louis Freeh, Director of the Federal Bureau of Investigation (FBI), has called wiretapping "one of law enforcement's most valuable investigative techniques." Freeh argues that wiretapping is crucial to the investigation of cases involving terrorism, espionage, organized crime, drug trafficking, public corruption, and violent crime. Without this technique, Freeh has testified, "law enforcement at the Federal, State, and local levels will be crippled." Not surprisingly, therefore, a number of public policy debates in recent years have centered around law enforcement proposals to preserve or expand government surveillance capabilities in light of technological developments.

This chapter addresses the privacy issues raised by new communications and computer technologies and the needs of law enforcement. The tremendous scientific and technological developments that have taken place in the last century have made possible today the widespread use and abuse of electronic surveillance techniques. Both proponents and opponents of wiretapping and electronic surveillance agree that the present state of the law in this area is extremely unsatisfactory and that the Congress should act to clarify the resulting confusion.

The Legal Framework

In important ways, electronic surveillance has always posed greater threats to privacy than the physical searches and seizures that the Fourth Amendment was originally intended to cover. To begin with, "electronic surveillance is almost inherently indiscriminate." Interception of a telephone line provides to law enforcement all of the target's communications, whether they are relevant to the investigation or not, raising concerns about compliance with the particularity requirement in the Fourth Amendment and posing the risk of general searches. In addition, electronic surveillance involves an on-going intrusion in a protected sphere, unlike the traditional search warrant, which authorizes only one intrusion, not a series of searches or a continuous surveillance. Officers must execute a traditional search warrant with dispatch, not over a prolonged period of time. If they do not find what they were looking for in a home or office, they must leave promptly and obtain a separate order if they wish to return to search again. Electronic surveillance, in contrast, continues around-the-clock for days or months. Finally, the usefulness of electronic surveillance depends on lack of notice to the suspect. In the execution of the traditional search warrant, an announcement of authority and purpose ("knock and notice") is considered essential so that the person whose privacy is being invaded can observe any violation in the scope or conduct of the search and immediately seek a judicial order to halt or remedy any violations. In contrast, wiretapping is conducted surreptitiously.

In 1967, in the landmark Berger and Katz cases, the Supreme Court ruled that electronic surveillance was a search and seizure covered by the privacy protections of the Fourth Amendment. In Berger, the Court condemned lengthy, continuous or indiscriminate electronic surveillances, but in Katz, the Court indicated that a short surveillance, narrowly focused on interception of a few conversations, was constitutionally acceptable if approved by a judge in advance and based on a special showing of need.

Responding to the Supreme Court's Berger and Katz opinions and to the arguments of law enforcement that wiretapping was a vital weapon in the efforts against organized crime, Congress, in 1968, authorized law enforcement wiretapping under a system of protections intended to compensate for the uniquely intrusive aspects of electronic surveillance. According to the Senate report, the legislation had "as its dual purpose (1) protecting the privacy of wire and oral communications and (2) delineating on a uniform basis the circumstances and conditions under which the interception of wire and oral communications may be authorized." The wiretap provisions were enacted as Title III of the Omnibus Crime Control and Safe Streets Act of 1968, so the federal wiretap law is still referred to sometimes as "Title III."

In brief, the legislation Congress enacted in 1968 had the following components: the content of wire communications could be seized by the government in criminal cases pursuant to a court order issued upon a finding of probable cause; wiretapping would be otherwise outlawed; wiretapping would be permitted only for specified crimes; it would be authorized only as a last resort, when other investigative techniques would not work; surveillance would be carried out in such a way as to "minimize" the interception of innocent conversations; notice would be provided after the investigation had been concluded; and there would be an opportunity prior to introduction of the evidence at any trial for an adversarial challenge to both the adequacy of the probable cause and the conduct of the wiretap. "Minimization" was deemed essential to satisfy the Fourth Amendment's particularity requirement, compensating for the fact that law enforcement was receiving all of the target's communications, including those that were not evidence of a crime. The showing of a special need, in the form of a lack of other reasonable means to obtain the information, was viewed as justification for the failure to provide advance or contemporaneous notice of the search.

In 1978, Congress regulated wiretapping in national security cases through another statute, the Foreign Intelligence Surveillance Act (FISA). This law authorizes the government to carry out electronic surveillance in the United States upon obtaining a judicial order (from one of a panel of Article III judges designated by the Chief Justice) based upon a probable cause finding that the target is a foreign power or an agent of a foreign power. FISA was intended to be used primarily in foreign intelligence and counter-intelligence cases and therefore did not offer some of the protections required under Title III. Most significantly, FISA does not require that the target ever be given notice of the surveillance, even after the investigation is closed, unless the government seeks to use the results in a criminal prosecution. In addition, for individuals who are not U.S. citizens or permanent resident aliens, the statute does not require probable cause to believe that the target is engaged in criminal conduct. Rather, it is enough that the target is an agent of a foreign power. Even for U.S. citizens, the statute allows surveillance where there is probable cause to believe that the person is engaged in clandestine intelligence activities on behalf of a foreign power, "which activities involve or may involve a violation of the criminal statutes of the United States."

A third major piece of legislation regulating electronic surveillance was enacted in 1986, when Congress made an initial response to the emergence of wireless services and the digital era with the adoption of the Electronic Communications Privacy Act (ECPA). Title III had been limited to voice communications, whether face-to-face or over a wire. ECPA extended Title III to include wireless voice communications and electronic communications of a non-voice nature, such as e-mail or other computer-to-computer transmissions. ECPA was intended to reestablish the balance between privacy and law enforcement, which Congress found had been upset, to the detriment of privacy, by the development of communications and computer technology and changes in the structure of the telecommunications industry. Among the developments noted by Congress were "large-scale electronic mail operations, cellular and cordless phones, paging devices, miniaturized transmitters for radio surveillance, and a dazzling array of digitized networks." Privacy, Congress concluded, was in danger of being gradually eroded as technology advanced.

In addition to the twin goals of privacy and law enforcement, ECPA sought to advance a third goal: supporting the development and use of these new technologies and services. Congress affirmatively wanted to encourage the proliferation of new communications technologies, but it recognized that consumers would not trust new technologies if the privacy of those using them was not protected.

ECPA made it a crime to knowingly intercept wireless communications and e-mail, but authorized law enforcement to do so with a warrant issued on probable cause. In ECPA, Congress also began to recognize the privacy implications of transactional data generated by communications systems.

ECPA established rules for the use of pen registers, which capture numbers identifying outgoing calls, and for trap and trace devices, which capture numbers identifying incoming calls. In addition, it set rules for law enforcement access to information identifying a subscriber of an electronic communications service. ECPA also eased certain procedural requirements for interception of wire communications by federal law enforcement officers.

When law enforcement officials discuss wiretapping today, they often hasten to emphasize how stringent are the privacy protections of the legal framework established between 1968 and 1986: that wiretaps are available only for the most serious cases; that authorization to conduct a tap is sought only when all other investigative techniques have failed; that applications are subject to rigorous judicial scrutiny; that wiretaps are conducted in such a manner as to minimize the interception of innocent conversations; and that parties whose conversations are intercepted are entitled to obtain after-the-fact judicial review of the authorization and conduct of wiretaps. Law enforcement officials cite these protections as a way of reassuring legislators and the public that the intrusiveness of electronic surveillance is well regulated.

There is substantial evidence, however, technological developments aside, that the protections initially established in 1968 and reaffirmed in 1986 are not working as intended. It appears increasingly apparent that components of the balanced legislative scheme have been watered down by Congress itself and by the judiciary:

(1) Wiretapping is no longer confined to violent and major crimes. Although Congress recognized in 1968 that wiretapping was an extraordinary technique that should be used only for especially serious crimes, the list of offenses for which wiretapping is permitted has been expanded steadily ever since -- from the original 26 in 1968 to 95 in 1996. The original list was largely limited to espionage and treason, violent crimes, and offenses typically associated with organized crime. The current list has been so expanded that wiretapping is now authorized for cases involving false statements on passport applications and loan applications or involving "any depredation" against any property of the United States. Further expansions are promoted in response to each new law enforcement concern that receives legislative attention. Wiretapping is used only rarely in cases involving homicide, kidnapping, or terrorism. In 1996, 71% of wiretaps nationwide were in drug cases.

(2) The yearly number of federal, state and local law enforcement wiretaps has gone up steadily, from 564 in 1980 to 1,149 in 1996. Wiretaps increased 9% in 1996 alone. Judges rarely deny wiretap applications. In 1996, only one wiretap application was denied; 1,149 were approved. For seven years in a row, 1989 through 1995, no judge, state or federal, denied a

single government request for wiretapping. In that period, judges approved 6,598 wiretap orders in criminal cases. There has been equally dramatic growth in the use of pen registers and trap and trace devices. In 1995, the law enforcement agencies of the federal Justice Department alone executed 3,414 pen register orders covering the telephone facilities of 7,899 persons and 1,558 trap and trace orders affecting the telephones of 3,902 persons. No judge has ever been known to deny an application for a pen register or trap and trace device, because the law states that a judge must approve any application signed by an Assistant United States Attorney (or higher-ranking government attorney) who certifies that the information likely to be obtained is relevant to an ongoing criminal investigation.

(3) While Katz indicated approval of wiretaps of short duration, the longest wiretap in 1996 lasted 420 days. The average length of intercepts has increased steadily, from an average of 21 days in 1980, to an average of 38 days in 1996. The average number of calls intercepted per wiretap has also increased steadily, from 1,058 per intercept in 1980 to 1,969 in 1996.

(4) The courts authorize electronic surveillance even when law enforcement agencies have not exhausted all other reasonably available techniques. In United States v. Garcia, for example, the Eighth Circuit held that electronic surveillance approval does not require the exhaustion of all normal investigative techniques. Representative of the judicial attitude is the conclusion of one court that the purpose of the statutory exhaustion requirement is "simply to inform the issuing judge of the difficulties involved in the use of conventional techniques."

(5) The minimization requirement also has not been strictly enforced by the judiciary. In Scott v. United States, the Supreme Court held that the complete recording of all conversations on a phone line belonging to the woman with whom the subject of the order was living was acceptable. Law enforcement agents in that case had made essentially no efforts to minimize the interception of nonpertinent calls, despite the high proportion of calls on the line that were nonpertinent. The Court justified this pattern of recording on the ground that the subject often used coded language in very brief conversations. In Scott, 40% of the conversations intercepted were relevant, but the lower courts have read the case as effectively eliminating the requirement to minimize the recording of innocent conversations. Scott's impact is illustrated by United States v. Ozar, where the Eighth Circuit upheld the "two minutes up/one minute down" technique recommended by the Justice Department, in which FBI agents listened to two out of every three minutes of every phone conversation. In Ozar, the government intercepted a total of 8,126 minutes of the defendant's telephone conversations, of which 223 minutes, or 2.75% were deemed pertinent to the ensuing charges. The Court of Appeals held that this was not a violation of Title III, not because the conversations were short and coded, as in Scott, but because they were lengthy and complicated.

(6) Defendants' after-the-fact challenges to the authorization or conduct of surveillance are rarely sustained. Between 1985 and 1994, judges nationwide granted 138 suppression motions while denying 3,060, for a 4.3% suppression rate.

(7) The FISA court in its entire seventeen-year history has never turned down a government electronic surveillance request. Little is known publicly about these taps, but the Justice Department has released figures showing that in 1996, the FISA court issued a record 839 orders, up 20% from the prior year.

Meanwhile, FISA has been used increasingly in criminal cases, for which it was not designed. The government does this by claiming that it is conducting parallel intelligence and criminal investigations and proceeds under the more flexible FISA standards. In another very troubling development, Congress recently authorized the use of FISA evidence in secret deportation proceedings, allowing the evidence to be introduced without disclosure to the respondent, thereby dispensing with one of the statute's key procedural protections.

Enhancements in Government Surveillance

In the long term, digital telephone technology will enhance the FBI's ability to collect, share and analyze information. Many of these enhancements will come without any FBI development effort, driven by consumer demand. In many ways, it is clear that this 1991 prediction by the FBI is coming true. While Section IV examines Congress' response to FBI concerns that new technology is making electronic surveillance harder, there are other ways in which new communications and computer technologies provide substantial advantages to law enforcement.

Wireless Services. In a host of circumstances where, in the past, persons would have used pay phones or not made a call at all, they now use cellular or other wireless phones, which are readily tapped at central switches. (It is normally far easier to identify a target's wireless service provider than it was to predict which pay phone he or she would use.)

Proportionately more wireless phones are tapped by law enforcement than traditional wireline phones. Indeed, law enforcement has been so quick to utilize this capability that in some urban areas cellular companies had been unable to accommodate simultaneously all of the law enforcement agencies seeking to tap cellular phones from mobile telephone switching offices, and therefore had to install additional capacity.

Location information. In the course of processing calls, many wireless communications systems collect information about the cell site (or the sector within a cell site) of the person making or receiving a call. Systems may even locate a cellular phone merely while it is turned on, even if it is not handling a call. The technology is proceeding in the direction of providing more precise location information, a trend that has been boosted by the rulings of the Federal Communications Commission in its "E-911" (enhanced 911) proceeding, which requires service providers to develop a locator capability for medical emergency and rescue purposes.

Wireless phone location information can be obtained by law enforcement. If it is a record collected and stored as part of the billing process, it can be obtained under current law by a mere subpoena. In 1994, three of the four manufacturers of cellular switches had developed the software capability to deliver location information to law enforcement immediately upon call completion.

E-mail and other on-line communications. E-mail is in some respects easier to intercept than regular mail. Indeed, since e-mail messages are often stored with a service provider for a period of time before they are read by the intended recipient (and even sometimes after they are read), e-mail is less transient than telephone calls and thus more vulnerable to interception. Law enforcement can intercept a person's e-mail and other Internet activity in real time, by monitoring the phone line that serves as most people's connection to the Net. This allows law enforcement, when it chooses to do so, to obtain an extraordinary window into a person's life. More readily, e-mail messages can be obtained from the host computer of the service provider. This is the method most commonly used by law enforcement to access e-mail. In this way, e- mail interception is easier than telephone interception: while a person might have one telephone number at home, a different number at work, and another when traveling on business or vacation, most people have only one e-mail address to which all their e-mail is sent, and where it is all subject to being accessed by the government.

Remote monitoring. Technology has freed law enforcement intercepts of the constraints of geography. Agents monitoring wiretaps do not have to sit hunched in vans outside the target's house. Instead, the intercepted communications can be transported hundreds or thousands of miles to a monitoring facility at a law enforcement office. It is now common in investigations spanning multiple jurisdictions to establish a single monitoring plant and transmit there in real time all intercepted conversations to be monitored, minimized, and recorded. The courts have held that a single federal judge can issue wiretap orders for telephones anywhere in the country, so long as the personnel listening to the conversations work in the judge's jurisdiction. The Drug Enforcement Agency forwards intercepts from many different investigations to a central facility in Utah, where they are transcribed and translated by military personnel.

Computer analysis. Law enforcement has recognized the informational richness of signaling and transactional information. Computer analysis is key to law enforcement exploitation of this data. Computers have made it possible for law enforcement agencies to analyze vast amounts of information about personal communications patterns far more easily.

Pen registers, which recorded the numbers dialed on a particular phone line, have been superseded by multiline dialed number recorders, and these, in turn, have been computerized, allowing agencies to automatically search for revealing patterns of calls. The DEA has developed an integrated system called TOLLS that will electronically load telephone call data from dialed number recorders into a mainframe system for matching and analysis.

Further computer analytic developments may be around the corner. Voice recognition technology, for example, would free law enforcement from the most labor intensive aspects of monitoring conversations, removing one of the biggest practical constraints on the number of interceptions made.

Telecommunications, of course, did not stand still after 1986. Indeed, the pace of change in technology and in the structure of the telecommunications industry accelerated and continues to accelerate. Behind the individual enhancements to surveillance capabilities identified above are five broad technological developments that profoundly challenge the assumptions made by Congress in 1968 when it first established the rules for electronic surveillance, and in 1986 when it reaffirmed those assumptions:

1) The dramatic development of the Internet has transformed all over again methods of gathering, processing and sharing of information, which had already been transformed by the computer itself. In 1981, fewer than 300 computers were linked to the Internet. In 1986, when ECPA was enacted, there were about 50,000. By June 1996, there were over 9.4 million host computers worldwide linked to the Internet, including users who connect to the Internet via modem. Some 40 million people worldwide can access the Internet. In commercial terms, networking has had enormous implications. The average number of electronic point-of-sale transactions in the United States went from 38 per day in 1985 to 1.2 million per day in 1993. Estimates for the potential of "Internet commerce" range up to "tens of billions of dollars by the turn of the century."

   The Internet is not like the telephone system, or the mail, or mass media. Rather, the Internet combines a much broader range of functions, serving not only the one-on-one functions of the telephone and the mail, but also the information functions of TV, newspapers and the library; the artistic functions of a movie theater and a museum; the political functions of a town meeting hall; the marketing and shopping functions of a mall; the organizing functions of door-to-door canvassing; and the social, even romantic functions of a nightclub or coffee house. As an intentionally open system of linked computers, the

Internet is inherently insecure. The dramatic development of the Internet as a networked global communications medium and the expansion in the range of transactions that occur on-line have produced a qualitative change in the nature of communications and, accordingly, in the nature and amount of the information that is exposed to both lawful interception and illegal intrusion or misuse.

2) Signaling information has become an increasingly rich source of information about habits of association and commerce. Congress in 1968 and again in 1986 assumed that there were two categories of data: content (which would receive the highest protection) and a category of minimally revealing dialing or routing information. However, in recent years, transactional data has evolved into a third, hybrid type, providing detailed information about a person's habits of association and commerce. Yet this "profiling" data was totally unprotected until 1986 and has since been subject only to the most minimal protection. On the Internet, this data gives a rich picture of a person's life. In a similar development in the area of voice communications, advanced signaling systems have also blurred the distinction between call-identifying information and call content. There is some concern that the development of packet switching may obliterate the distinction between signaling data and communications content. In some cellular and other wireless telephone systems, this signaling data includes location information, potentially turning wireless phones into tracking devices. Law enforcement is increasingly turning to transactional or signaling data as a source of investigative importance.

3) The rapid expansion of wireless services, which are increasingly used not just by the wealthy and in business applications, but by ordinary citizens for personal conversations, has made electronic communication almost totally flexible and constantly available, yet also more insecure. The number of wireless customers has gone from 92,000 in 1984 to 44 million by the end of 1996. Moreover, wireless transmission is no longer important only for voice communication, but is becoming increasingly important for data transfer. Wireless modems and wireless local area networks are linking computers and transferring data that could include proprietary information, medical records, and financial data. Wireless links are increasingly serving as gateways to the global information infrastructure. While offering attractive advantages of flexibility, wireless communications are less secure than traditional landline communications.

4) Control over technology has shifted away from the hands of government and a few monopolies. Telephony itself is now characterized by competition and rapid innovation, producing an environment with many new products, services and features, and many new service providers. State-of-the-art encryption technology is no longer subject to government monopoly. Users can now affirmatively choose encryption technology that will enhance their privacy and protect the security of their data against criminals. The Internet was designed from the outset as a decentralized medium for rapid transmission of information, and has evolved to a state of unprecedented openness. Barriers to participation are low; anyone with a computer and a modem can be a

publisher. Services and even entirely new infrastructures are developing rapidly in response to user demands. Government efforts to control the development and spread of technology become harder to sustain.

5) The globalization of communications technology and networks is breaking down national borders. One of the great strengths of the Internet is that it can be as easy to send an e-mail message to New York as to Nairobi. The information infrastructure is now global, as are the markets for telecommunications products and services. On the one hand, the irrelevance of borders means that government controls over information and technology become harder to maintain. On the other hand, enforceable privacy protections have not yet emerged for the global information infrastructure.

ECPA was intended to establish rules for government surveillance in the digital world. In many respects, it has proven to be a durable statute. However, technology has evolved in ways not contemplated when ECPA was enacted. In drafting ECPA, Congress assumed that it would be adequate to extend to electronic communications the constitutional conclusion that underpinned Title III in 1968: that capture of electronic communications would not be an unreasonable intrusion if there were stringent ex parte judicial review before the fact, minimization during a search, and equally stringent adversarial review after the investigation had been completed. That assumption, however, was made when few if any foresaw the development of the multiple forms of activity that are carried on today in "cyberspace." The interactive nature of the Internet, with the rapid emergence of features such as home banking, telecommuting and even telemedicine, has produced an environment in which many people spend hours each day "on-line." In this context, to intercept all a person's electronic communications means a lot more today than it did in 1968 or 1986. These developments call for an examination of the effectiveness and coverage of ECPA.

A first step toward examining ECPA would be to assess how the rules it set for governmental access to e-mail and other computer communications are working. Unfortunately, however, there is no publicly available data on which to base such an assessment. While the wiretap provisions of Title III require very detailed reports on interception of voice communications and interception of e-mail in transit, there is no similar requirement for collecting and publishing information on the extent of government access to e-mail and other electronic communications while they are in storage with service providers incident to transmission, by far the easier and presumably the more common means of government's accessing electronic communications.

This deficiency should be corrected by amending ECPA to require that courts and prosecutors submit reports on orders sought and granted for electronic communication access under 18 U.S.C. ? 2703, for inclusion in the Administrative Office reports on wiretapping. Until such a change can be enacted, Congressional committees should exercise their oversight authority to obtain such data from the federal agencies and the major service providers.

Another issue that needs to be re-addressed is whether one of the key protections established in 1968, the minimization rule, can be applied to non-voice communications. Minimization means that law enforcement is not supposed to record non-relevant communications. At the time ECPA was enacted, it was assumed that this was impossible in the e-mail context: law enforcement must get all the communications to and from a target, and read each one to determine if it is relevant. In 1986, in fact, the Senate Judiciary Committee expressly addressed this concern and suggested that minimization should be conducted by the initial law enforcement officers who review the intercepted communications. The committee stated that "[T]hose officials would delete all non-relevant material and disseminate to other officials only the information which is relevant to the investigation." This solution has been criticized as unrealistic. Actually, it is not that different from what happens in the case of ordinary telephone wiretaps, since the initial law enforcement personnel who monitor voice intercepts conduct an initial review of each conversation to decide whether to record it or not.

Technology, however, may offer a solution, producing more effective minimization than is available in the context of voice communications. Whether law enforcement accesses e-mail from the telephone company (or access provider) while in transmission, or from an e-mail service provider while it is in storage incident to transmission, it may be relatively easy for the service provider to perform the minimization. The service provider can use screens or filters to select from the e-mail messages to or from parties identified in the order only those containing certain key words or phrases that would be identical to those used by monitors in the voice context. As the investigation proceeds and law enforcement learns more about the patterns of the target, the interception can become more discriminating.

Another set of assumptions are being challenged by the profound changes occurring as a result of the Internet. These concern the degree of protection from governmental access one can justifiedly expect with respect to transactional records held by third parties. In 1976, the Supreme Court in United States v. Miller ruled that individuals had no constitutionally protected privacy interest in business records that were held by a third party. Miller involved checks held by a bank, and the rationale of the case assumed a world of paper records, yet the holding in its broadest implications has been applied unquestioningly to the electronic world. Thus, in 1979, the Court in Smith v. Maryland ruled that the use of a pen register to collect the phone numbers dialed on a surveillanced line did not implicate Fourth Amendment interests.

ECPA responded to Smith by requiring a judicial order for pen registers and trap and trace devices. For transactional information relating to e-mail and other electronic communications, ECPA required a subpoena, a warrant or a court order. In 1994, Congress recognized that transactional data associated with e-mail and other computer communications was emerging as a hybrid form of data, somewhere between addressing information and content, and was becoming increasingly revealing of personal patterns of association. Therefore, Congress set a higher standard for access to transactional data regarding electronic communications and eliminated subpoena access. Congress should examine the Justice Department's interpretation and application of the new standard to see if it is adequate or should be strengthened. Such an examination must give adequate attention to the communicative, associational nature of the transactional data itself in an online environment.

Finally, reexamination of ECPA must question the assumption that there is a distinction between the communication of content and its storage. In an era when people work for "virtual companies" and conduct personal, political and business lives in "cyberspace," that distinction is increasingly blurred.

The growth of online commerce, politics and relationships, the shift to distributed, networked computing, the growth of the World Wide Web as an information source, and the ready ability to encrypt records stored with third parties, call into question the application to the Internet of concepts developed for governmental access to business records in a relatively static, paper-based environment and may radically change the legal notion of what is a reasonable expectation of privacy.

It is time to reconsider how the lines have been drawn between records entitled to full Fourth Amendment protection and records under Miller that fall outside the protection of the Fourth Amendment. There are now essentially three legal regimes for access to electronic data:

i) the traditional Fourth Amendment standard, for records stored on an individual's hard drive or floppy disks;

ii) the Title III-ECPA standard, for records in transmission;

iii) a third standard, the scope of which is probably unclear, for records stored on a remote server, such as the research paper (or the diary) of a student stored on a university server or the records of an employee stored on the server of the employer.

As the third category of records expands because people find it more convenient to store records remotely, the legal ambiguity grows more significant. Are the records stored on such a server accessible by mere subpoena? Are they covered by the "remote computing" provisions of ECPA? If the records were seized from the individual's hard drive or floppies using a warrant or subpoena, contemporaneous notice would be required. If the records were seized in transmission, a court order would be required, but the interception could proceed secretly. If the records were seized from a third party, notice might be delayed. Do these distinctions make sense? Is the delay or denial of notice for stored records acceptable any longer? Conceptions of the Fourth Amendment developed in a 20th century world of paper records may not be applicable to 21st century technologies where many of our most important records are not "papers" in our "houses," but are "bytes" stored electronically and accessed remotely at "virtual" locations.

While some technological developments have made electronic surveillance easier, more intrusive or more revealing, the FBI in the early 1990's began to complain about the ways in which technological developments were making law enforcement interception more difficult. These difficulties were often encompassed by the term "digital telephony," although digital transmission itself was not really the problem. In fact, there were a number of problems. Some of the difficulties related to the rapid growth of wireless systems, which are easily tapped at the central switches but did not always have the capacity to accommodate multiple surveillances. Others were related to the increased competition in the telecommunications industry, which meant that a target could use two or more service providers, making one-stop surveillance impossible. Some problems arose due to services and features that put more control in the hands of users. During the 1994 hearings, the FBI voiced concerns about a number of these problems, some of which existed in analog systems, but which had become more common in digital switches. Among them were problems intercepting calls rerouted through call forwarding services and the inability to identify the destination of calls made using a speed dialing feature. Some problems had to do with physical changes in the networks. For example, the FBI anticipated increasing trouble in covertly isolating the communication stream associated with a particular target as multiplexed transmission technologies and fiber cables replaced the paired copper wires that traditionally had been associated uniquely with each customer.

Congress responded to these technological developments by enacting the Communications Assistance for Law Enforcement Act of 1994 (CALEA, sometimes referred to as the "digital telephony" legislation). CALEA requires telephone companies to ensure that new technologies (and some old technologies) do not impede law enforcement interception of communications. The legislation mandates, in effect, that carriers must take steps to ensure that the broad technological trends in the industry do not eliminate law enforcement access to communications of targeted individuals.

In adopting CALEA, Congress explicitly stated its intention to preserve the balance among the three interests that had guided the drafters of ECPA in 1986: law enforcement needs, privacy, and technological innovation. Congress accepted the FBI's assurances that the legislation would preserve the status quo in terms of law enforcement surveillance, without expanding government capabilities. Congress stressed specifically that the surveillance requirements of CALEA should be narrowly interpreted. Congress also required carriers to change their systems to protect the privacy and security of communications not authorized to be intercepted. To ensure that implementation did not block technological innovation, Congress prohibited the FBI from dictating network or equipment design standards. Finally, Congress also amended some provisions of ECPA to heighten privacy protections.

However, since CALEA was enacted, a struggle has been underway in which the FBI, on behalf of law enforcement generally, has attempted to broadly interpret the requirements of CALEA, by dictating system design and mandating, nationwide, certain capabilities in excess of traditional interception practices. The most notable and troubling aspect of this campaign is the FBI's effort to use CALEA, in contravention of explicit assurances during the drafting process, to require cellular phone companies and other wireless service providers to have location tracking capability built into their systems for law enforcement purposes. The FBI is also claiming, for example, that CALEA mandates interception of certain conference calls after the targeted facility has been dropped from the conversation, thus continuing the surveillance against parties and facilities for which no judicial approval was granted. Seeking to exploit the increasing value of signaling information, the FBI has argued that CALEA requires the configuration and delivery of a signaling channel that includes detailed message notifications about the targeted facility. The FBI maintains that this configuration and delivery should be performed whether or not there is a call in progress and for facilities not identified in the surveillance order. In a provision with far reaching implications, anticipating the adoption of packet switching protocols that could obliterate the distinction between signaling and content, the FBI and industry have proposed allowing carriers to deliver communication content to law enforcement under a mere pen register order, depending once again on law enforcement to sort out the signaling information from the content.

CALEA was based on the dual premise that (i)Title III and other laws authorizing electronic surveillance have strict legal requirements and (ii) those requirements are being stringently enforced by the courts to protect privacy. As suggested above, this premise is becoming increasingly tenuous. If privacy protections afforded by the wiretap laws are not being strictly enforced, then the foundation of CALEA falters and the legislation becomes far more threatening, requiring as it does the ubiquitous adoption of features in the nation's telephone systems to ensure ready government access.

The premise of CALEA would also be negated by legislative weakening of the wiretap standards. Already the Justice Department has successfully won Congressional repeal of the provision extending ECPA to wireless data transfers. The extension of ECPA to wireless data transfers was one of the privacy enhancements adopted in CALEA with the intent of balancing privacy concerns with law enforcement needs. In addition, in its proposed anti-terrorism law forwarded to Congress in 1995, the Clinton Adminisiration sought numerous weakening changes in Title III, including: (i) weakening the sanctions against illegal wiretapping, (ii) facilitating the procurement of roving taps and warrantless taps, and (iii) creating exemptions from the carefully crafted privacy protection standards of the Foreign Intelligence Surveillance Act. Although many of the Clinton changes were not enacted, the Justice Department has continued to pursue them and has proposed others that would loosen the privacy standards of the wiretap laws.

As discussed in Section VIII, many of the proposed changes in the wiretap laws should be rejected on the merits. However, the fact that CALEA now requires telephone companies to design their systems to facilitate law enforcement surveillance is an additional reason to oppose any weakening of the wiretap standards. If the Executive Branch and Congress wish to fulfill the intent of CALEA, they should strengthen, not weaken, the privacy protections of Title III, ECPA and FISA. Unless these laws, in light of judicial interpretation and continuing technological developments, offer meaningful protection to privacy, the foundations of CALEA will be eroded.

During the Bush Administration, the Justice Department urged Congress to adopt legislation that would have created de facto licensing authority over the development and deployment of new communications technology. Telecommunications companies and civil liberties groups opposed the legislation, arguing that any legislation should be narrowly crafted to address identified problems while providing for public accountability and protecting privacy and not interfering with the innovation and competitiveness that have fueled the digital revolution. After hearings and consultations with industry, privacy groups, and law enforcement, Congress rejected the broad approach originally proposed by the FBI. Instead, with the strong support of the FBI, Congress enacted CALEA, which established minimum functional requirements intended to preserve rather than expand law enforcement access to communications, and deferred to industry to develop solutions.

CALEA requires telephone companies to design (and in some cases retrofit) their networks to ensure that law enforcement agencies can carry out electronic surveillance on advanced digital equipment and services. Three of its four requirements are intended to preserve law enforcement access. These pertain to (1) the interception of call content; (2) the interception of call-identifying information; and (3) the delivery to law enforcement of intercepted call content and call-identifying information. In contrast, the fourth requirement of CALEA, section 103(a)(4), requires carriers to protect the privacy and security of communications not authorized to be intercepted.

Congress intended that, in the first instance, common carriers and equipment manufacturers, not government agencies, would develop publicly the details for implementation of these assistance requirements. Congress expected that this approach would temper law enforcement demands with considerations of privacy and innovation, as well as cost and competitiveness. If industry failed to produce a standard or if any agency or person had concerns about the standard, the legislation gave the Federal Communications Commission the authority to develop an appropriate standard, taking into account the need to protect privacy and to promote innovation.

A distinction should be drawn between what CALEA mandated as a minimum national standard for law enforcement access versus what expansions in surveillance capability will be available to law enforcement as a result of market-driven technological developments.

Before CALEA, some changes in telecommunications technology were making law enforcement surveillance harder, while other changes were making surveillance easier or more productive. CALEA was intended to "preserve the status quo" by ensuring that technological developments did not erode law enforcement access to call content and identifying information. Congress did not intend to impede the development of technology that makes surveillance easier or more fruitful, nor did it intend to deny law enforcement the authority to take advantage of those developments.

Congress left intact the existing authority under 18 U.S.C. ? 2518(4), which authorizes law enforcement to take advantage of all technological developments enhancing surveillance capability and requires companies to make available whatever advanced capability they have. But Congress did not mandate the nationwide ubiquitous installation of every technologically possible surveillance enhancement. Instead, Congress mandated the nationwide availability only of certain minimum features, based upon its understanding of past surveillance practices as described in the CALEA hearings and based upon the FBI's description in the CALEA hearings of what its needs were.

In some respects, the checks and balances Congress wrote into CALEA have worked as intended. The FBI published in the Federal Register, under a notice and comment procedure, a capacity notice that was widely criticized and withdrawn. The FBI published a second capacity notice revealing much more data about historical surveillance patterns, but that second notice also raised serious questions which the Bureau must address in finalizing the capacity requirements. In terms of capability, industry bodies drafted "safe harbor" technical standards to provide the detail necessary to translate CALEA's broad functional requirements into network and equipment specifications. The FBI had extensive input in the standards process, articulating law enforcement's desires and pushing hard for an expansive reading of the requirements.

Unfortunately, the FBI's participation went beyond the consultation intended by Congress and instead amounted to an effort to dominate the standards process and dictate specific surveillance features. Nonetheless, as of October 1997, industry had largely rejected FBI demands for surveillance features that, in contravention of the clear intent of CALEA, would expand the government's electronic surveillance capability beyond its current reach. In two respects, however, industry acceded to FBI demands for features that would go beyond the status quo.

(1) Location information. Industry yielded to FBI insistence that cellular and other wireless systems be designed to provide information on the location of their customers as they make and receive calls. This involves capturing and delivering to law enforcement the signals that identify a wireless telephone user's location for call processing purposes. It is clear from the legislative history that Congress did not intend to impose geographic location information as a CALEA requirement

with respect to cellular or other wireless systems. Concerns with "location tracking" were initially a major source of opposition to the legislation, so the FBI was eager to disavow any interest in location information at an early stage. Thus, early in 1994, the FBI expressly assured Congress that CALEA did not mandate provision of location information, and nothing in the legislative history suggests that any of the changes made as the legislation proceeded through the drafting process were intended to bring location information within the scope of CALEA requirements.

(2) Packet switching. In a decision that has potentially far-reaching implications for the future of telephony, the Internet and government surveillance, the proposed CALEA implementation standard issued in July 1997 would allow telecommunications companies using "packet switching" to provide the full content of customer communications to the government even when the government is only authorized to intercept addressing or signaling data.

Despite indications that it is feasible to provide signaling information separate from the content in a packet switching environment, the proposed standard would allow companies to deliver the entire packet data stream, including call content, when law enforcement is entitled to receive only dialing or signaling information under a pen register order. Such orders are issued without probable cause and without the discretionary review accorded to full call content interceptions.

The proposed CALEA standard relies on law enforcement to sort out the addressing information from the content, keeping the former but ignoring the latter. This approach, were it followed, could totally obliterate the distinction between call content and signaling information that was a core assumption of ECPA and of CALEA itself. It also would violate section 103(a)(4) of CALEA, which requires the telecommunications industry to protect communications not authorized to be intercepted.

In the old analog systems, law enforcement agencies authorized to receive signaling information were provided with access to the target's entire line, including content. With subsequent developments in technology, the signaling data was carried on a channel separate from the call content.

In this respect, technology itself enhanced privacy, creating an environment in which a law enforcement agency conducting a pen register could receive only information it was entitled to receive. Absent CALEA, packet switching might have reversed that privacy enhancement. However, CALEA imposed on the industry an affirmative obligation to protect privacy. Yet, the proposed industry standard initially failed to ensure that law enforcement agencies receive only the information appropriate to the level of authorization in hand.

Another capability sought by the FBI, but rejected by industry as of November 1997, was the ability to monitor all conversations during a conference call initiated by a targeted facility, even if the targeted facility is on hold or has hung up from the call. It is questionable whether law enforcement has authority under the particularity requirement of the Fourth Amendment and Title III to intercept communications involving only non-targeted facilities just because a targeted facility initiated a conference call.

A number of the enhancements sought by the FBI were related to the Bureau's attempts to exploit transactional data. In legislative terms, the FBI tried to force more information into the definition of the CALEA term "call-identifying information." The plain language of CALEA and the legislative history indicate that "call-identifying information" means the numbers dialed by a subscriber to direct a communication, or other signaling information that serves the same call routing purpose as the dialed digits.

This includes the switch-based information equivalent to a seven or ten digit phone number that directs a call when a voice dialing or speed dialing feature is used. The term likely includes information indicating that the party under surveillance has terminated a call by hanging up. However, the FBI argued that this term includes much more. For instance, at various points in the CALEA implementation process, the FBI argued that carriers must build in the capability to provide not only location-related information on wireless phone users, but "location-related updates during calls."

The Bureau also asked for detailed "call progress" tones relating to both the target of the investigation and persons with whom the target is communicating, and messages during three-way calls that would indicate when a party, who is not the target of the surveillance, drops off a three-way call. Further, the FBI sought "voice message waiting" tones to notify the government when a surveillance target has a voice mail waiting and feature status messages that would notify the government in real time when a surveillance target changes his or her mix of service features.

Both Congress and the Federal Communications Commission (FCC) have oversight roles to ensure that CALEA is properly implemented in a way that preserves the crucial balance between privacy and law enforcement powers.

CALEA requires the FBI to obtain annual appropriations for implementing the law. This has allowed the House and Senate Appropriations Committees to examine the issues posed by implementation and to withhold funds until they are satisfied that implementation is proceeding appropriately.

In 1995, the first year after CALEA was enacted, Congress declined to appropriate any funds for implementation.

In 1996, Congress established a CALEA Compliance Fund but blocked the FBI from expending any funds until it had submitted a detailed implementation plan.

In 1997, after reviewing the implementation plan, both Houses expressed concern about the lack of priority in the FBI's plan. The Senate Appropriations Committee declined the Administration's request for $100,000,000. Instead, the Committee directed the FBI to create a working group with the purpose of creating "a more rational, reasonable, and cost-effective CALEA implementation plan."

The Committee recommended that no funds be expended for CALEA implementation until the working group provided a plan satisfactory to the Committee. The House-Senate conference committee on the fiscal 1998 appropriation for the Department of Justice came to a somewhat different resolution. The conference agreement, which passed the Congress and was signed into law, included no additional funding for CALEA implementation, but the report noted that there had been recent discussions between the Committees on Appropriations, the Justice Department and representatives of the telecommunications industry.

As a result of these discussions, the conference report stated an agreement had been reached, which included a commitment by industry and law enforcement to provide to the Committees on January 4, 1997 cost estimates for the deployment of "the solution," along with a timetable for deployment and signed agreements from two carriers or equipment manufacturers (presumably to begin development of the solution).

The FCC has ample jurisdiction to ensure that CALEA implementation protects privacy. The most important source of the FCC's jurisdiction is section 107 of CALEA, which authorizes the Commission to intervene to establish an implementation standard if the industry standard-setting process fails to produce an acceptable standard. In that event, the FCC is required to ensure that the standard protects the privacy and security of communications not authorized to be intercepted and achieves other specified public policy goals, including promotion of technology innovation.

Any party, including public interest groups, may seek a proceeding under section 107 to challenge CALEA implementation. Also, section 105 of CALEA requires that carriers ensure that any interception within their switching premises be activated only in compliance with a court order and with the affirmative intervention of an individual officer or employee of the carrier. These provisions give the FCC ample authority to reject elements of the FBI-industry implementation standard that go beyond preserving the status quo and that do not adequately protect privacy. Attention also needs to be given to law enforcement compliance with the new language in the pen register and trap and trace section, requiring the use of reasonably available technology that limits pen registers and trap and trace devices to the collection of "dialing and signaling information used in call processing."

CALEA imposed on the nations's telecommunications systems an unprecedented new obligation: to design their systems and services with the objective (along with all their other objectives related to provision of quality service) of ensuring the government's ability to carry out electronic surveillance. It was the judgment of Congress that wiretapping was a law enforcement capability worth preserving. And Congress had before it the acknowledgment of industry representatives that, unless action was legislatively forced, the electronic surveillance capability might be lost or substantially diminished as a result of technological development. However, Congress fully recognized the dangers to privacy and technological innovation inherent in what it was mandating. Therefore, Congress wove throughout CALEA a series of limitations, and it established a series of checks and balances, lodging in a number of entities authority to influence or control the implementation of the law.

Thus, CALEA spelled out four capability requirements. These four requirements, while phrased in general terms, are nonetheless exclusive; anything that law enforcement would want to require under CALEA has to fit under one of these four requirements or it cannot be mandated. Further, Congress specifically excluded certain capabilities. It specified that carriers have no obligation to ensure the ability to unscramble encrypted communications when the user controls the encryption keys. It specified that a given carrier has no responsibility to continue monitoring when a target using cellular roaming moves out of the carrier's service area and into the service area of another carrier.

The legislation denied to law enforcement any authority to dictate system design. Instead, the legislation defers to industry to establish standards. Any publicly available standard adopted in good faith to implement the requirements of the law constitutes a safe harbor. Companies are deemed in compliance with the act if they comply with the industry standard. Law enforcement cannot unilaterally declare a standard deficient. If law enforcement is not satisfied with the industry standard, it must petition the FCC to adopt a different standard, and the FCC's latitude is limited by a specified set of criteria that must guide the development of a standard.

The concept of "reasonableness" appears throughout the legislation. Carriers are obligated to make available only such call-identifying data as is "reasonably available." The FCC may grant an extension of time for compliance if compliance within the specified period is not "reasonably achievable."

A court can order compliance only if alternative technologies or facilities of another carrier are not "reasonably available" to law enforcement for implementing the interception and only if compliance is "reasonably achievable." Carriers are not required to bear the costs of retrofitting equipment installed before January 1, 1995 if compliance is "not reasonably achievable."

Congress also included in CALEA mechanisms of public accountability. Capacity requirements must be adopted only after a public notice and comment proceeding in the Federal Register. Technical standards for implementing the capability requirements have to be "publicly available." Funding is subject to the annual appropriations process, with hearings, reports, and enacted laws. The Attorney General is required to issue periodic reports on implementation.

As a series of checks and balances, CALEA placed authority over implementation in a number of hands. Thus, industry bodies develop the standards. Upon the petition of industry, law enforcement or any other person, the FCC can develop a superseding standard. The FCC was also granted the authority to issue extensions of the compliance deadline, and to determine that compliance is not reasonably achievable with respect to a certain service or carrier. The courts have jurisdiction over compliance proceedings.

Congress has control through its appropriations committees, which must annually appropriate funds for compliance and therefore can use the power of the purse to control how the legislation is being implemented. The Judiciary Committees and the Commerce Committees, as the authorizing committees, can always revisit the legislation and amend it as circumstances change and in light of experience.

For the CALEA legislation to work in a balanced fashion, the limitations and reasonableness provisions written into law by Congress must be invoked and the entities with responsibility for overseeing the implementation of the statute must choose to exercise their authority to preserve the intended balance. The FBI has substantial resources and the politically powerful anti-crime rhetoric at its disposal, and it has the ability to mobilize state and local law enforcement to promote its position. Thus, the FBI will dominate the implementation process unless the other government institutions exercise the authority granted them under the statute to promote the counterbalancing values of privacy and innovation.

In this sense, CALEA is merely one more manifestation of the on-going efforts in our democratic society to regulate the police and national security powers of the government. Congress, deeming it necessary to preserve an electronic surveillance authority, can legislate limits and controls, but those limits must be enforced and the controls must be exercised by the executive and regulatory agencies, future Congresses, and the courts.

Illegal electronic intrusion into computer networks is a rapidly escalating crime problem. White collar criminals, economic espionage agents, organized crime groups, foreign intelligence agents, and terrorist groups have been identified as "electronic intruders" responsible for penetrations of American computer networks. It is estimated that the Pentagon's computers are subject to hackers' attempts 250,000 times a year.

The United States Government relies upon the National Information Infrastructure (NII) for the efficient, uninterrupted flow of electronic information for air traffic control, military communications, energy distribution, public safety, and other essential government programs and services. Intelligence and industry forecasts indicate the United States is just beginning to realize the potentially damaging effects and extent of the computer crime problem. On balance, the advantages of more widespread use of cryptography outweigh the disadvantages.

Newer communications media are inherently insecure. Wireless telephones have great advantages in convenience compared with wireline counterparts, yet, since wireless phones transmit over the airwaves, eavesdropping is easier not only for curious neighbors but also for burglars identifying potential targets and industrial spies stealing trade secrets.

Similarly, decentralized computer networks such as the Internet have low barriers to entry, are much less expensive, are more robust and can be used to accomplish a far greater variety of tasks than the proprietary networks of the past, but, again, at the expense of intrinsic security. The vulnerabilities of the national and global information infrastructures have been recognized not only by the FBI, but also by the Defense Science Board Task Force on Information Warfare-Defense and by the President's Commission on Critical Infrastructure Protection.

The losses to date from inadequate system security are enormous. In one series of transactions in 1994, an international group of criminals penetrated Citicorp's computerized electronic transfer system and moved about $12 million from legitimate customer accounts into their own accounts in banks around the world. In 1996, after a comprehensive study, the National Research Council concluded, "Of all the information vulnerabilities facing U.S. companies internationally, electronic vulnerabilities appear to be the most significant."

Given these inherent vulnerabilities, widespread use of encryption to protect communications and stored data is essential to prevent fraud and other forms of crime in the digital age. At the same time, encryption poses challenges to law enforcement and national security agencies, which have raised the specter of criminal suspects' undecipherable stored information or voice communications. This has led to a vigorous legislative debate over control of encryption technology.

In some ways, the encryption debate has been a conflict between two competing models of security, one in which private individuals, businesses and governments choose from a variety of encryption options to protect their security, and another wherein the federal government assumes the primary responsibility for protecting personal and business as well as governmental security through government-promoted weaknesses in encryption technology.

While there are law enforcement equities on both sides of the encryption issue, the centralized model of security based on government-controlled encryption weaknesses is incompatible with certain defining characteristics of the digital communications revolution: decentralization, competition, globalization, and the dynamics of decreasing cost and increasing computing power that have put more control and more choices in the hands of end users.

The Executive Branch's various efforts to impose a centralized model of security on a decentralized medium have delayed full realization of the Internet's economic, personal and democratizing potential. They have also hurt the competitiveness of American computer companies by prohibiting export abroad, thereby inhibiting in the U.S. the use of strong encryption that is already available overseas. At the same time, given the already widespread proliferation of user-controlled encryption technology, the centralized model cannot offer assurances of achieving the desired law enforcement access. Strong non-escrowed encryption is and will continue to be available to those who want it. There are currently hundreds of encryption products available worldwide. This led the National Research Council to conclude that, on balance, the security-enhancing, crime-preventing benefits of encryption outweigh the impediments to law enforcement.

Globalization is a key factor, and the global market has rejected all government proposals to control encryption technology. U.S. proposals in 1993 for government agencies to serve as key escrow agents were immediately rejected by business and individual users as involving an unacceptable level of vulnerability. More recent approaches that depend upon government licensing or "registration" of escrow agents or other forms of government control of decryption mechanisms (including proposals to require key recovery features as a condition of receiving public key certificates) are also not achieving market acceptance.

The type of ubiquitous, near-instantaneous key escrow, key recovery, or key management "infrastructure" sought by the U.S. government is so complex, so vulnerable, so expensive and/or so cumbersome -- so fundamentally at odds with user needs -- that it will not by accepted by users.

Yet the market alone will not address all of the privacy issues posed by encryption. While it seems clear that most businesses and individuals will not trust the government or government-dictated private structures to hold their keys, it also seems clear that under some encryption applications, particularly those involving stored data, some users are interested in securing a means to recover their encrypted data if they lose their own key. Market-based efforts to address this problem -- responses to user needs -- are resulting in a range of key escrow, key recovery, or "trusted third party" systems for decryption assistance.

These are quite different from the systems proposed by the Administration under its legislative proposal, which is voluntary in name only. These user-driven, user-controlled data-recovery or key escrow arrangements will offer law enforcement an opportunity to satisfy many of its basic access needs for stored data.

As the market develops key recovery arrangements, government agencies will be seeking access to those keys for law enforcement and national security purposes, to decrypt seized files and communications intercepted under the wiretap laws. Government efforts to access stored keys will pose obvious privacy concerns. Given the centrality of encryption to privacy and security in the digital age, there is a strong argument that escrowed encryption keys and key recovery assistance should be entitled to greater protection than that traditionally accorded to so-called "third party records."

The Fourth Amendment may have stronger application to especially sensitive information such as a decryption key entrusted to a third party under an escrow arrangement. Disclosure of keys, even escrowed keys, also raises serious questions under the Fifth Amendment's protection against compelled self incrimination.

Encryption will play a central enabling role in the protection of privacy in the digital age. Government attempts to access keys or decryption assistance will raise important privacy interests. Reliance on the courts to sort out the issues will produce a possibly long period of uncertainty and conflicting decisions. Legislative action setting clear privacy standards for government access to keys and decryption assistance held by second or third parties would be far preferable. Such legislation should include standards that prohibit escrow agents from providing keys or decryption assistance except in conformity with a court order issued upon a finding of probable cause and a showing that there is no feasible alternative of obtaining the plaintext, and should require minimization in the use of the key or assistance.

Protecting Wireless Communications

In the network of networks that comprises the telecommunications "system" of today and the future, it is no longer appropriate to look at wireless telephone systems as distinct from wireline systems or to look at the telephone system as separate from the Internet. The increasing use of wireless communications services, the seamless integration of wireless and wireline networks, and the importance of wireless data links heighten the urgency of ensuring the privacy and security of wireless communications. In this context of a global communications network increasingly dependent on wireless links, it is a serious invasion of privacy to eavesdrop on wireless telephone conversations. Wireless eavesdroppers are invading the privacy not only of the person who is using a wireless phone, but also of anybody else who is in the conversation using an ordinary landline telephone. As wireless telephones become more ubiquitous, scanning threatens the privacy of all telephone users.

Encryption will play an essential role here too, for securing over-the-air links. But it is clear that there is a need for legislative improvements clarifying both the prohibitions against unauthorized private interception and the legal standards for governmental access to wireless transmissions.

Location information. Wireless telephone systems are developing the capability to provide more refined location information on wireless phone users. Nonconsensual government monitoring of location through a wireless phone implicates privacy interests. Since wireless telephones are regularly carried into places where a person has a reasonable expectation of privacy, Congress should clarify the law by requiring a warrant based on a showing of probable cause for nonconsensual governmental access to real-time wireless telephone location information.

Wireless data transfers. At a time when wireless local area networks are proliferating and when wireless data transmissions could be used for everything from proprietary data to medical records, it is not clear that wireless data transfers are protected to the same extent as wireless voice communications. The status of legal protection for wireless data transfers has a confused history, leaving it unclear whether they are currently protected by ECPA. An industry and privacy task force concluded in 1991 that wireless transfers of data might not be covered by ECPA, and recommended that coverage be extended. In 1994, in CALEA and with the support of the Administration, Congress passed a provision making it clear that the privacy of wireless data transfers was protected by ECPA. But less than two years later, in the anti- terrorism act of 1996, Congress repealed the provision on the basis of the Justice Department's claim that the 1994 amendment was inappropriately overbroad. This confusion should be resolved by appropriate legislative language extending the privacy protections of ECPA unambiguously to wireless data transfers.

Interception devices. ECPA made it a crime to manufacture, sell, assemble, possess or advertise any device that is "primarily useful" for the interception of wireless telephone conversations. Unfortunately, the effectiveness of this provision is quite limited, since it is difficult to prove that a device capable of intercepting cellular and a range of other frequencies is "primarily useful" for prohibited interceptions. Congress should delete the word "primarily," at least as it affects manufacture, sale, assembly, and advertisement.

The manufacture and import of scanners equipped or readily alterable to receive transmissions in frequencies assigned to the "domestic cellular radio telecommunications service" are prohibited under section 302(d) of the Communications Act. However, since the enactment of this provision, a new category of services called "commercial mobile radio services" has been created, into which cellular, as well as additional mobile services at different frequency ranges, such as personal communications systems (PCS), have been added. The law does not appear to prohibit manufacture and import of devices equipped to scan these frequencies. Congress should extend the section 302 prohibition to the parts of the spectrum used for PCS and other wireless telephone communications.

The balance among the interests of law enforcement, privacy and technological innovation has come under challenge in recent years. Steadily growing numbers of wiretaps, longer and longer surveillances intercepting more and more communications suggest that the wiretapping laws are not working as originally intended to constrain the use of this highly intrusive technique. These developments point to the need for amendments to the law to re-establish the balance Congress originally sought. Until such corrective amendments are enacted, it would be premature to consider proposals to further expand the scope of, or weaken the privacy protection standards in, the wiretap laws.

Unfortunately, the focus of the legislative debate recently has been in the opposite direction, on proposals to give the government greater latitude in wiretapping. As noted above in Section VII, the Justice Department sought and obtained repeal of one of the privacy protections that were adopted in CALEA. Further, the President sought in his terrorism legislation a series of other changes in the wiretap laws that would have weakened the sanctions against illegal government wiretapping; weakened the standards for so-called "roving taps;" and expanded the availability of warrantless taps in "emergency" situations. While these other changes were ultimately rejected, they were considered and debated without attention to counterbalancing proposals to enhance privacy.

The Clinton Administration has continued to support these and other changes in the wiretap laws. In July 1996, the Department of Justice submitted to Congress a report recommending eight amendments to the federal electronic surveillance laws, including the change in the statute's exclusionary rule, the loosening of the standard for "roving taps," and additional authority for emergency wiretaps without judicial approval. The report stated that "several other proposed amendments are under consideration by the Department, . . . [which] are expected to be submitted to Congress at a later time."

By far, the most dangerous change the Administration proposed was an amendment to Title III to allow courts to receive evidence obtained in violation of the wiretap law. When Title III was adopted, Congress included a statutory exclusion rule, calling it "an integral part of the system of limitations designed to protect privacy." The Administration proposal, although sometimes described as a good faith exception, would require a person to prove "bad faith" on the part of the government, before evidence will be excluded for violation of the law - an almost impossible undertaking. The Administration's 1995 proposal was not limited to situations where law enforcement officers relied on a technically defective warrant.

The Supreme Court has already held that the statutory suppression or exclusion rule in Title III is not to be applied to technical violations. The Administration proposal would apply to all provisions of the wiretap law, including those governing the conduct of the government after the warrant is issued. Thus, it would remove the only real incentive against violating such central protections as the minimization and evidence preservation rules. The Administration argued that the proposed change would merely apply to wiretaps the same standard applicable to other searches. However, the constitutional presupposition of Title III is that special, heightened standards are necessary for electronic surveillance because of its unique nature.

If amendments to the wiretap laws are to be considered, then it must be in the context that gives equal weight to an examination of issues from a privacy perspective. It should be clear from the discussion in Section II (B) that amendments are necessary to repair the damage done by judicial interpretation. Specifically, it is time to strengthen the minimization rule and to clarify the requirement that law enforcement exhaust other techniques before seeking an interception order. Other changes are necessary as well:

Transactional data. Advanced signaling systems for voice communications have blurred the distinction between call identifying information and call content. Currently, the standards for governmental access to signaling data under what are known as "pen registers" and "trap and trace devices" require a court order, but the statute puts the judge in a purely ministerial role: the sole function of the judge is to determine whether the signature of an Assistant United States Attorney is on the application. One improvement would be an amendment requiring that the judge exercise discretion and only approve the request upon finding, based on a showing by the government, that the information sought is relevant and material to an ongoing criminal investigation. As argued in Section VII, above, one type of transactional data, namely real-time location information generated in wireless telephone systems, implicates such serious privacy interests that Congress should clarify the law by requiring a warrant based on a showing of probable cause for nonconsensual governmental access to such information when obtained on a real-time, tracking basis. In light of the growing significance of transactional and signaling data, it is time for Congress to examine more generally the implications of government access to and analysis of all forms of such information for subscriber profiling purposes.

Roving wiretaps. The Justice Department has proposed loosening the standard for so- called roving or multi-point wiretaps. Roving taps (taps placed on a phone line other than the line subscribed to by the target of a surveillance order) are considered especially sensitive because they often entail tapping the phone of someone who is not the subject of an investigation and not suspected of any involvement in criminal conduct. The Justice Department argues that the current statute requires the government to show the subjective intent of the subject to evade interception. The Department argues that it should be enough that the subject's actions have the objective result of thwarting interception. If Congress changes the standard for roving taps, it should add to the law an explicit prohibition against interception of the conversations of innocent third parties, so that such conversations would be outside the scope of the warrant. While this conforms to stated Justice Department policy and the few lower court decisions, it would be desirable to write the principle into the Title III statute.

Emergency wiretaps. Title III allows the use of wiretapping without court approval in emergency situations involving immediate danger of death or serious physical injury, threats to the national security, or organized crime. In such cases, an application for a court order must be filed within forty-eight hours. The Administration has recommended expanding this emergency authority to include terrorism cases that do not involve an immediate danger of injury or threat to the national security.

More appropriate than the Administration's proposed change would be a careful reexamination of the Title III emergency exception itself. The emergency exception was enacted in 1968. Now, given the pervasiveness of faxes, wireless telephones, and e-mail, it is hard to understand why it would ever be impossible or even difficult to reach a federal judge to obtain prior approval for electronic surveillance. It should be noted that in 1977 the Federal Rules of Criminal Procedure were amended to allow for telephonic submission of search warrant applications and affidavits in emergency situations, with procedures for contemporaneous recording of the oral testimony supporting probable cause.

Limiting use of FISA in criminal cases. In most FISA cases, since the target is never notified of the existence of the surveillance, there is never an opportunity for after-the-fact adversarial review of the legality of the taps. Even if there is a criminal investigation and notice is provided, the adversarial hearing is inadequate because the target is not allowed to see the affidavit that provided the basis for the order. The increasing use of FISA intercepts in criminal cases suggests that FISA is turning out to be a bigger than expected exception to ordinary wiretap procedures.

In espionage cases involving U.S. persons, long after it is clear that the subject is suspected of engaging in espionage, and long after there is adequate basis to open a criminal case and obtain a wiretap order under Title III, the FBI continues to proceed under a FISA order, maintaining that the investigation serves a dual purpose of counterintelligence and criminal investigation. This is directly contrary to the intent of FISA.

FISA should be amended to exclude from any criminal trial evidence obtained from a FISA surveillance after there was probable cause to believe that a crime was being committed. This will require the FBI to obtain a

Title III order at the appropriate time, making the wiretap subject to the higher standards applicable to Title III intercepts.

International Issues

The Internet is a global medium. One of its great strengths is the ease with which it spans the globe: information flows as effortlessly from New York to Nairobi as from one building to another in Washington, D.C. Moreover, a communication from New York to Nairobi might travel through the United Kingdom and five other countries one day, but through France and five different countries the next.

In this global context, it has been said, the U.S. Bill of Rights is a local ordinance, meaning that the U.S. constitutional guarantees (and the procedures of the U.S. wiretap laws) offer no privacy protection against foreign government interception of the communications of U.S. citizens that cross national borders.

As U.S. law enforcement agencies become more active abroad, and as they engage in more joint operations with foreign police organizations, the line blurs between intelligence agencies and law enforcement agencies. Greater attention will have to be paid to the rules governing electronic surveillance abroad.

For both the Internet and traditional telephony, new rules need to be developed to govern U.S. surveillance abroad and the increasing extent of joint international operations, which currently take place in a legal no-man's-land. It has been held that the U.S. wiretap statutes have no extraterritorial application.

Congress should address this gap by extending the court order requirements of Title III and FISA to interceptions of communications by the U.S. government abroad for use in U.S. criminal cases.

U.S. government agencies, particularly the FBI, have been promoting the adoption of CALEA-type standards on an international scale. In 1994, the "Barrett Commission" in Australia, crediting the FBI's leadership, supported the development of "international user requirements" as the most effective means of "international cooperation to ensure that law enforcement's needs are taken into account in the development of new technology."

In 1995, the Council of the European Union adopted a set of interception requirements for telecommunications systems, similar to the requirements developed by the FBI, and urged member states to implement the requirements with respect to systems and service providers in their own countries. Efforts were also undertaken to urge non-EU countries to adopt the requirements.

In 1997, the Telecommunications Standardization Sector of the International Telecommunication Union, upon a motion by Australia, adopted a resolution directing all its standards groups to consider the EU surveillance requirements in their standards development. If the U.S. government is promoting surveillance standards for systems abroad, it should be U.S. policy to also promote world-wide adoption of privacy protections at least as strong as those in the United States.

The U.S. government has been less successful in promoting international adoption of key recovery for encryption. Despite the Administration's best efforts, international bodies have not endorsed key escrow solutions. The OECD Cryptography Policy Guidelines specifically do not endorse key escrow; rather, they cautiously propose that "national cryptography policies may allow lawful access to plaintext or cryptographic keys".

Nonetheless, as market-driven key escrow arrangements emerge, Fourth and Fifth Amendment concerns about what standards will govern access to keys take on international implications, because governments will be seeking access to keys escrowed outside their territory. If commercial key escrow systems achieve acceptance in the United States, foreign governments are likely to seek access to escrowed keys and decryption assistance, raising the question of standards to be applied when a foreign government seeks cooperation of U.S. authorities.

To regulate any assistance provided to foreign governments seeking access to escrowed keys or decryption assistance in the United States, and to prevent the disclosure of decryption keys or decryption assistance to foreign governments that do not respect privacy and other human rights or provide due process, Congress should adopt statutory rules that include strict court order standards. The rules for a foreign request should have to satisfy three basic criteria:

1) the foreign government should comply with the treaty and other standards normally governing the provision of U.S. legal assistance to that government;
2) the foreign request should have to meet a standard at least as high as U.S. law enforcement agencies; and

3) standards should be in place that prohibit the disclosure of keys or decryption assistance for political offenses or other activity that would be protected under the U.S.

First Amendment, or to foreign governments that do not adhere to minimum standards of due process and privacy protection. Communications privacy is a bedrock constitutional principle, and electronic communications must be protected through strong privacy legislation implementing the Fourth Amendment's requirements. For the past quarter century, the law of this nation regarding electronic surveillance has sought to balance the interests of privacy and law enforcement. The uses of new technologies, however, are always outpacing the law, often in ways that threaten privacy, and also in ways that limit law enforcement's effectiveness. Other changes in technology offer the possibility of enhancing privacy. Still other changes increase surveillance capabilities.

Consequently, Congress has been required periodically to examine the legal framework for protecting privacy while ensuring that law enforcement has the necessary and appropriate capabilities. It did so in 1968 when it responded to widespread eavesdropping by prohibiting wiretapping without a court order. It did so in 1986 with the adoption of ECPA, which extended the protections and authorities of Title III to e-mail and cellular telephone communications. It did so again in 1994 when it responded to law enforcement concerns about the impact of new technologies by enacting CALEA, which required telecommunications carriers to ensure that their systems could accommodate government surveillance.

As exemplified by the Internet, the digital communications technologies are flexible, decentralized, networked, open and interactive. They merge voice, data, and images. They eliminate distinctions between what is kept in the home and what is stored with third parties. They generate large quantities of easily captured transactional data, combine wireless and wireline systems seamlessly, and place choices and control in the hands of users. Their economics are characterized by competition and innovation. They are global in reach. The explosion in the amount of information transmitted and stored electronically and the emergence of a form of online existence for both businesses and individuals have produced a qualitative change in the nature of communications and, accordingly, in the amount and nature of the information that is exposed to intrusion, interception and misuse. A re-examination of the wiretap laws must take into account these defining features of the digital revolution.

Such a review should also consider the overall balance between the technical and legal capabilities of government and the technical and legal status of privacy protections. Piecemeal amendments to the surveillance laws in response only to government concerns will inappropriately upset the balance. Any amendments to the wiretap laws must be narrowly crafted to ensure that they do not erode privacy protections, and must be balanced by other, privacy-enhancing amendments. New technologies enhance the ability of law enforcement to intercept and analyze communications and track individuals. Many of these enhancements are coming about without government intervention, as the unintended consequences of market-driven changes in technology. Existing law allows law enforcement to take advantage of these developments. As technology enhances surveillance capabilities, the legal standards for government use of these new technologies must be increased to adequately protect privacy.

Government efforts to control the development of technology to preserve its communications surveillance capability must be carefully circumscribed. Merely as a practical matter, the rapid and decentralized changes occurring in technology are likely to outstrip government efforts at control. The most notable case in point is encryption: there seems to be no way to limit the spread of virtually unbreakable encryption. Changes in technology since 1994 when Congress adopted the CALEA legislation pose equally difficult problems, while also creating opportunities for enhancing privacy. Congress and the FCC should restrain FBI efforts to use this legislation to obtain surveillance capacities that go beyond the status quo.

The legislature must continually strive to develop rules that keep pace with technological developments. The process never reaches a point of final repose, but there are clear steps that should be taken now to reestablish the balance between privacy and government surveillance powers.

6

Information Fair Use

Over the past few years, various forces have pushed for measures to expand the rights of intellectual property holders at the expense of other speakers and listeners. Unfortunately, these ill-conceived measures have watered down time-honored standards that protected freedom of expression, including the doctrine of fair use.

Fair use should not be unduly limited on the pretext of preventing illicit traffic of intellectual property. At the very least, fair use should be applied to the electronic world to the same extent as with other media (such as newspapers and books). No special intellectual property regimes or "conditions" should be imposed for information in electronic media.

The right to free speech is widely recognized as one of the most fundamental principles in a civil society. Article 19 of the Universal Declaration of Human Rights states:

> "Everyone has the right to freedom of opinion and expression; this right includes freedom to hold

> opinions without interference and to seek, receive and impart information and ideas through any media and regardless of frontiers."

Similar language can be found in the International Covenant on Civil and Political Rights, the European Convention for the Protection of Human Rights and Fundamental Freedoms, and many other human rights accords. However, while this principle has survived countless attacks throughout history, and despite its acceptance in most of the world, a new threat to free speech has emerged -- not directly from governments, but from newly empowered intellectual property holders. Over the past few years, various forces have pushed for measures to expand the rights of intellectual property holders at the expense of other speakers and listeners.

Unfortunately, these ill-conceived measures have watered down time-honored standards that protected freedom of expression, including the doctrine of fair use. Despite considerable opposition, these proposals have been incorporated within multinational treaties and have formed the basis for new intellectual property legislation throughout the globe.

The expansion of Intellectual Property rights significantly threatens free expression. The fair use doctrine, for example, has fostered creativity, innovation and knowledge. It has allowed scientists to exchange ideas freely and to develop exciting new technologies. Fair use has enabled artists to enrich our cultures in a variety of media. It has immeasurably aided teachers in the education of our children. This chapter will examine the history of fair use, measure its value in the free marketplace of ideas, and propose steps to preserve the doctrine in the digital age.

Legal Background

The fair use doctrine balances two competing interests: the protection of free speech rights and the protection of authors' and artists' works from exploitation. Under this rule, individuals may legally make use of copyrighted materials, depending upon the extent of material used, the purpose of the use, and other similar factors.

The following version of the doctrine as incorporated into American law spells out most of the key principles behind fair use and provides a suitable starting point: "The fair use of a copyrighted work ÿ for purposes such as criticism, comment, news reporting, teaching (including multiple copies for classroom use), scholarship, or research, is not an infringement of copyright. In determining whether the use made of a work in any particular case is a fair use the factors to be considered shall include-

"(1) the purpose and character of the use, including whether such use is of a commercial nature or is for nonprofit educational purposes;

"(2) the nature of the copyrighted work;

"(3) the amount and substantiality of the portion used in relation to the copyrighted work as a whole; and

"(4) the effect of the use upon the potential market for or value of the copyrighted work."

This doctrine applies to a broad range of activities. Generally, expression may be protected if it is "sufficiently imbued with elements of communication." Courts have also applied fair use to new technologies as they were developed. For example, based on the principles of fair use, videocassette recorders (VCRs) and similar appliances that could be utilized for piracy purposes are not illegal as long as they are also "capable of substantial noninfringing uses."

Recently, judges have begun to grapple with how to apply fair use and similar principles of free expression to new digital media and technologies. A large percentage of these decisions have come from the United States, where a disproportionately large number of intellectual property holders (ranging from high-technology firms to entertainment conglomerates) are based and where a plurality of computer users still reside.

American courts have applied free speech doctrines with equal force to discussions carried out with the use of computers, including the Internet. Most significantly, in Reno v. American Civil Liberties Union, the U.S. Supreme Court struck down several serious restrictions on Internet speech. The High Court found that that speech on the Internet was entitled to the highest Constitutional Protection -- protection which was, at least, the equal of that provided to the printed word.

The American decisions recognize that expression can take on a digitized form and that computer language is itself a form of speech. Most notably, two U.S. Circuit Courts of Appeals have held that encryption software was protected by the free speech provisions of the Constitution and struck down restrictions on its export.

While the courts have generally cast a skeptical eye on governmental restrictions on digital speech, several recent developments have cast doubt on the future of fair use. These developments threaten to create a regime of private restrictions on speech. Over the past few years, intellectual property rights holders have attempted to strengthen their hands through the adoption of new treaties and international accords, the most important of which was created under the auspices of the World Intellectual Property Organization (WIPO) in Geneva.

The WIPO treaty's treatment of the issue of "circumvention" is especially problematic. The treaty requires signatory nations to prevent people from breaking through anticircumvention devices (such as copy protection codes on software) with the intent make illegal use of a protect work (e.g. piracy). The pact covers many forms of modern media (which are encoded in some way or other), including computer software, compact discs (CDs), digital video discs (DVDs) and electronic books.

A number of developing nations, particularly those in Africa, were successful in amending the treaty to allow its adherents to carve out exceptions (such as fair use) to the anticircumvention rule. Moreover, the rule itself was drawn in such a way as to theoretically allow circumvention, so long as the circumventer is making legal use of the protected work.

The WIPO treaty, of course, needed to be implemented on the national level with legislation. Unfortunately, the new pact does not require signatory nations to apply any of the traditional copyright defenses to circumvention, such as fair use. Countries can fully comply with WIPO standards by completely banning circumvention, which would render fair use all but impossible to the average person.

The very first piece of legislation came from the United States in the form of the Digital Millennium Copyright Act (DMCA). The DMCA was portrayed as the logical result of the WIPO treaty. Its supporters saw it as a natural extension of globalization and as an important element of U.S. trade policy, which would benefit American entertainment conglomerates and other large intellectual property rights holders. In reality, the United States went far beyond what the WIPO treaty required. The DMCA broadly prohibits people from providing any device that is meant to circumvent a technological measure that controls access to a copy protected work. But where the WIPO agreement allowed signatory nations to include many exceptions, the U.S. statute provided very few exemptions, such as the creation of new software to allow copyrighted material to be used on other machines. Moreover, because these exceptions are so narrowly worded, consumers effectively have far fewer rights to fair use than they did prior to the DMCA's passage.

Essentially, this means that you can still buy a copyrighted work, but if that work is encoded in some way, such as computer programs, compact discs and Digital Video Discs (DVDs), your rights may be fundamentally limited. You may not make "fair use" of your favorite movie or album (assuming it is in digital form), even for salutary purposes such as commentary or news reporting. You may not make copies of it (even for backup purposes). You may not play it on any platform you choose (such as on your home computer rather than using a stand-alone player). You may not look "under the hood," i.e examine the underlying code and operation, of that work that you bought (software package or otherwise) to see how it operates, even if there is a problem. You might have been able to do all of these things in the pre-digital era, but in the New World envisioned by the DMCA, all of these free speech rights must take a backseat to preventing even the theoretical possibility of piracy.

The DMCA affords copyright holders almost completely control over subsequent uses of the work, including fair use. Once the copyright holder employs an anti- circumvention tool like encryption -- even weak encryption-- than the user who foils it or merely discusses how to foil it becomes liable for a violation of the law.

These provisions allow large intellectual property holders to restrict competition, innovation and the spread of knowledge-- the very purposes for which the copyright laws were created.

Despite strong opposition from a diverse coalition of organizations, including the Electronic Frontier Foundation, the Computer Professionals for Social Responsibility, the Electronic Privacy Information Center, the Modern Language Association and the US Catholic Conference, the DMCA did become law. Since then, the DMCA has begun to produce the results feared by its opponents. One such case arose when a Norwegian teenager (who wished to play DVDs on his Linux computer) created a program named DeCSS. This primitive program interacted with the encoding scheme contained on DVDs and allowed users to view favorite movies on computers using the Linux operating system, but was ill designed for copying entire DVDs. When 2600 magazine reported on DeCSS and included links to the program on its website, the Motion Picture Association of America (MPAA) sued the magazine's publisher under the DMCA and won at the trial level. A similar suit has been filed against dozens of computer users in California, and more court action is likely.

DeCSS is just one of several technologies that have fueled widespread debate over the diminution of fair use.

A number of entertainment conglomerates have filed suit to prevent the use of other new computer programs (such as Napster and MP3.com) that allow individuals to trade music files online. Many of the arguments raised by the plaintiffs are similar to the ones used against videocassette recorders--that these devices will foster piracy. While many of the lawsuits against MP3.com have been settled, one court recently levied fines against the company that amounted to over EUR 100 million. In the Napster case, the presiding judge issued a harsh decision that essentially silenced ordinary computer users by forcing them to prove (at the outset) that their speech had not been copyrighted by someone else.

The Napster case raises several troubling issues. At the outset, it is worth noting that Napster is used to trade both copyrighted and non-copyrighted material. Like the VCR, Napster can be used for both legal and arguably illegal purposes.

As a service provider, Napster is being held liable for the "infringing" uses. Under this theory, Napster is responsible for monitoring all of the traffic on its site. Given the sheer impracticality of determining which of millions of users are violating copyright laws, Napster would have to shut down, even if the courts only order it block infringing uses.

Indeed holding Internet Service Providers and other conduits liable for illegal content will lead to a general chill on free expression as the providers are forced to engage in whole sale monitoring and censorship of their users. In the U.S., the DMCA has been already become a sword of Damocles held over the head of fair users to prevent the spread of knowledge and has created a form of private censorship.

In Reno v. ACLU, the U.S. Supreme Court has noted that "the growth of the Internet has been and continues to be phenomenal. As a matter of constitutional tradition, in the absence of evidence to the contrary, we presume that governmental regulation of the content of speech is more likely to interfere with the free exchange of ideas than to encourage it."

The DMCA has had precisely that effect of interfering with the "free exchange of ideas."

Meanwhile, intellectual property holders are rushing to implement DMCA-type measures around the world. For example, several weeks ago, the Australian government introduced the Copyright Digital Amendment Bill 2000, which mirrors the DMCA's harsh standards regarding anticircumvention and other limits on fair use.

Not surprisingly, the bill is generating considerable controversy (as the DMCA has in the United States) because of its potentially harmful effects on free speech.

These efforts are not confined to industrialized nations; the proponents of these bills are pushing for tougher intellectual property measures in developing countries, often with little regard for free expression values.

Fair Use in Practice

Fair use should not be unduly limited on the pretext of preventing illicit traffic of intellectual property. At the very least, fair use should be applied to the electronic world to the same extent as with other media (such as newspapers and books). No special intellectual property regimes or "conditions" should be imposed for information in electronic media.

Fair use is not a "problem," as many of its detractors suggest. Furthermore, it is misleading to claim that fair use doctrines allow the "destruction of intellectual and cultural property." The fundamental goal of intellectual property laws is to prevent the unfair exploitation of artists; there are other sets of rules (both civil and criminal laws) regarding any potential "destruction of intellectual and cultural property." Attention should instead be focused on overly broad intellectual property laws that endanger free speech. The doctrine of fair use represents a partial and time-honored solution to this dilemma. To understand why this is the case, it is important to revisit the reasons why fair use principles were created in the first place, and what effects these principles have had.

Fair use has allowed artists of all types to enrich our culture with their views of the world around us. Consider the work of painters like Andy Warhol, who composed numerous works with such images as Campbell's Soup cans and photographs of Marilyn Monroe-images that were protected under intellectual property laws.

Consider, too, the work of Jean-Michel Basquiat, who paid homage to musicians like Miles Davis by including lyrics to their (copyrighted) songs in his paintings. Without fair use, these artists might have been branded as outlaws. Unfortunately, this specter of legal liability (through new ill-conceived intellectual property laws) may jeopardize the work of more recent artists, many of whom now use the digital domain as a medium for their creative endeavors.

Furthermore, many artists are actually benefiting from the new technology. Musicians such as Prince, Limp Bizkit and the Offspring have embraced software (like Napster) that allows Internet users to trade music files online. While some forces in the music industry have shunned these programs, many other artists are thrilled by the emergence of Napster and its cohorts, because it has increased interest in their work. For new artists, fair use of the songs (via music-trading software) has led to heavy publicity, a lucrative recording contract, and massive sales (indeed, the album sales for one Internet savvy group have gone from zero to nearly half a million copies). These benefits have also been felt by more established groups. At a recent hearing in the United States Congress, Sixties rock veteran Roger McGuinn testified that the trading of music files through the Information Superhighway had apparently led to higher attendance at his concerts, greater awareness of his musical exploits, and more sales of his records. Indeed, a recent study (by Jupiter Communications) suggests that the use of Napster and other similar products has actually led to higher sales for the music industry, not less. The recording industry has itself admitted that sales of CDs have been rising for years, even after the advent of MP3.com and its cohorts.

These examples also underline that there are many new ways for content creators to get paid for their recordings that do not require stringent intellectual property regimes. Dean Varian from the University of California-Berkeley pointed out in a recent article that "the current business model for music distribution is unlikely to survive. But this doesn't mean there will be no music; it just means the business will have to change." For example:

"[Best selling novelist] Stephen King is trying a 'ransom' model. He has released two chapters of a book and will release the rest if fans send in enough money. [Heavy metal band] Metallica ÿ could experiment with variations on the same theme: release 10 seconds of a new song, pledging to deliver the rest only if listeners send in the required ransom. For extra motivation, fans who contribute could receive special treatment -- autographs, coupons for T-shirts, a lottery ticket to meet the performers, or some other benefit that would encourage them to contribute rather than get a free ride."

Moreover, since computer programs themselves are a form of expression, it should come as no surprise that computer scientists, journalists and other individuals have attacked the DMCA and its global counterparts as an attack on their right to free expression.

The fair use doctrine promotes education. It generally provides that "the purpose and character of the use, including whether such use is a commercial nature or is for nonprofit educational purposes" (emphasis added) should be taken into consideration. If the fair use doctrine did not exist, it is likely that many teaching materials (such as textbooks, instructional films and so forth) would either be unavailable, too expensive, or not produced altogether, due to the potential legal liability. Fair use has allowed teachers to do their work and help new generations appreciate aspects of world cultures without undue fear of lawsuits.

For these reasons, it is not surprising that many educational groups oppose attempts to curb fair use. Several of these organizations have stated: "As technology and society's use of it continues to evolve, the need in the library, scholarly and educational communities for an appreciation of both information proprietors' rights and user privileges like fair use is expected to intensify.

— "We will work to extend the application of fair use into digital networked environments in libraries and educational institutions by relying on it responsibly to lawfully make creative use of information;

— "We will resist relying on any proposed code of conduct which may substantially or artificially constrain the full and appropriate application of fair use; and

— "We will encourage our members to reject any licensing agreement clause that implicitly or explicitly limits or abrogates fair use or any other legally conveyed user privilege."

Fair use promotes global communication and the spread of knowledge throughout the world. The disappearance of fair use will curb technical discussions of important public and scientific issue. The attacks on 2600 magazine for its reporting of DVD-related software may be a troubling portent of things to come. These effects will be felt most strongly on the Internet. If the fair use doctrine did not exist, Internet users might be prevented from discussing matters of communal interest. In addition, many Internet service providers may begin censoring content of their subscribers' websites, e-mail messages, or chat room discussions, for fear of liability. This result would run counter to past precedents that protect analogous activities in the non-Internet context.

The fair use doctrines were also created to promote science. Fair use helps ensure that new technologies can be developed and used without undue fear of an intellectual property lawsuit. Past legal precedents clearly indicate that such devices as videocassette recorders may be distributed legally so long as they have some legitimate uses under intellectual property laws. Without fair use in place, many such technological advances will never get beyond the drawing board, for fear of potential legal liability.

Indeed, we have already begun to see these problems appearing in the DVD arena, where intellectual property holders have launched lawsuit after lawsuit over a single, primitive program, which was designed to help consumers watch their lawfully obtained movies on their own computers.

A number of distinguished scholars in their testimony have expressed fears that new intellectual property laws will prevent them from speaking freely about a whole host of scientific discoveries. Indeed, during his testimony in the DeCSS trial, Professor David Touretzky of Carnegie Mellon University worried aloud that a ruling against 2600 would preempt his ability to discuss his works, saying, "I've been programming computers since I was 12 years old, and I'm very concerned when events take place that threaten my ability to express myself." These expert views sharply contrast with the arguments from opponents of fair use, who often suggest that stronger intellectual property laws will encourage innovation (through the profit motive). On the contrary, the elimination of fair use is far more likely to chill academic discourse and stifle the development of new technologies.

The elimination of fair use and the new intellectual property rights that have been accorded to holders in the developed world will have particularly detrimental effect on developing nations. In the new economy, no resource is more valuable than information. But the new laws which protect information that previously would have been available for use will quickly price information and the products developed with that information out of the reach of the developing world.

These problems have already cropped up in the realm of patent law. Pharmaceutical firms have sought stringent patent protections that allow them to charge consumers several times more than the free market price. In particular, these patent laws have had a cruel and tragic effect on developing nations by pricing drugs to combat AIDS out of the reach of millions of the people who have AIDS or are HIV positive.

As a result, many people are unable to afford the drugs they need, and are often forced into illegal behavior in order to get the treatments they so desperately require. Ironically, while patent laws are supposed to prevent piracy, the harsh economic consequences of these intellectual property regimes have created new incentives to engage in such illicit activity.

Similar problems have already arisen in other areas of intellectual property law. Observers have noted how copyright and trademark protections have provided entertainment companies with economic windfalls worth billions of Euros every year. Part of the reason for this windfall is that the intellectual property-based fees can vastly inflate the costs to consumers for items like CDs, videotapes, DVDs, computer programs, and so on. Moreover, the profits gained from these monopolies help finance entertainment company lawsuits against potential competitors and innovators, which, in turn, can keep the prices for many products at a high level. This system for entertainment distribution has led to problems even in relatively prosperous countries, where several government officials have sued these corporations for price-gouging.

The hardships visited on prosperous countries by the erosion of fair use pale in comparison to the problems faced by developing nations. Given the limited economic resources that these countries possess, we in the developed world are asking for far too much when we ask these nations to strengthen intellectual property rights enforcement measures beyond what already exists. Indeed, the liberalization and relaxation of unnecessarily harsh intellectual property laws might greatly benefit these countries by lowering the cost barriers to the technology they need to grow.

Scholars and advocates have cited intellectual property laws as one of the biggest barriers to the exchange of informational and technological resources. In an open letter to the WIPO, nearly a dozen organizations (including Departamento de Informatica-UFPE, Computer Professionals for Social Responsibility, Consumer Project on Technology and many others) warned that the new WIPO pact would create "an enormous chilling effect on the development of new information technologies." It should come as no surprise that some 30 African nations had proposed alternative language to counteract these effects. Similarly, as noted economist Dean Baker points out,

"[The United States] has worked hard to extend U.S.-style copyright and patent laws throughout the developing world. These are extremely costly forms of protectionism. Copyright protection can raise the price of items like compact disks or videocassettes, which sell for a dollar or two in a free market, as high as thirty dollars.

Similar, patent protection can raise the price of pharmaceuticals, which may sell for one or two dollars per prescription in a free market, to hundreds or even thousands of dollars per prescription. It is inaccurate to describe a trade policy that tolerates or promotes this sort of protectionism as 'free trade.'"

For example, consider the plight of mainland China, which is still struggling to enter the Information Age. Its people can ill afford to pay the prices charged by Western corporations for such items as computer software, CDs, and DVDs-prices that are fostered by strong intellectual property schemes. It should come as no surprise that the Chinese government is pushing users to develop and adopt indigenous open source products (such as Red Flag Linux) in part to avoid having to purchase similar goods from the West (such as Microsoft Windows) that are considerably more expensive, largely due to copyright, trademark and patent restrictions. Many Chinese citizens aren't willing to wait for these efforts to bear fruit, and have resorted to piracy in order to fulfill their needs. These problems are not limited to mainland China alone; they have arisen in many parts of Africa, Asia and other parts of the world.

Yet proponents of new intellectual property conventions make the disingenuous claim that their measures are necessary to protect the "cultural, artistic and scientific heritage of developing countries, including traditional and indigenous information", and that new intellectual property rights are needed to make this "heritage" more available.

Outright theft of information can be and is protected by preexisting laws. There may be a need for more vigorous enforcement, but the laws are adequate.

The plain fact is that most of the supporters of this "heritage" theory are actually not from developing countries, but represent large intellectual property holders in industrialized nations. Thus, these "heritage" based suggestions should be viewed with a degree of skepticism.

Some have suggesting allocating a "symbolic percentage of fees received on private copies (unrecorded supports and reading devices) to subsidize developing countries access to international index works" protected by intellectual property laws. These proposals need to be very carefully examined and raise a host of troubling questions.

— In developing nations, who will foot the bill? Average citizens? Non-commercial entities? Corporations? The government? Some other entity?

— Will these fees have the effect that intellectual property holders expect? The China example suggests that this set of proposals may be counterproductive because they will encourage piracy and spur governments in emerging nations toward quasi-protectionism.

— Will these fees also be imposed on already-developed nations? To what extent?

A disturbing new threat to fair use and free expression has arisen in the form of proposals to extend intellectual property protections for the first time to mere facts or data. Specifically, legislation has been introduced in the US , and treaties have been proposed that would apply quasi-copyright protection to public facts that have been collected in some way. The advent of sophisticated computer technology has made it possible to aggregate public facts into databases that can easily searched and correlated with other databases. The parties who create these databases are surely entitled to some protection for their compiled works. If, for example, an organization were to compile the intellectual property decisions of World Trade Organization into a unique form on a CD-ROM, others could legitimately be prevented from simply duplicating the CD and offering it for sale.

But these new database protection schemes would go much further. They would give the parties, who create these databases of public facts, an ownership interest in the fact themselves. The data base owners would have proprietary control over the decisions themselves. Fair use of these facts would not be permitted.

These proposals would remove public information from the public domain. They would seriously impede scientific research, the discussion of public issues and educational exchanges. Data ranging from stock prices, to sports scores, to decisions of public bodies, to governmental satellite images that are used to protect the environment and promote sustainable development could be removed from the public domain.

They would have a particularly onerous impact on journalists, who would be chilled in their ability to report on public facts, which may have been compiled into a proprietary database.

According a property interest in facts would also inevitably drive up the cost of obtaining those facts with a devastating effect on developing nations. Finally, onerous database protection laws that fail to protect fair use will also significantly harm the Internet. A central characteristic of the current Internet is the easy and inexpensive availability of information. The Internet can be a democratizing medium that puts information in the hands of the rich and poor. The database protection schemes will concentrate information in the hands of those who can afford to pay inflated prices for knowledge.

The preservation and expansion of the doctrine of fair use is essential to the preservation of free expression in the 21st Century. It is key to future economic development in many nations. Governments should respect the need for broad access to information and knowledge. Policymakers must resist the temptation to curb the well-established principle of fair use.

The World's lawmakers should be leery of calls to harmonize levels of protection and access worldwide along the line of the DMCA and should recognize these devastating effect those efforts may have a detrimental impact on developing countries.

The WIPO Treaty, itself, needs to be amended to specifically require that the signatory nations include fair use and other freedom of expression doctrines in any their intellectual property legislation. Any new treaties should contain similar provisions.

A global alliance needs to be created to advocate for these principles. This conference presents a unique opportunity to begin forging an alliance between the non-governmental in the developed world, who have been fighting to protect fair use and access to information and technology and between governmental and non-governmental forces in the developing world. We need to begin to coordinate our interests and to work toward the common goal of protecting fair use and access to information. Different proposals have been made to restrict the "fair use" exception in a digital context. Digitization provides tools to detect private digital copying of a protected work and to limit it. This may allow title-holders to prevent practices that have been important for educational and scholarly purposes. Given the power conferred by the technology, "fair use" exceptions established by the law may become inapplicable and substantially affect access to information, particularly in developing countries. The protection of databases, as established or proposed in some jurisdictions, may aggravate this problem. The development of new principles for the application in this context of "fair use" needs to be considered, including possible approaches to deal, under special rules, with the case of developing countries.

The digitization of information and the development of computer networks, such as Internet, are posing a new and far reaching challenge to copyright. The way in which it is finally resolved may have important implications for the access to and the use of information worldwide.

The main technological change behind this "new revolution" (G-7 Ministerial Conference, 1995), are improvements in data storage, manipulation and transmission of data. With digitization, all kinds of data and copyright works may be recorded and compressed in the same, binary, format. While this allows to reproduce copies without any degradation (every copy is perfect), developments in software permit to manipulate data, images, voice, make "sampling" and otherwise alter works by interactive techniques.

The power of digital technology has transformed the way creators work and how authors and publishers deliver copyright works. It has blurred the lines between copying and reading, sale and reuse, performance and viewing a work. The digitization of works -which are broken down to 0s and 1s- affects the very notion of what constitutes a "copyright work", as well as other key legal concepts such as "author", "originality" and "infringement". Underlying these developments is the capacity of the new technologies to create unauthorized, perfect and costless copies.

In addition, as a result of the explosive growth of the Internet, any work may be distributed worldwide, essentially instantaneously and at an insignificant cost.. Data transmission is no longer limited to a one-to-one basis, but one-to-many or even one-to-all basis. Internet, thus becomes a "broadcasting" system.

The growth of the system and the improvement of transmission techniques challenges the market position of several industries and services, including those related to voice transmission, radio broadcasting, phonograms, publishing of literary works and computer programs.

These developments have polarized the opinions on the ways in which copyright law should react, in order to protect the producers and suppliers of different kinds of works while preserving the interest of the public, particularly in relation to research and education..

Some authors and industrial groups have argued that copyright only requires minor changes in order to adapt to the new technological changes, particularly with respect to the scope of exploitation rights and the extent of the "fair use" exception. This was for example, the position held by the U.S government in its "White Paper on Intellectual Property and the National Information Infrastructure". Said paper argued that "no more than minor clarification and limited amendment" of the Copyright Act were necessary, in order to strengthen the rights of the copyright owner, particularly by clarifying and "dematerializing" the concepts of "fixation", "distribution", "transmission" and "publication". The only major change deemed to be necessary was the introduction of a sui generis right to supplement copyright protection for data databases.

For other scholars, however, copyright, which was born to respond to the problems posed by printing, and was later adapted to audiovisual works, needs to be reconceptualized in the digital era. The copyright subject-matter has evolved over time from symbolic representations of sensual matter to the sensual matter itself, and from works passively received by the audience to works which interactively engage the audience".

According to some views, the "right to prevent copying" (as conferred under copyright) should be replaced by a "right to prevent access" to a work. Other have argued, in contrast, that the exclusive rights granted by copyright, which are becoming "outdated and irrelevant", could be replaced by mere rights to obtain a remuneration.

Since on-line access to subject-matter may be allowed only to those who agree to pay for it and comply with various restrictions regarding use, the need for property rights at all in a digital environment has also been questioned. Payment for access may be guaranteed by way of automatic, on-line, debiting of a credit card account or a bank deposit account. Developments in the technology should make it possible to 'lock' the digital data constituting the subject-matter to which access is allowed. In addition, it should be possible to detect and trace any subsequent unauthorized uses of the access subject-matter, and to automatically debit an account by way of a contractually agreed right to compensation for the unauthorized use.

The debate on the protection of copyright for digital works has taken place in a context of expansion and strengthening of authors' protection. Like in the area of patents, in the field of copyright there has been a fundamental shift from a system originally based on non-commercial considerations -the benefits that the society may derive from creative authorship and the dissemination of ideas- to a "law of misappropriation" the ultimate objective of which would be to protect the commercial value of creative outputs. The encouragement of investment and the availability to the public of their results would be sufficient to justify the awarding of monopoly positions . Whatever copyright may have rested upon in the past, "the primary goals of copyright are now economic considerations". Under the new, dominant conception that has emerged in response to changes in technology and market trends, the primary concern is rewarding investors, rather than the encouragement of individual creation and the public dissemination of knowledge. As stated by David,"even if the rethoric of argument occasionally appeals to notions of justice and equity, modern economic analysis, and its characteristic preocupation with questions of efficiency, now set the terms for policy discussions about the protection of intellectual property".

Limitations to exclusive rights

Despite the above referred trend, there has been consensus so far that the purpose of copyright is not to ensure the holder a maximum economic return, but to balancing authors rights to obtain a fair return and society's interest in access to and use of information.

More than 100 years ago Numa Droz, one of the founders of the Berne Convention, already stated that "limits to absolute protection are rightly set by the public interest".

In order to reach such balance, copyright laws have normally incorporated a variety of limitations to the authors' exclusive rights, in particular reproduction.

The exclusive reproduction right was defined in Article 9 of the Berne Convention. Paragraph 1 provided that authors of literary and artistic works have the exclusive right of authorizing the reproduction of their works "in any manner or form" . These broad terms were interpreted to cover all methods of reproduction (e.g. drawing, lithography, offset and other printing processes, photocopying, recording), including those that were unknown at the time of adoption of the Convention.

Paragraph 2 of the Convention balanced such exclusive rights by stipulating that

"It shall be a matter for legislation in the countries of the Union to permit the reproduction of such works in certain special cases, provided that such reproduction does not conflict with a normal exploitation of the work and does not unreasonably prejudice the legitimate interests of the author".

Almost every copyright law based on the "authors rights" conception has contained exceptions for copying for personal use (scientific, educational or other private use), archival copying, library use, education, freedom of news reporting and reporting of current events.

These limitations are generally formulated as specific exceptions for particular uses or situations defined in advance. Thus, though the right to prevent unauthorized reproduction of a protected work has been one of the pillars of copyright protection, exceptions were carved in most national laws for private or personal use. These exceptions, however, have not generally allowed for reproduction which might seriously affect the author's primary market. The exceptions have, therefore, been limited in different ways.

In Europe, for instance, these limitations normally include the following conditions:

— Copies should be made of mere parts of the work. Complete works may be copied only where originals are not available on the market.

— Copies may be produced by reprographic processes only, because those copies are of lesser quality.

— Only single copies may be reproduced. Copies may not be used for other than private purposes and not be given to third parties.

— The private use must be intended by the copier himself or the copier must act in a non-commercial way.

— If there are exemptions for the benefit of libraries and archives, those institutions must be accessible to the public and act in a non-commercial way.

— The legitimate interest of the right-holder must be taken into account".

Under Anglo-American copyright law, exceptions are generally formulated on a case-by-case basis, and are grounded on the application of broad general principles. The exceptions refer to acts of 'fair dealing' or 'fair use', such as copying for purposes of research, teaching, journalism, criticism, parody and library activities.

A good example is the U.S. doctrine of "fair use" which only provides general legislative guidelines and largely leaves to courts the task of elaborating what is permissible on specific instances. "Fair use" is defined as an equitable rule of reason that permits copyrighted materials to be used under certain conditions without the consent of the copyright owner . Such conditions, according to section 107 of the U.S Copyright law as developed by case law, include:

— The purpose and character of the use, including whether the use is commercial or for non profit educational purpose, transformative and productive or duplicative ;

— Whether the original work is published or unpublished (taking material from an unpublished work weighs against a finding of fair use).

— The nature of the copyrighted work (the scope of fair use is broader for factual works than it is for works of fantasy);

— The amount and substantiality of the portion used in relation to the copyrighted work as a whole (the greater the taking of copyrighted material, the weaker the claim of fair use); and,

— The effect of the use on the potential market for or value of the copyrighted work .

The application of the general guidelines provided by the US law and the lack of a complete and precise list of exempted acts, has made it difficult to articulate the fair use doctrine in particular cases , but has provided a flexible framework to adopt solutions as new technologies have emerged. In Europe, despite the progress made in the harmonization of different aspects of intellectual property laws, the issue of fair use gave rise to many divergent regulations. EU member countries shown little willingness to abandon their own conceptions about the extent of limitations to the reproduction right. This led to sometimes contrasting solutions in different countries. For instance, in the case of reprography and private copying in particular, solutions ranged from a straightforward ban on private copying to legalization without compensation of rightholders.

The analysis of the law of other countries, including developing countries, also show considerable divergences and, in some cases, uncertainty about the exact scope of the exception to the reproduction right .

The status and scope of the "fair use" exception came under scrutiny and controversy as a result of the development and diffusion of digital technology. As mentioned, this technology has substantially modified the way creators work and how authors and publishers deliver copyright works.

It has, on the one hand, increased the power of copyright owners to control copying, the sale of copies and public transmissions of works, and it has also extended such power to reading, reusing copies and viewing protected material. On the other hand, digital technology permits to create unauthorized, perfect and costless copies, and the almost instantaneous and worldwide distribution of protected works through computer networks. These developments have created new pressures to review the availability and scope of a "fair use" exception and to internationalize the copyright system. The "fair use" doctrine, it is argued, is justified when the transaction costs are too high and prevent copyright owners and users to entering into a copyright license such as in the case of library photocopying or home videotaping. But technologies exist today that enable copyright owners and users to negotiate individual licenses for electronically stored works at a low cost. This may be done, for instance, through a "Copyright Clearence Center" that collect and administer royalties for each individual use.

In addition. given the international reach of computer networks and the diverging legal solutions existing at the national level, reproduction acts that may be subject to the rightholder´s consent in one country may well be covered by a "fair use" exception in other countries. This has been viewed by copyright industries, some legislators and policy makers as a serious threat to the economic basis of copyright exploitation.

The concerns about the status of fair use in a digital context led in some countries to the establishment of national ad hoc commissions, the preparation of reports, the enactment of new legislation and the negotiation and adoption of two new international treaties. In a number of judicial decisions the impact of digital technology on fair use was also specifically considered.

In the United States the issue of the future of fair use was addressed by the "National Information Infrastructure Task Force's Working Group on Intellectual Property Rights", chaired by Bruce A. Lehman, the U.S. commissioner of patents and trademarks . A "Conference of Fair Use" ("CONFU") was established, but it collapsed as a result of disagreement on the extent of the "safe harbor" for fair use . Libraries and other groups expressing the users' views defended the room for lawful uses of copyrighted works by individuals, libraries, and educational institutions in the digital environment. US Congress passed in October 1998 the "Digital Millennium Copyright Act" (DMCA) and has under consideration two bills (the "Collection of Information Antipiracy" and the "Consumer and Investor Access to Information Act") for the protection of data bases developed under quite diverging philosophies on the desirable extent of protection.

In Canada, a "Copyright Subcommittee" examined whether the fair dealing provisions should apply and whether criteria should be introduced to provide guidance to the use of works on the Information Highway. The subcommittee observed a high level of dissonance among submissions representing both users and creators regarding the current state of the fair dealing provisions in the Canadian Copyright Act.

Submissions from creator's groups generally argued that, given the ease of reproduction of works on the Information Highway, fair dealing should be excluded as a possible defense in order to restore some balance of control for copyright owners. Submissions from users requested greater clarity in the application of the fair dealing provision and argued that there should be criteria such as are currently found in the U.S. law.

The European Commission prepared a "Green paper" where it argued that the change brought about by digital technology must be taken into account when we consider the right of reproduction in a digital environment. Where the technology does not allow copying to be prevented, a valid response may continue to be that levies should be charged on the equipment and recording medium, and private copying be declared permissible. But where there is the technical means to limit or prevent private copying, there is no further justification for what amounts to a system of statutory licensing and equitable remuneration.

"Without a harmonized response to these questions there may be difficulties with the Internal Market if a right-holder from another Member State with more protective legislation refuses to allow digital works or other protected matter to be brought into his territory where they originate in other Member States where digitization does not require the consent of the right-holder.

"The scope of the reproduction right is a separate question, because so many exceptions have been made by Member States under Article 9(2) of the Berne Convention. Careful consideration will be needed in order to determine which of these exceptions can continue. An example of the sort of difficulty which arises is the question of matter disseminated in digital form. There will also have to be a review of the legality of private digital copying, given that the technology allows this kind of copying to be monitored, prevented or limited.

"A situation in which private copying is legal in some Member States and not in others will create serious difficulty. The fact that private copying is authorized in certain Member States means that some operators will be afraid to allow access to their services there. The technical arrangements needed to control private copying cannot be made compulsory in Member States which authorize private copying, but will be required in other Member States. These differences will place barriers in the way of trade in the relevant equipment".

The European Union gave, in 1991, an important step in the direction of reducing the scope of limitations to exclusive reproduction rights in the area of software. Given that copies of digital works can be identical to the original, the EC Computer Programs Directive narrowly tailored exceptions to such rights. Similarly, the EC Directive on Data Bases, limited reproduction for private purposes only to non-electronic databases (article 6.2.a).

Moreover, in order to address the problems of copyright in digital works, the adoption of a new European Directive on the "Harmonization of certain aspects of copyright and related rights in the Information Society" is under consideration. The draft Directive permits Member States to exempt from the reproduction rights copies for non-commercial archiving or conservation purposes by libraries and universities, and in respect of ephemeral fixations made by broadcasting organizations by means of their own facilities and for their own broadcasts.

The Member States are also permitted under the draft to provide for limitations to the reproduction rights where the use is for the sole purpose of illustration for teaching or scientific research, and this is subject to both acknowledgment of the source and the provision of fair compensation of right-holders. Also excludable is the use of excerpts in connection with the reporting of current events, as long as the source and, if possible, the author's name is indicated, and to the extent justified by the informatory purpose and the objective of illustrating the event concerned.

Other exemptions in the draft Directive include quotations for purposes such as criticism or review, provided that they relate to a work or other subject matter which has already been lawfully made available to the public, that the source and, if possible, the author's name is indicated, and that their use is in accordance with fair practice, and to the extent required by the specific purpose.

National courts have also taken into account the effects of digital technology on the extent of permissible fair use in deciding particular cases relating to various categories of digital works . For instance, in Germany the Federal Supreme Court acknowledged that the interests of authors are affected increasingly as a result of the development of technology. The Court addressed, in particular, the problems raised when articles are entered into public archives on the day of their publication and on-line users may order these articles also the same day.

Though this leads to a situation where archives may compete with the original publication itself, the Court argued that the availability of information is essential in a modern society, and considered a mandatory royalty sufficient to take care of the interests of authors in such cases. The perceived need to adapt and strengthen copyright law to the digital environment was also the driving force for the negotiation and adoption of two World Intellectual Property Organization treaties in 1996. The preamble to the WIPO Copyright Treaty (1996) proclaimed

"the need to maintain a balance between the rights of authors and the larger public interest, particularly education, research and access to information, as reflected in the Berne Convention".

Article 10 of the WIPO Convention included a specific provision on limitations to exclusive rights, modeled on, but on its face more restrictive than article

9(2) of the Berne Convention and article 13 of the TRIPS Agreement. According to the WIPO Convention,

(1) Contracting Parties may, in their national legislation, provide for limitations of or exceptions to the rights granted to authors of literary and artistic works under this Treaty only in certain special cases that do not conflict with the normal exploitation of the work and do not unreasonably prejudice the legitimate interests of the author.

(2) Contracting Parties shall, when applying the Berne Convention, confine any limitations of or exceptions to rights provided for therein to certain special cases which do not conflict with the normal exploitation of the work and do not unreasonably prejudice the legitimate interests of the author.

In the Berne Convention there was no limitation that the States shall "confine" the exceptions to those meeting the three-step test introduced by article 9(2).

Challenges to the Fair Use Doctrine

Though the described developments have eroded the status and scope of the fair use doctrine, it survived and has obtained and specific recognition in the WIPO Copyright Treaty, as mentioned. However, new challenges to the application of the doctrine emerged from new fronts:

— the development of protection technologies (generally known as "rights management systems" or "rights management technologies") and the express regulation of "circumventing" devices or services that may be used to defeat technical means of protection (such as "password codes" for computer programs, encryption or scrambling for cable programming, videocassettes, CD-ROMs and DVDs);

— the extended use of contract law to control access to and the use of digital copyright works; and

— the development of a sui generis form of protection, for databases.

Available technologies permit right-holders to control access by third parties to works in digital form. Once accessed, it is also possible to monitor and regulate their use. This in-built protection can be more effective than any intellectual property rights protection, and may deprive the fair use doctrine of any concrete value. With the effective use of such protective technologies, title-holders may enjoy "virtually absolute control over their works, unencumbered by the limitations embodied in copyright law".

Technologies designed to prevent third parties from unauthorized access to and use of digital works may permit right-holders to control, monitor and meter every possible use of a work. If strengthened by the legal prohibition to defeat them, such systems create new and powerful means to prevent reproduction, including for fair use, and other acts.

Recent legal developments have precisely moved in that direction. The referred to WIPO Treaty incorporated, under the influence of the US government and US motion picture industry, a new international norm to regulate technologies likely to circumvent technological protection to digital works. Article 13 states that

"Contracting Parties shall provide legal protection and effective legal remedies against the circumvention of effective technological measures that are used by authors in connection with the exercise of their rights under this Treaty or the Berne Convention and that restricts acts, in respect of their works, which are not authorized by the authors concerned or permitted by law".

In the USA, the already mentioned DMCA enacted, among other things, to implement the WIPO Copyright Treaty obligation to provide legal remedies against circumvention of technological protection, went a step further. The DMCA prohibits the manufacture, sale, or importation of technologies that can be used to circumvent technological protection for copyrighted works. The Act (article 1201) proscribes devices or services that

- are primarily designed or produced to circumvent;
- have only limited commercially significant purpose or use other than to circumvent; or
- are marketed for use in circumventing.

The DMCA includes a number of acts that will be exempted from the reproduction right. However, the Act transforms the fair use doctrine from a flexible common law "safe harbour" to a system of narrow, specific exceptions to exclusive rights , modeled on the European approach on fair use. The DMCA also narrows down the fair use doctrine since it reverses the traditional presumption of fairness that attaches to non-commercial uses. Under the DMCA, the Congress gave the Library of Congress -a congressional agency- rulemaking authority to promulgate by October 2000 exceptions to the anticircumvention prohibition if users of a certain class of works are or are likely to be adversely affected by the prohibition. Those exceptions must be revised every three years thereafter.

Since copying of a work may be a fair use under certain circumstances, the DMCA does not prohibit the act of circumventing a technological measure that prevents copying . However, as indicated, devices primarily designed to circumvent controls protecting the title-holder reproduction are banned (section 1201).

The act of circumventing a technological protection measure to gain access is prohibited. Fair use is not, under the DMCA, a defense to the act of gaining unauthorized access to a work, since this is a violation on its own right.

Preventing access can de facto impede copying. It cannot be copied what cannot be accessed. Even after legitimate access, users may be technologically unable to make copies, given the ban on devices primarily designed to circumvent. Title-holders may also bring acts of copying under the ban on access, by requiring users to re-access a work for every use.

Commentators seem to agree that the DMCA entails a significant departure from the US legal tradition in relation to fair use, which was based on a case-by-case fundamentally equitable balancing of private and public interests. Moreover, many fear that

"Because the anti-circumvention rules makes circumvention of access controls and independent wrong, it has the potential to convert copyright into an absolute form of protection that it was never intended to be. To the extent protected technological measures are actually effective in controlling access to copyrighted works, they will, as a practical matter, preclude all uses of copyrighted works not authorized by copyright owners, including fair use and other excepted uses that the law in legal theory permits. By reinforcing technological protective measures with legal sanctions for their circumvention, the anti-circumvention rule may, in practice, wipe away many of the exceptions and exemptions to copyright protection that Congress has provided for balance".

Based on the mentioned electronic fences , title-holders are in a position to prohibit use or to seek payment for any use of technologically protected works. They can, in fact, supersede any rules allowing for fair use.

Since digital distribution systems permit right-holders to directly interact with users and to determine the conditions for access to and use of works, the massive use of contracts on terms and conditions dictated by suppliers is another ingredient of the threat to fair use and, more fundamentally, to copyright law as such. The enforcement of "shrink wrap" licenses for software and of pre-determined conditions attached to the commercialization of other digital works illustrate this threat.

It has been observed that fees charged for electronic information licenses (which give libraries or schools permission to use materials) are generally higher than prices for the equivalent books or periodicals. The costs of information, particularly scientific books and journals, has been reported to increase by 10 percent or more annually..

Though the enforcement of unconscionable contractual terms may be denied by courts, or subject to antitrust or misuse doctrines , the asymmetry in the contractual relationship may lead to overriding fair use and other statutory limitations to copyright. An electronic agreement that governs access and use for every user looks like an exclusive right rather than a bilateral license. As noted by Cohen,

"if society values the fair use limits on copyright protection, it would be entirely logical to forbid or limit the ability to contract around them -particularly where the terms are non-negotiated and bind large numbers of consumers".

Finally, the fair use doctrine (and corresponding exemptions under continental law) can be restricted as a result of the development of a sui generis regime foı databases.

Databases are protectable, under copyright, as compilations. In principle, however, only those databases that meet the copyright originality test are protectable. In other words, the simple compilations of data are in the public domain.

The European Council Directive 96/9/EC, developed a new, sui generis, form of protection for any database if it is shown that qualitatively and/or quantitatively a "substantial investment in either obtaining, verification or presentation of the contents" has been made (article 7).

The EC Directive provides for an "extraction right", i.e. the right to prevent "the extraction or reutilization of the whole or substantial part, evaluated quantitatively or qualitatively, of the contents of the database" (art. 7).

This Directive provides a conspicuous example of the emerging paradigm of IPRs protection, whereunder the main goal is not to protect creativity and ingenuity, but investments. Databases are, in effect, protected under the sui generis right without requiring originality in the selection or arrangement of their contents. In accordance to the European Commission, the main feature of the Directive is

"to create a new economic right to protect the substantial investment of by a database marker. Considering the considerable investment of human, technical and financial resources necessary to create a database, and given that those databases can be copied at a much lower cost than that of their development, such legal change is important. Unauthorised access to a database and the extraction of its contents are thus acts which can gave grave technical and economic consequences".

The Directive's sections on the sui generis right define two categories of restricted acts: extraction and re-utilization. The right applies to the whole or a substantial part of a database, which means that an insubstantial part is not protected. Protection lasts for 15 years, and that period may be renewed if there has been substantial new investment.

The Directive defines exceptions to the right which are similar to those existing in the chapter on copyright, but, in view of the volume of information in such databases, the exceptions are generally limited to the right of extraction. The sui generis right is conferred in addition to the other existing rights. The Directive does not prescribe, but only authorize, Member countries to provide exceptions for the cases of extraction for "private purposes", "teaching or scientific research", "public security or an administration or judicial procedure" (article 9). Moreover, Member countries may limit the exception relating to teaching and research to "certain categories of teaching and scientific research institution".

In the USA, the Supreme Court decided in Feist Publication Inc. vs. Rural Telephone Services that information consisting solely of facts arranged in a straightforward manner (an alphabetical arrangement of telephone suscribers' names and numbers) were not "original works of authorship" within the meaning of the Copyright Act.

This decision was viewed by some authors as endangering the vitality of the U.S information industries:

"To a nation that counts information as an important asset and a principal export, the outcome is (or should be) extremely worrisome".

After Feist, a bill (the "Collection of Information Antipiracy Bill") was introduced into US Congress in order to expand protection for databases, based on the model of unfair competition rather than property. With the purpose of offering a less restrictive, alternative regulation, a second bill (the "Consumer and Investor Access to Information Act") was also introduced.

The adoption of new regulations on databases may limit the scope of fair use, particularly for scientists, libraries and educational institutions. For instance, under the U.S "Antipiracy" Bill, making available or extracting information for non-profit educational, scientific or research purposes would constitute a "fair use" only if those acts do not materially harm the primary market of the database maker .

The development and diffusion of digital technology has an ambivalent impact on copyright protection. On the one hand, this technology allows the making of perfect and costless copies of copyrighted works, thus expanding the scope for unauthorized reproduction. On the other, it permits right-holders to detect and limit such reproduction. Standardized contractual schemes can reinforce or supplement the technological protection.

The fair use doctrine and similar limits on the scope of copyright protection incorporated in most copyright laws and relevant international treaties, have played an important role in promoting the dissemination of knowledge and the creative arts.

Access to information is the foundation of a democratic society. Copyright must ensure a sound balance between the authors' and the society's interests. There is no reason to think that giving copyright owners greater control over the reproduction and use of their works in the digital environment will result in greater benefit for the public.

While the potential negative effects of free-riding on authors and the copyright industry need to be taken into account, the combination of electronic fences via the use of "rights management systems", the use of contract law and the development of a sui generis protection for databases, may effectively reduce or eliminate the ability of researchers, authors, critics, scholars, teachers, students and consumers to find, to quote for publication or otherwise make fair use of information.

Current technical and legal developments may result in growing barriers to the access to all types of information, which will be increasingly channelled through digital networks. Such barriers are likely to affect not only technology, but also general factual information, as well as scientific knowledge, including information in the public domain.

The adoption of anti-circumvention measures, such as under the DMCA, and the displacement of copyright by contract can make illusory any fair use exceptions contained in copyright law. If the legislative model developed in the USA on anti-circumvention measures and the European approach on data bases become internationalized, the access to and fair use of works may be restricted on a global scale. This may widen the large technological gap that today separate developed and developing countries.

7

E-Commerce Policy Strategies

The global dimension of the net requires new approaches to formulating the policy infrastructures needed to achieve the full potential of the net. Commerce must invest in the development of these policy infrastructures and governments must support these new approaches; It is argued that in the absence of an effective balance between commercial needs and social requirements it will be difficult to achieve universal access. The Internet Law and Policy Forum is working on how such a balance might be devised.

The global information infrastructure creates a space the dimensions of which are nearly impossible to imagine. The combination of computers and related technologies with the dimensions of bandwidth provided by the multiple technologies of fiber optics, cellular, microwave and satellite transmission define an environment that will envelope our earth and, regardless of the risks of cultural degradation which are inherent in such a phenomenon, become an essential aspect of the lives of many humans, and certainly nearly all who live in urban environments. For those citizens of this planet, there is no question that accessing digital information will become an essential utility, equal or greater in value than the essential resources of harnessed power, water, and sanitary and civil living conditions. Information in electronic form, and the infrastructure on which that information is created and transported (and valued as an asset in the global electronic marketplace), is becoming a further asset by which the development of an economy will be evaluated.

Distinguished from the resources of power and water, however, information is not a natural resource. Instead, it finds its origin in the creative activities of humankind. In our writing, coding, processing, banking, artistic creating and other activities that produce intellectual capital, information (and its inherent value to facilitating economic development) has already evolved during this century as a resource for which its distribution is not governed by the pragmatics of its physical location, but by the policy structures and legal systems which define the rights of ownership, and the rights to protect ownership, in the information.

Information is, without question, an economic resource. In considering the challenges of achieving access to information, we must recognize and accept that the world's economies and nations have already positioned and waged enormous battles over the governing policy structures. The recent negotiations within the World Intellectual Property Organization (WIPO), both those which succeeded and which failed, illustrate the scale of the debates.

But the recent convergence of technologies which are fostering the vision of a global information infrastructure, and in particular the Internet, is distinguished by a characteristic that is often overlooked in the policy debates. The reality of this global space is that virtually all of its infrastructure is itself the private property funded by capitalism. In those nations in which the telecommunications infrastructure has been a responsibility of the state, we are witnessing its privatization at an amazing pace. In nations lacking significant communications infrastructure, we are seeing 'generation-skipping' in the investments--copper wiring is being bypassed for fiber, if not for cellular or satellite delivery. Such choices are occurring only upon the investment of private capital in the solutions--the investments must yield acceptable rates of return in order to induce the investment in the first instance.

The same is true for the software, networking tools, payment systems and other ?building blocks? which are becoming the required elements for conducting global electronic commerce—innovation is being spurred by the expectation of returns superior to investments that might be made in more traditional lines—manufacturing, construction or financial investments.

The situation presents us with an essential truth--a truth which must be taken into account throughout our consideration of the laws and ethics of cyberspace. It is a truth which the authors of the science fiction which first imagined cyberspace realized long ago. Quite simply, cyberspace does not exist, and the global electronic marketplace will not mature, if their function and operation will not produce acceptable profits to those who place their capital at risk. Moreover, taking account of the pace of development, investment and innovation which characterize the evolution of the global information infrastructure, the time periods in which the acceptability of those profits is to be measured are being compressed. Time, volume and velocity are simply being evaluated differently with respect to investments for cyberspace. The pressures for measurable performance and return are unparalleled--the impact of private sector capitalism cannot be under-estimated.

The demands are creating, across the infrastructure, an appetite for information which is becoming stronger with each failed investment in the technologies; as William Gates has observed, 'content is everything.' Criteria for the investments are being defined only in terms of the ability of the resulting products--whether hardware, infrastructure or software--to facilitate new revenue. But, regardless of the quality of the technology, what has become apparent is that the information, and its quality for entertainment, education, commerce, government or research, must be valued by the consumer or user if the technology is to be turned on and utilized.

Consequently, the information is becoming the economic currency—the global coin of the realm of cyberspace. And, as an asset with economic value, in digital form, information becomes even more defined by its monetary characteristics than by its values for education, research or development. The pressures of capitalism are thus also placing tension on how those creating the Internet and the tools for empowering digital access to information consider the complex, challenging demands for answers to the legal, ethical and policy frameworks that are as essential to the evolution of a global electronic marketplace as the technologies themselves. Compromised by the expectations for appropriate returns on investment, we have seen the first generation of the Internet blur the libertarian philosophy of its creators—'let there be no rules'—with the economic demands of the capitalists—'let there be no rules which impair the potential for adequate return'.

The resulting mantra has left much of the global community with the perception the Internet and its potential are endangered by a lawless attitude, without ethical values or social integrity, which is being accelerated by the forces of capitalism. Hence, many fear the Internet; governments, responding to fear, are investing enormous resources into the development of policy and regulatory structures which endeavor to eliminate those fears.

The objective of the exercise, in fact, is to endeavor to improve access by allowing cultural, political and social values to be considered and weighed in the process of achieving the best possible environment for accessing, for proper purposes, the greatest portion of the available information. In so doing, the predictability of the electronic space (and the risk of sanctions for non-compliance) is hoped to increase its desirability as a functioning resource to all.

But, contrary to perceptions, the defining forces of capitalism, and their pressures for results, are consistent with the calls of those seeking predictability within the global dimensions of cyberspace. The existence of clear, articulate standards, and in particular the existence of legal certainty regarding the consequences of using the technology for executing commercial transactions, is fundamentally essential to realizing a marketplace. This need for certainty began in the layers of standards which define the infrastructure itself—the rules which describe how data elements combine into packets, how networks connect, how data is transported and how applications interface.

Today, the debates around which, among others, this conference is convened, only begin to introduce us to the last layers—the legal and policy structures which will provide true inter-operability. But the need for these structures to be disciplined into predictable, certain rules is equally imperative. Without clarity throughout the full structure, the environment is dysfunctional. Without functionality, capital has no interest. This scenario, in fact, accelerates a different type of risk—the risk of marginalization. If we are to discuss pursuing universal access to digital information, we must commit to understanding the importance of a predictable legal infrastructure to facilitating that objective. Here is where the needs of a global community and the needs of capital investments converge. In nations and economies in which there is an absence of certainty and predictability in the legal consequences from the commercial use of the global information infrastructure, capital will not be attracted. In those circumstances, capital will move elsewhere, thus risking the marginalization of the subject economies even further.

The resources of the World Bank and other facilities committed to economic development will be insufficient. Time, volume and velocity will continue to have their expected consequences and drive capital toward the environments in which certainty and the potential for an adequate return on investment are most likely to be closely associated.

The global dimensions of the Net require us to consider new approaches to formulating the policy infrastructures that are required, including the legal system elements which, despite diversities in cultural and legal structures, provide a sufficiently harmonious environment for predictability to exist without regard to national sovereignties. This should not be the sole responsibility of governments and inter-governmental organizations, although they possess (and are demonstrating) the competence to respond. For example, OECD, UNCTAD and UNCITRAL are already hard at work on projects which are responsive to the needs for consistent, foreseeable legal frameworks.

However, taking account of the potential appeal of increased returns on their investments, commerce (and the sources of capital) can realize significant benefit from investing in the development of the infrastructure of law and policy that can sustain, and facilitate, universal access. What is required to attract that investment? More than mere capital resources are necessary; as well, governments must be prepared to seriously consider the work product of any initiatives within the private sector and, as appropriate, to cooperate with those efforts. This strategy presents an entirely different paradigm than the traditional model which characterizes much of the law-making processes of the world.

Even in advanced democracies, the paramount function of government is to provide the venue for governance. Yet much of the rhetoric from governments regarding how the legal structures for the Internet will be designed calls for self-regulatory work products to be significant in the architecture. The expectations for industry leadership are surprisingly consistent among developed, western nations. But the questions remain: what invites private sector investment in law and policy development? what invites government to take that investment seriously?

Nearly a decade of experience with facilitating electronic commerce has provided us with some insights into the strategies that must be adopted. Successful standards development, whether for technology or for policy, requires the following key (but not inclusive) attributes. First, the issue being considered must arise from the need of the marketplace for the problem to be resolved--solutions must be market-driven. Second, there must be agility to the process.

The participants must commit resources sufficient to allow a timely, focused effort. Significant policy issues, if not resolved quickly, have the capacity to exhaust the human resources which are invested; timetables, administered with discipline, must be pursued. Third, those involved in the process must be both the relevant stakeholders and, as well, must have sufficient critical mass to assure that the resulting work product will acquire some level of market acceptance. Fourth, there must be sufficient resources committed--financial, time and human in nature—to reflect the seriousness of the parties to achieve a meaningful result. Finally, there must be defined, transparent processes to assure the integrity of the means by which the solutions have been achieved.

Process is tremendously important to the challenge of earning from governments a deferral of their inherent jurisdiction to regulate the integrity and operations of the marketplace. At the global level, if the objective is to produce work product which may be 'imported' into national or regional legal structures or market functions, the parties must commit to defining, publicizing and adhering to the steps by which experts are engaged, input received and support for the resulting output achieved. The legal and policy structures which will govern the marketplace for digital information assets will not be built as a single system; rather, it will be constructed from 'building blocks' which must, in turn, be assembled into systems that align to the cultural, economic and ethical dimensions of the varying marketplaces in which electronic commerce will be conducted.

Accordingly, experience suggests that governments will have tremendous curiosity in the process by which self-regulatory solutions have evolved. Critical is to evaluate the need for, and fully embrace the opportunity for, government review and input of the work. The Net demands new models of conduct; our experiences, even to this 'early' date, suggest that the formal structures will simply not keep pace. But governments and commerce find a mutuality in their desire to achieve progress; what is required is to incorporate the attributes of successful process into authentic models that can allow governments to either defer to regulatory products developed within commerce (such as widely accepted model agreements, commercial codes of conduct, innovative dispute resolution mechanisms) or, as appropriate, to accept and enact into law model regulations which facilitate a harmonized environment. The resulting predictability thereby overcomes the reluctance of capital to invest in market growth and innovation.

But 'self-regulation' is not sufficient; governments will only defer and give respect to that 'self-regulation' which is effective in operation. Thus, clarity must be accompanied by a) the existence of well-defined standards for when behavior is unacceptable; b) articulate means by which to exercise due process for determining a violation; and c) meaningful sanctions to be imposed (and an agreed result as to what authority may impose those sanctions). For the private sector to effectively exercise its potential to invest in regulatory frameworks which accelerate predictability in the marketplace, the stakeholders must be prepared to commit to developing complete solutions within each incremental step of the process.

During 1996, a consortium of over 20 multi-national businesses invested in a pilot project to determine the potential for self-regulation. Operated under the name of the Internet Law & Policy Forum (ILPF), this project has endeavored to demonstrate the capacity of industry, in collaboration with government, to create a neutral venue in which the stakeholders of the Internet could convene and seek to develop harmonized solutions to the challenging legal and policy questions. Central to the strategy is to leverage private sector investment in order to produce work product which normalizes the marketplace and provides to economies entering the global marketplace of cyberspace the tools and resources to put in place appropriate legal and policy systems to give to private capital the necessary investment incentive.

Today, the sponsors of the Forum are evaluating the success of their exercise and making choices regarding the suitability of further investment; regardless of their decision, the needs of the global community, and the opportunities for private sector leadership, remain vital to how we design in the coming months the strategies for responding. The legal and policy structures required are essential to avoiding marginalization and, in that avoidance, we leverage capital to achieve progress toward universal access.

8

Information Access: Role of Society

The advent of information and communication technologies coincides with increasing demands for public access to government information. The tools of the Internet provide a vehicle for improved information sharing among branches of government as well as with the public. Many governments today operate in an environment of ever-increasing public need and declining, or at best, stable revenue streams. Citizens, taxpayers and all sorts of government constituents and special interest groups are crying out for increased government accountability. They want government to improve services, cut waste, streamline existing activities, and provide greater public access to information.

The use of the Internet is already beginning to change the way government operates in response to these constituent mandates. Government use of the Internet has the potential to provide better government service. As reported in the *PIPER Letter*, "when government delivers information, in many cases it is delivering the government service itself. This new interactive medium, with its built-in measurements and feedback loops, allows government to 'relate' to individual constituents with a new depth and frequency. It can add an entirely new dimension to government's relationship to its stakeholders."

Attitudes to democracy will be a key driver in the level of openness and accessibility to information provided by government. Such a process would define all programmes government-wide, aid in collecting meaningful data, provide universal access for citizens to information, and ultimately offer a relatively simple mechanism for the provision of many state services at a much lower cost to the taxpayer.

The Commonwealth of Kentucky's Web site contains a goal statement which is a concise example of the philosophy and commitment governments are making to Internet technology as a way of improving government service: "Our goals are to:

— Develop the Commonwealth's public sector communications network as a widely accessible, affordable infrastructure resource which can be used to break through the barriers traditionally imposed by geography, demographics, or ability to pay.

— Provide the capability to transport information in any electronic form (voice, video, data, image or radio) among public sector agencies, educational institutions, economic development interests and governmental institutions."

The Internet offers a unique opportunity to streamline the delivery of government services, enhance communication with its citizenry, and serve as a catalyst for empowering citizens to interact with government.

The growth in popularity and ease of access to the Internet appears to coincide with pressures from public interest groups and some legislatures for more access to public information.

The need for some governments to embrace this new technology is in part driven by the legislative mandate that all agencies provide public access to information. Meeting the requirements of this mandate often proves difficult using the *ad hoc* methods and controls of the past. Despite the passage of freedom of information legislation in many countries, there is still a resistance to sharing information by people within government who want to limit access to their data.

The control of information is an elitist perspective. However, according to novelist Tom Clancy, "the more information available to the average person, the greater the synergy that develops from it." If implemented, the tools of the Internet provide a method for improving the sharing of information with the public, as well as improving the efficiency of internal communications. Proper use of the technology will increase opportunities for citizens to participate in government by voicing their opinions and concerns.

The development of the World Wide Web (WWW) has created a platform-independent mechanism for the transfer of documents, the ability to search large databases, to enter basic transactions, and even the ability to run applications.

Governments are often frustrated in their efforts to co-ordinate and manage information by the wide variety of hardware and software platforms owned within the public sector.

Internet technology offers a unifying platform on which the collection of data for internal and external use can be built. It has been adopted by hundreds of thousands of content providers and tens of millions of users. The presence of a large user community makes a compelling case for the preparation of an information framework that takes advantage of this technology.

In a very short period of time, many government officials will realise that the growth of Internet technologies will have a major impact not only on how information is presented to the public, but on how business is conducted among government agencies and the general public. Internet technology may set the stage for the online public services of the future.

In order to understand the context in which governments are likely to develop public information, the research reported in this chapter includes a review of the Internet's origin, its rapid growth and the technologies that influence its character and utility. Governments will also need to understand the internal and external factors that may affect the establishment and operation of a government Web site.

An overview of current Internet issues gives content providers an insight into potential change. Current issues include changes to the telecommunications infrastructure, security and privacy, copyright protection, and universal access.

A stakeholder analysis looks at those affected by the creation of a government Web site and their possible attitudes or values. Internal to the organisation are the legislature, and individual government agencies. External stakeholders - potential customers of the information presented - are the news media and the general public.

The origin of the Internet in 1969 can be traced to cold war research. The United States Department of Defense Advanced Research Projects Agency (DARPA) set out to create a robust mechanism for computer-based communications. The original network was called ARPANET. Its objective was to construct a communications network able to withstand disruptions that would take place in the event of nuclear war. The network was designed to allow multiple destination paths and to enable lower-level communications software to utilise alternative paths at will. In addition, the network offered a built-in mechanism for load balancing as well as the ability to bypass inactive circuits.

Initially the Internet provided four basic network services: remote access (Telnet), file transfer (FTP), mail, and news. To promote education and research activities, access was generally free.

The concept of a free public network, rather than a private, commercial one, was a clear part of the culture surrounding the network. Academics and students used the network to exchange information, to share software, and to discuss and debate issues. During the 1970s, other academic organisations around the world began to construct similar networks to ARPANET using the same software available in the United States.

The military, in particular, realised that it would need to create a more secure network than the experimental ARPANET. The military wanted to maintain its own secure telecommunications system and also maintain links to the public networks. To make this possible, an *internetting* project was initiated to link together these networks; hence the name the Internet.

An inter-networking protocol was developed to work with the original transmission control protocol. This combination of transmission control and an Internet protocol, abbreviated to TCP/IP, is the dominant standard for computer-based communications today. The benefit of the TCP/IP standard is that it is supported by virtually every computer and software manufacturer in the world.

Whether the intention is to publish material or services for world-wide access or to confine them to an organisational environment, a wide choice exists in hardware and software. By enabling a rich interconnection of computing and communication environments, TCP/IP offers a simple mechanism for communicating from both present and future information systems.

By 1986, the National Science Foundation (NSF), an independent government agency established to promote science and engineering, had taken the lead role to put together a high speed backbone with a transmission rate of 1.5 Megabits per second (Mbps). It established a mechanism for regional and local commercial providers to offer access outside government and academic communities.

Government subsidies helped to support the technology while demand grew. By 1989, backbone speeds were increased to 45Mbps. In April 1995, NSF support for the Internet backbone was withdrawn and the Internet is now operating using commercial telecommunications providers.

The level of traffic generated on the Internet has been growing rapidly. One of the most remarkable features of the Internet is the flat fee policy. In the flat-fee model, users are charged for the size of the 'pipe' or maximum rate of transmission rather than the actual amount of data transmitted. For modem users, of course, charges may be based on connect time. While allowing users open access to any site, the Internet enables world-wide communication without the overhead of a toll system similar to the long distance telephone network now in place.

The institution of long distance charges on the Internet would be impractical, since it would be impossible for users to predict the charges resulting from a given connection. Other key factors contributing to the growth of the Internet are its:

— Ability to link physically dissimilar networks;

— Role as the world's *de facto* electronic mail system;

— Use of public domain protocols (standards) that are universally supported by manufacturers;

— Growing acceptance by mainstream business and society (*.com* domain hosts established by private corporations have long surpassed *.edu* domains established by universities in the US);

— Two-way communication, whereby one can be both an originator and a consumer of information; and

— Ability to realise dramatic gains in the functionality of existing computer systems.

Surveys conducted on a regular basis show an exponential increase in the growth of Internet hosts, networks and domains. A host is simply any computer with a TCP/IP address, although not all addresses have full Internet access. For example, the three largest online service providers, America OnLine, CompuServe, and

Prodigy, offer Internet access to their combined total of ten million subscribers. The number of hosts associated with their service is a relatively small number that does not reflect their large subscriber volume.

Until its discontinuance in April 1995, it was possible to document the traffic on the NSFNET backbone. Figures indicated that the amount of data moving across the backbone also grew rapidly. "Total NSFNET traffic grew from *195 million* packets in August 1988 to almost *24 billion* in November 1992, a 100-fold increase in four years. During November 1992, the network reached its first *billion-packet-a-day* mark." The last traffic measures available in April 1995, showed a monthly total of 59 billion packets. Twenty one percent of those packets were generated by the World Wide Web, making it the largest single Internet service.

It is difficult to determine the actual number of Internet users, but growth rates are clearly high. International Data Corporation estimated the total number of users in the US alone at 8 million in January 1996. A more recent study estimates nearly 20 million users at the end of 1997, with predictions that there may be five times as many worldwide by the year 2000.

The World Wide Web and the Internet are commonly considered to be synonymous. "In actuality, the Web is a collection of protocols and standards used to access the information on the Internet. On the other hand, the Internet is a physical medium used to transport the data. The World Wide Web defines and unifies the 'languages' used to retrieve data on the Internet."

The World Wide Web was introduced in 1991. Developed at CERN, a particle physics research centre in Switzerland, the WWW is a distributed hypertext system that operates on a client/server model. Web servers store available documents as plain ASCII text. These documents contain markup tags and follow a standard known as Hypertext Markup Language (HTML). The hypertext feature of HTML provides support for linkage instructions, or URLs (Universal Resource Locators), and allows direct access to pages on other Web servers.

In contrast to earlier connection-based protocols, the Web permits a seamless connection to any Internet address. The client programs that run on the user's computer, providing access to the Web, are known as browsers. The Mosaic browser, written for graphical user interfaces, became the prototype for many imitators, such as Netscape Navigator. This software family supports a mixture of text, sound, graphics, images, video, animation and binary (executable) files.

The information provided to users by Web servers is not limited to static files. Several methods exist to forward requests to other server processes that are able to extract information from large database systems and format it for the user. This technique permits simple transaction processing and is the foundation for electronic commerce via the Internet.

Software developers have been working to advance the capabilities of the Web by creating special viewers. For example, there are special viewers for *Postscript* documents or for executing multimedia presentations. Viewers are usually given away free by software developers, in hopes of marketing their development system. For the past two years, Sun Microsystems has been promoting an Internet development system called *Java*, that permits platform-independent software to be executed directly via the Web. More elaborate software tools, such as three-dimensional virtual reality generators, require far more bandwidth than the standard text-based Web page. With enhanced display features, the Internet is an attractive marketing medium with a wide global audience.

The ultimate value of the Internet to government operations and constituent interests might best be demonstrated when viewed in terms of the available options to collect and distribute information:

— *Point to point*: A single user sends a message to a single receiver.

  Government examples: a citizen provides an opinion to a legislator on a prevailing policy issue; a government agency notifies a client of a grant-award the same day they approve it.

— *Point to multipoint*: A single user sends a message to a number of specific receivers.

  Government examples: a foreign business requests information concerning economic development opportunities within the country, and the request is sent on to a number of potential business partners; a national development committee sends project updates to public and private sector participants.

— *Point to server broadcast*: A single user sends a message to a server that makes the message available to any user interested in that topic area.

  Government examples: during a severe storm, emergency management officials can get real-time storm updates provided by the meteorological service; government agencies can sponsor forums for collaborative work on policy and programme issues.

— *Point to server narrowcast*: A single user sends a message to a server that makes the message available only to an authorised group of users.

  Government examples: persons seeking professional licenses may check the status of their application; government agency administrators may exchange confidential information.

— *Server broadcast*: A server contains stored information. This information is broadcast in the sense that the server provides this information to any requesting client. Users can observe this information anonymously.

  Government examples: a citizen can access the government's Web site; a public sector organisation provides a single point of contact for its customers to access its programmatic activities.

— *Server narrowcast*: A server provides information to only a specific set of authorised users.

  Government examples: the judiciary provides a dedicated, subscription-based server for the dissemination of court decisions; practising lawyers can subscribe to the judiciary server for access to information as soon as it becomes available.

Environmental Monitoring

As participants on the Internet, governments will need to be aware of national Internet-related issues. If the Internet becomes an effective means to distribute information, the viability of the technology will be a public concern. Current issues of concern to developers of Web sites include changes to the telecommunications infrastructure, security, copyright protection, and universal access. The evolution if not resolution of these issues will impact the future development of available information services and will have an impact on the appropriateness of this medium for government.

Telecommunications Infrastructure

The condition of national (and international) telecommunications infrastructure is a critical determinant of the viability and utility of government Internet-based services. It has therefore been the principal focus of state attention in deliberations about the Internet.

Deregulation has been seen as a key tool in many countries seeking to upgrade their telecommunications infrastructure. However, a balance of state and market will still be required in many circumstances, though with the state taking a more promotional than regulatory role. The experience of the United States is indicative of the political difficulty in balancing state and market.

Due to the prior interests of Vice President Al Gore, the Clinton Administration was instrumental in focusing public attention on the idea of a future National Information Superhighway in 1994. The administration produced a *Strategic Planning Document* that placed the highest priority on information technology because "any nation that dominates information technology will be a leading superpower of the 21st century."

The administration sees an active role for government, citing the prior success of the state in the development of a High Performance Computing and Communications (HPCC) programme, sponsored legislatively by then Senator Gore in 1986. This program was responsible for the development of the high speed (45Mbps) Internet backbones that are in place today.

However, the continuing federal budget deficit combined with opposition from congressional Republicans to government interference in the free market process has limited activities to existing research projects.

Although these projects involve US$2bn-worth of federal research funds, this is a scant commitment when applied to a nationwide communications infrastructure. In 1996, the US Congress passed The Telecommunications Act.

The act attempted to reduce government regulation and control, recognising that communications technologies had advanced to the point where the transmission medium no longer defines the type of service. The act did not provide government funding for constructing an infrastructure.

Futurists such as George Gilder and Microsoft's Bill Gates speak enthusiastically about what they expect to be a communications revolution that will take place over the next ten years. They believe that a convergence of telecommunications services will occur as each form of communication is converted from analogue to digital format. However, this revolution can only take place if the economic and political environment is conducive to support the expansion of the telecommunications infrastructure.

By placing responsibility for managing the Internet backbone with telecommunications companies, the commercialisation of the Internet is likely to accelerate and a period of change and competition is underway. Of course, that is not a guarantee that competition will continue to be the norm. There is a high cost associated with building independent data networks that reach every household. The consolidation of competitors may restore local monopolies that restrict the range of services available to the public.

The large infrastructure investments increase the likelihood that competitors will merge until several massive communication service providers dominate the industry. The providers might be far different from traditional communications providers, as the experience of television indicates.

While AT&T dominated the telephone industry before its break-up in 1984, it controlled only the transmission medium, not the content. Broadcast television stations have, in effect, controlled the use of their channel license and in so doing have concentrated on the lowest common denominator for programming.

Cable operators, although forced to provide limited public access on their systems, have followed a similar path and while many systems routinely advertise more that 100 channel capability, a large percentage of these channels are dedicated to pay per view and premium entertainment services.

The danger of entertainment-oriented system design is that it allows for a high speed channel in one direction only, thereby limiting information providers to those organisations who control the source of the high speed data stream.

In the US, then, there has been a massive expansion of the telecommunications infrastructure, but the interaction of government and commerce remains an area for conflict, with a continuously shifting boundary of responsibilities. The same outcomes of conflict and shifting responsibilities are seen world-wide, and they will ultimately determine the extent to which an infrastructure exists to support government use of the Internet.

Security and Privacy

To support commercial and governmental transactions the Internet must offer a secure environment in which such transactions can take place. In a packet switched network the precise path from one site to another is unknown; therefore, the possibility exists for those packets to be examined, imitated, or diverted, resulting in the loss of personal information that may be used to commit fraud. The developers of Internet software have been working to construct secure transaction systems. However, public trust remains low, and some government agencies have also become involved.

The development of secure network systems using large key cryptography has been opposed by law enforcement officials in a number of countries, notably the US. US government regulations, for example, have prohibited the export of cryptography technology since World War II. The fear is that if criminals obtain technology from which information cannot be decoded, it would be impossible for law enforcement officials to track their activities. Government security agencies have asked that a second key be available that would permit the equivalent of government wiretapping. However, the global nature of the Internet makes it highly unlikely that a security system with a *back door* known only to the US government will be universally adopted. In addition to security, an increase in electronic commerce as well as other types of transactions raises concerns about privacy. The information collected about users in an all-digital environment is potentially immense and the ability to develop personal profiles from past transaction records could result in instances where life and health insurance are denied or employment is refused because of such profiles. The full impact of participating in an electronic marketplace that can be monitored and analysed has yet to be fully understood.

Copyright Protection

The ease with which digital information can be replicated has threatened the viability of conventional copyright laws. Information is no longer bound to a physical object such as a book or a vinyl disk that is difficult to reproduce. Digital information can be replicated with no loss of quality. Software tools can be used to modify or transform content from one form to another. The material may be transmitted quickly to any location on the network.

At the same time, there needs to be a further clarification of what constitutes fair use. Fair use has traditionally allowed the transfer of material purchased and has allowed the purchaser some degree of ownership over the material. However, many software and content developers have taken the position that only the original purchaser has any right to use material and has no right to transfer it to others. If this concept had been applied to books, there would be no libraries, and books would have to be burned rather than sold or given to others.

Universal Access

If access to the Internet becomes essential for conducting ordinary day-to-day business, then it will be necessary to ensure that the average citizen has such access. The doctrine of universal access has, for example, been behind regulatory efforts to maintain low local phone rates at the expense of business users who pay the bulk of long distance charges.

The strategy has been successful in a number of countries, with near universal access for phone services being achieved in many of the industrialised nations. At present, the costs of obtaining Internet access are too high to bring about universal access and the computer systems used are too difficult to set up and manage.

The minimum functionality that will constitute access has been changing and will continue to do so. On the one hand, access is becoming easier, with options to use TV sets for display and alternate access methods such as satellite and coaxial cable. On the other hand, data transfer requirements continue to rise with the complexity of online materials. Universal access, therefore, is a moving target. Whilst access rates are likely to improve, universal access is still a long way off. So, if governments are going to encourage use of the Internet for access to information and services, then there is a corresponding obligation to ensure that public access points exist throughout the country.

Stakeholder Perspectives

Information systems are social systems, and Web sites are no exception. Therefore, when planning Web site development, there needs to be a clear understanding of the social milieu within which that site exists. This understanding is best created through an awareness of the different stakeholder groups who have a stake in the Web site. The identity of these stakeholder groups will differ from country to country, but typical groups include: senior political figures, the legislature, and public sector organisations within government; and the news media and citizens outside government.

The interests of these groups will differ from situation to situation, but there follows an example of stakeholder identity and interests taken from the State of Connecticut in the US.

Senior Political Figures

In Connecticut these include the Governor, Lieutenant Governor, Secretary of State, Attorney General, Comptroller, and Treasurer. As elected officials they all have an interest in some level of participation in the development of a government Web site. First and foremost, they wish their constituents to perceive that they are managing their responsibilities. Failure to participate might be seen as an omission that reflects poorly on their office. Hence, not surprisingly, all of these offices have begun to develop Web sites.

In addition, the Secretary of State, who has responsibility for recording and publishing basic State and municipal data, implementing the State Election Laws and promoting voter registration, will wish to offer a volume of online information related to the administration of the office.

The Legislature

The most sought after legislative information is the status of proposed legislation. In pre-electronic form, this information is typically made available directly from the offices of the legislature or by subscription to a private information service.

Making this information available electronically via the Web can reduce the number of routine queries that legislators receive. They would be able themselves to use the service from home or office, and would find this beneficial since they need access to State information to understand the programmes they are creating and funding.

Not surprisingly, several legislative Web sites have been sponsored by the Connecticut legislature and by its two major political parties.

Public Sector Organisations

The State Library is the official State archivist and has been actively seeking to make information such as General Statutes available for online searches. This agency views the development of the Internet as an electronic extension of the library.

Internet technology has the capacity to span both the function of the traditional library in maintaining historic information and the capacity of the media to provide current information as soon as it is generated. Libraries have an important role to play in ensuring that there is universal access to online information by placing access terminals within their facilities.

State agencies are required to provide public access to non-confidential government databases. The law requires that agencies provide the information in whatever format it is requested by the user.

The State's Office of Information and Technology has required agencies to submit lists of public access databases in order to construct a mechanism for public access to electronic information. The hardware and software independence granted by Internet technology provides an opportunity to address this requirement via the creation of Internet servers containing copies or subsets of existing databases.

Public sector organisations have other reasons for adopting this technology. It has internal uses as well as external ones, and government agencies have been using 'intranets' for meeting agendas and minutes, procedural manuals and regulations, internal staff contact details, training materials, bulletin boards, etc. Agencies can also prototype their external applications as intranet applications.

Thanks to the benefits they bring, Web sites have been developed by a substantial number of Connecticut State agencies. For example, the Department of Economic Development (DED) has responsibility for promoting industrial development within the State.

Tourism is a major industry that benefits from low cost exposure, and promoting tourism is already a predominant activity on a number of government Web sites. DED has a major interest in the development of an attractive, easy-to-use site that features the benefits of visiting and living in the State.

News Media

The media would like to see as much raw data available on government Web sites as is possible, since this makes their background research work quicker and easier. They also have a commitment to freedom of information, to which the Internet is often seen as a major contributor. In Connecticut, for example, a news media editor chairs the State Council on Freedom of Information. Media sources also themselves provide information via Web sites.

Citizens

The general public has a stake in how its government functions. Those most interested in government activities will want as much detail as possible about specific programme areas. Welfare claimants want information about how, where and what to claim; job seekers want ready access to employment information; business people want information on government regulatory and promotional measures; and so on. In addition, citizens in general want to receive information about the performance of government, but also want to provide information about their viewpoints by participating in political discussion. It is therefore important that Internet-enabled applications should provide the opportunity for input from citizens to government, as well as presenting static material as an output from government to citizens.

Web Site Creation

There are any number of serious and compelling reasons for governments to create a presence on the Internet.

However, the online environment is a dynamic and challenging arena and *'doing it'* and *'doing it well'* require two very different levels of planning and collaboration. This is particularly true where governments seek to create a single and integrated Web presence. Such an approach has much to recommend it. Compared with a 'free for all' approach in which Ministries, departments and agencies all create their own separate sites, the integrated path is:

— more customer-focused,

— easier to use,

— cheaper to create, and

— less likely to create inconsistencies and duplications.

However, governments tend to be a loose affiliation of large and small, geographically diverse and programmatically unique organisations. Developing an all-inclusive and consistent representation of a many faceted organisation can be a daunting task - online or off. Before evaluating specific efforts at creating a presence on the Internet, an examination of the principles for information delivery on the Internet will provide a useful framework for analysing those efforts.

Information Delivery Principles on the Web

The World Wide Web has achieved explosive growth in activity, traffic, data, servers and information. However, the ability to produce high-quality, meaningful information, with low levels of 'noise' and redundancy is still in its infancy. Harder still, for government efforts, is to be able to craft good information and then use it to

(a) invite citizens to take a more active role in their government, and

(b) improve planning, policy analysis and decision making in government operations.

According to John December,

> "Ultimately, the challenge for a Web information provider is to acknowledge the dynamic nature of Web information and recognise that information quality is not just a set of outward characteristics or design decisions, but a part of a continuous process in which content and presentation are adjusted to meet user needs. Webs that more completely articulate information so that it can become knowledge may be the key to the Web's continued growth."

One of the key elements which was evident in analysing the Internet efforts of US State governments, is the extent to which these governments' Web presentations appeared to have a very direct focus on user needs. With regard to general content and style considerations, a key distinction seems to be:

— whether the government was presenting itself as a functional bureaucracy to its users/customers, i.e. 'This Is What We Do', or

— whether the government tried to view itself as a user/customer would, i.e. 'How May We Help You?'.

The latter approach does not presume that a user has a significant amount of institutional knowledge about the organisation itself (i.e. knows exactly which agency or functional unit can solve his/her problem).

Rather, the better government presentations anticipate a lack of knowledge of the organisation and assume a 'subject matter' approach to guide the user to the appropriate topic or subject matter area, and only then to the organisational unit which can help solve the problem.

The following methodology can be generally applied in the development process of a Web site. However, one can use these principles in a ıeverse-engineering sense to evaluate, analyse, contrast and compare existing government Web sites:

- *Audience*: Is it clear for whom the Web site is intended: government employees or user/customers (constituents, special interest groups, etc.)?
- *Purpose Statement*: Is there a statement of the site's purpose or a clear articulation of the reason for and scope of the site's existence?
- *Objectives (list)*: Does the Web site meet the specific goals of the purpose statement?
- *Web Specification*: Is there a clear sense of organisation regarding what pieces of domain information will be presented as well as any technical or policy limitations on that presentation?
- *Domain Information*: What is the breadth and depth of the knowledge and information in the subject domains presented in the Web site?
- *Web Presentation*: How well have both style and content elements been used to present the information delivered to the user?

Evaluation Criteria

It was beyond the scope of the present research to cover all six of the areas just listed in its evaluation of the Web sites of forty-eight US State governments. Instead, the main focus was on evaluation of site design and page layout. The sites were therefore evaluated on the basis of seven key criteria.

Table 1

Description of Key Criteria Used to Evaluate Presentation of US State Government Web Sites

Criterion	Description
Retrieval Time	Time to download page(s)
Readability	Use of background colours and texture
Flexibility	Options available to users
Semantics	Coherent use of symbolic
Aesthetics	Coherent style to help users focus on content
Layout/Organisation	Context cues: page length, layout, and typography
Advanced display features	Use of image maps, forms, multimedia, virtual reality, or other

Site Design And Page Layout Concepts

Beyond the conceptual framework of the Web site is the actual presentation of the information itself. How well is the site organised? Web site users are most comfortable with a sense of predictability and structure. According to the *Web Style Manual* created by the Yale Centre for Advanced Instructional Media, "The users' perceptions of and assumptions about the organisation of your World Wide Web (WWW) site can have a major impact on the usability of your page and site design. Proper World Wide Web (WWW) site design is largely a matter of balancing the structure and relationship of a menu or 'home pages' and individual content pages or other linked graphics and documents. The goal is to build a hierarchy of menus and pages that feels natural and well-structured to the user, and doesn't interfere with their use of the Web site or mislead them."

Government Web presentations were evaluated with regard to their *overall* site organisation.

Individual page design is also very important. Page designers are advised to employ a universal grid, or template. Grids and templates make use of standard headers, icons and navigation tools to improve the legibility of the page. This page layout standardisation also gives give a consistent look to the presentation and allows the user to identify easily and quickly what the subject matter is and who is responsible for maintaining the page.

Examination of Web sites revealed a number of home page presentations with common design problems, exemplifying problems described in *HTML and CGI Unleashed*:

— *The Page from Outer Space*: A general lack of navigation and information cues.

— *The Monster Page*: A page with long access time required.

— *Multimedia Overkill*: A page with overly complex information and texture.

— *Uneven Page*: A page with an uneven information structure.

— *Meaningless Links*: A page with a lot of links which fail to add meaning to the information presented.

— *Clown Pants*: A page where units of meaning are scattered haphazardly.

Web Site Results

At the time of evaluation, forty-eight US State government Web sites were assigned an overall rating between 0 and 5 (*0=none, 1=poor, 2=fair, 3=good, 4=superior, 5=excellent*) using the seven general criteria mentioned above. Admittedly, this was a subjective exercise. If time had allowed, a more scientific approach would have been used to minimise the individual bias of the survey, such as a group scoring model. Web sites also change continuously, and the results presented will not necessarily reflect site style and content at the moment this chapter is being read.

The results of the evaluation process appear below and, in fact, generally follow a normal distribution curve. Twenty-seven of the forty-eight were given a rating of three, or 'good', which is considered to be average. Eight sites were deemed to be 'superior' and four sites were considered to be 'excellent' examples of what a government presence on the Internet should be. No government site received a ranking of one.

In addition to the key criteria used to evaluate the Web sites, another thirty specific features and subject matter 'domains' were identified that might be present on a site. The inclusion of an item indicates that the site designers have at least presented the topic. As might be expected with a new technology, the level of detail provided varies significantly among the sites. No standards exist for the format of material and many sites will be substantially redesigned as they are developed.

The universe of features is a useful demonstration of the prevailing level of technical and content-related issues. Generally, the features list addresses what government home page designers felt was significant to include in the site whether or not they had the capacity to implement it fully.

The most common component is e-mail feedback which indicates that some level of user interaction is supported by the site. The State agency directory feature is a close second. This generally provides a guide to State agencies via tables of each government organisation with departments, staff and phone numbers. This function is comparable to the government information pages of the telephone book; however, the technology allows for more flexible presentation of information.

By appearance, traditional organisational breakdowns of government - the executive (71%), legislative (60%) and judicial branches (44%) - are in keeping with expectations, given their respective magnitudes and/or service delivery responsibilities.

Traditional State government marketing areas - i.e. tourism promotion and economic development - were also in the top half of features found. As one might expect, primary and secondary education, colleges and universities and libraries - subject areas State governments tend to point to with a sense of 'pride' - also make the top half of the features list.

Certain features which tend to be resource-dependent - either human or technical - are scattered throughout the list. The use of site-specific search engines (38%), a very useful feature, is likely to grow as government sites increase in importance (and traffic volume), and as resources are made available to maintain and upgrade them.

Another very useful feature, the What's New page (42%), simply tracks additions, deletions and revisions to specific site pages. As the government sites grow, this indexing feature will become more and more labour intensive - but also more and more necessary. Help pages (21%) have been developed to varying degrees. Again, as these sites grow in popularity or necessity, help features will have to expand accordingly.

In addition, there are two other site design parameters which are important from an administrative management perspective:

— a 'date of last revision' indicator, and

— a page counter.

Thirty-four of the forty-eight sites include a date of last revision feature. This feature provides a vital cue to users about the age of the material which they are viewing. Despite controversy, the page counter feature is a necessity when constructing a site. Much has been written about the validity of what constitutes an actual 'hit' on a specific page. Current research demonstrates that most hit rates are dramatically overstated. However, applying a 'log scale' perspective provides a sound simple basis for measuring the benefits of maintaining specific subject matter within a Web page presentation or of reallocating resources to another area of promise. Despite this, only fourteen of forty-eight sites used page counters within their presentations.

The first step in the development of any government-wide strategy towards a Web site is the recognition of a need for a uniquely identifiable presence on the Internet. For some governments, Web presence has developed in an ad hoc, organic way that creates many different sites, each of which presents government information on the World Wide Web.

These multiple sites are in many cases redundant and lack a co-ordinated framework for linking among them. In these situations, there may be a perceived need for both a single point of 'official' access for the government and a co-ordinated approach to managing the content available through the official home page.

The objectives of this integrated approach are to:

— Establish a master or welcome government home page for accessing all government information which is available on the World Wide Web.

— Make the government Web site and pages with official links from it appear as consistent in format, inter-linkages, and functionality as possible.

— Ensure information available through the government Web site is structured in such a way that users can logically and quickly step through it to the specific information they need.

— Provide quality assurance in preparing information for the government Web site and all organisations or agencies linked to that site.

The government's Internet address may well be registered in the name of one public agency. That agency is a logical point at which to construct the mechanism for management of the site. In order to represent the interests of the previously-discussed stakeholders, the agency would be well advised to appoint an Advisory Committee that would enforce the standards developed to manage the site and major links. The work of this committee is discussed below.

Major goals to be achieved through the implementation of a government Web site are:

— To build a user-friendly place on the Internet available to citizens for access to and dissemination of government information and services.

— To gain the experience necessary to build a foundation for improved access to government information and delivery of services through the use of information technology.

— To promote the country to the rest of the world in a manner that enhances tourism, economic development opportunities and other national or regional interests.

The administration of the government Web site on the Internet requires the formation of a general framework upon which government information is built. The Welcome Page is meant to be the highest level of reference or menu with the subsequent Domain Home Pages or menus branching from that to describe the resources of government. The highest level should be identified by the official government domain address.

Welcome Page: The Welcome Page is defined as the single access point at the apex of the government Internet information hyperspace. This page contains a list of the available high-level Information Domains, online cross-references off to Domain Home Pages for these subject categories, and some instructional information for getting started.

Domain Home Page: A Domain Home Page is the first home page linked to by each subject category listed on the Welcome Page. The Domain Home Page provides an overview, context and/or index to that particular subject category, online cross-references (or hyperlinks) to specific information covered under that subject category, and instructions (if needed) for continuing down the information tree.

Related Home Page: Related Home Pages are defined as any additional pages that are not a Welcome Page or a Domain Home Page. For example, individual government agency presentations.

Because the government Web site will be widely accessed by many users, both within and outside the public sector, it is important that there be in place a mechanism to structure and monitor the content and organisation of the Web presentation. The mechanism will ensure that the site represents an accurate, overall picture of the resources of government rather than one that is piecemeal, misleading, or incomplete.

The establishment of a government Web site Advisory Committee can provide the policy direction and the framework required to develop and manage the implementation of the site. Members can include representatives from both the internal and external stakeholders, and it should be recognised that additional stakeholders are likely to step forward as the Web site evolves.

The Advisory Committee can take responsibility for the oversight to develop the format, content and organisation of the Web site. It can also develop a co-ordinated approach to the structure, organisation, and location of government agency Web pages and their linked contents within the government's overall Web presence. However, the Advisory Committee would not be responsible for specific approval or authorisation of content for a particular government agency's pages. That function is best left to the individual agencies.

Web site assessment should be an ongoing activity of the Advisory Committee and the government agency charged with site responsibility. The assessment can be based not only on how well contributing government agencies have met with published guidelines, but also on how well the government's efforts compare to other national government sites. This will require a continuous monitoring function to survey, report and act on other government Web sites.

Assessment of the government's own site should recognise that static sites are unlikely to hold the attention of users and that Internet methods and practices are changing rapidly. It is not likely that the methods of 1998 will be satisfactory even five years from now. By continually re-evaluating the potential of the technology, projects can be developed that extend its reach to a wider range of information and services.

The World Wide Web introduces new concepts of presentation, delivery and organisation into the business of providing government information for public use. The necessity to organise the information into a coherent whole often runs counter to existing government cultures, where individual government agency ownership of programmes and their related information prevents co-ordinated efforts to publicise or evaluate the work of government.

The development of a Web site will assist in defining the many linkages that exist between government agencies, which are often poorly defined in the real world. It will make evident areas of duplication and overlapping responsibility. It will demand greater government accountability, and greater objectivity in the justification of decisions. It will change the culture from *need to know* to *right to know*.

In these many ways, then, a Web site will change the way that information flows within government, and between government and citizens. By changing information flows, the site changes the balance of cultures, of relationships, and of power. As such, site development must be recognised as a political process as well as a technical one. Indeed, it is likely that the main barriers to Web site development and exploitation by government will be political rather than technical.

In technical terms, an integrated approach to government Web site development requires the establishment of a co-operative process that encourages the collaborative exploration of information technologies and the development of common system design and implementation standards, including data standards. While it will not be fiscally practical to convert every legacy application to the new standard, conformance with uniform system requirements could more easily be made a part of every new or rewritten system.

The establishment of a properly constructed government Web site represents a start toward a real or perceived flattening of the bureaucracy. The democratic attitudes of the citizenry, and the existence of channels for expression of those attitudes, will be a key driver in the level of openness and accessibility to information provided by its government.

Where a democratic environment exists the Internet is likely to be used as a tool that can enable the publication of details about all government programmes, the collection and dissemination of meaningful data about those programmes, the provision of universal access to information for citizens, and ultimately the development of a relatively simple mechanism for the provision of many government services at a lower cost to the taxpayer.

Conversely, where a democratic environment does not exist the Internet is likely to be seen by government more as threat than opportunity. In such cases, Internet-enabled applications are less likely to be exploited. Where government is attempting to created a single, integrated Web presence, it can try to find incentives that will encourage the participation of its constituent agencies. Such measures can include:

— *Technical*: provision of space for pages on a central Web server; funding for telecommunications infrastructure within government.

— *Consultancy/advice*: centrally-provided assistance with the process of planning, developing and maintaining Web pages.

— *Training*: awareness training for senior staff; technical training for Web authors and site managers; access training for government staff and citizens.

— *Regulation/legislation*: treating email correspondence with the same priority as posted letters; digital signature legislation to give email the same legal force as paper documents; freedom of information legislation that includes electronic formats.

Appendix-I

2nd UNESCO International Congress on the Ethical, Legal and Societal Challenges of Cyberspace

The Congress INFOethics'98, held in Monaco from 1 to 3 October 1998, was opened by the Representative of the Director-General of UNESCO, Mr Henrikas Yushkiavitshus, Assistant Director-General for Communication, Information and Informatics and by the Representative of the Minister of State of the Principality of Monaco, Mr Jean Pastorelli. It was attended by 160 participants from 66 countries including lawyers, government officials, technicians, academics and the media. Twelve international intergovernmental and non-governmental organizations were represented at the Congress. The debates proceeded as planned in six sessions each illustrated by short video clips prepared by the Institut National de l'Audiovisuel (INA), France. A report on the results of a UNESCO Virtual Forum on Information Ethics that took place from October 1997 to April 1998 was presented by its co-ordinator, Mr Rainer Kuhlen, University of Constance (Germany). The closing speech was delivered by Ms Vigdis Finnbogadóttir,

Chairperson of the World Commission on the Ethics of Scientific Knowledge and Technology and former President of the Republic of Iceland.

The Congress was chaired by the President of the German Commission for UNESCO, Mr Peter Canisius. A total of 28 speakers from 23 countries participated in the six discussion panels. The discussions were moderated by representatives from six international organizations. The six moderators prepared a report and conclusions on the discussions in their respective sessions and presented them to the plenary at the closing session of the Congress. On the initiative of the Chairman, a drafting group prepared a statement proposing possible lines of action that the Organization could consider to follow up on the issues discussed during the Congress.

The organization of this event benefited from financial support from the Government of Monaco, the Agence pour la Francophonie (ACCT) and some National Commissions for UNESCO. The Direction de Tourisme et des Congrès de Monaco provided the physical facilities for the organization of the Congress.

Content

There was general agreement that it is useful that UNESCO continues to follow up on the different ethical and societal aspects of the applications of new information technologies particularly when it concerns the challenges of open access to the contents disseminated through the electronic information media.

The themes and topics selected for the Congress were considered pertinent and concrete. Participants appreciated that enough time was allocated under each theme for discussion. Most of the presentations were very substantive and of high quality and were followed by animated debates with the participants from the floor.

The conclusions of these debates, as well as the final statement issued by the Congress, can serve as a basis for future UNESCO action in the field of INFOethics in its domain of competence. These reports are summarised below.

Roundtable 1: Information in Public Domain

To further develop information in public domain through activities that:

— improve access to public information itself;

— provide freedom of access to means of accessing and processing information - to computer software;

It was noted that attempts by commercial software producers to control the distribution, adaptation and use of software through the application of copyright laws are being countered by free software groups which develop new software through collective efforts and share the results freely with users.

— Increase the role of the public sector in making electronic networks (principally the Internet) accessible to all on equal terms.

The free software movement represents an attempt to counter the influence of commercial interests in what should also be the public domain.

— Raise awareness of the state responsibility to formulate and implement new kinds of policies to deal with information in cyberspace.

The rapid growth of the Internet has given rise to a number of problems for the solution of which some have proposed more state intervention, while others pointed to the need of establishing principles of freedom in cyberspace similar to those of freedom of the sea established in a much earlier era.

— Provide guaranteed access to the benefits of the Information Society for all humankind.

Discussion of the respective roles of the private and public sectors in the development of the Internet tends to focus on such problems as inequality of access to information and the abuse of the new media for criminal or antisocial purposes.

Roundtable 2: Multilingualism

The national authorities, UNESCO and other international organizations are encouraged to watch that the world balance be maintained in matters concerning access and production of information on the Internet by:

— developing multilingualism on the Internet;

— developing intelligent linguistic systems (recognition of languages, automated translation, TAO, etc.), together with the adoption of techniques for the drafting of original articles so that they are correctly translated by machines;

— participating in the implementation of a world policy for character coding and for information input-output procedures;

— encouraging the diffusion of cultural heritage;

— promoting less used languages, either because they are in 5characters different from Latin, or are spoken by fewer people, or are not representing the language used in public administration (i.e. indigenous).

It was considered that, if the present trend in the Information Society is maintained, English will definitely become the international and business language; some European languages will be used regionally and for specialized communication all other languages will be exclusively used for local communications.

Some predict that from 5 to 6 thousand of currently used languages only about one hundred will survive, which will lead to serious social, cultural and scientific consequences. There will be no real cultural and social exchanges as long as English is the only communication language on the Internet. This situation creates citizens of a " second zone ", discriminated populations. The overabundance of information on the Internet makes it also difficult to find the information that is accurate and of quality.

Roundtable 3: Privacy and Confidentiality Rights

Because the new communication technologies bring considerable challenges and opportunities to protect privacy, there is a need to increase trust and reliability in information networks, especially by:

— applying Article 12 of the Universal Declaration of Human Rights as the basic starting point to build an international campaign to boost privacy issues into the international agenda and make it more prominent. Prominence of the matter will make parties involved more accountable for the way in which they treat personal privacy.

— working with organizations at the regional level to reach regional agreements on key privacy issues that can later be worked into a global consensus;

— identifying companies, organizations and institutions that comply with Article 12 to promote the incorporation of privacy safeguards into institutions' daily practices;

— encouraging international organizations, like UNESCO, to raise awareness of this matter through international meetings so that civil society and government officials can grasp the full implications of privacy related challenges;

— promoting work that is addressed to build agreed upon standards of what is acceptable and what is not from a citizen's personal privacy point of view.

Roundtable 4: Proprietary and Security Rights

It was suggested that UNESCO pursue the following follow-up actions:

— the strengthening of the role of libraries in support of users seeking orientation in the growing complexity of the information world including support via cyberspace (the Internet);

— the definition and promotion of "fair use" of information technologies and their essential components;

— the protection with respect to Intellectual Property Rights of human heritage from excesses of "privatisation";

— the identification of important issues overseen so far, such as Collective Property Rights of Indigenous People, and implementing such rights;

— the refusal to accept that definitions and practices concerning "property" be continuously extended to reduce public access and free flow of information for the benefit of a few individuals or organizations at the public's expense and, especially, institutions concerned with education, science and culture.

Some additional remarks were made concerning other possible actions:

— to study the process of how developments of the flow of information influence moral aspects, intellectual property, privacy and responsibility (i.e. ISO 9000 "quality" measures/processes may provide means for this analysis);

— to add UNESCO's contribution to the Russian resolution presented to the UN concerning "Breakthroughs in the field of informatisation and telecommunication in the framework of international security";

— to protect basic rights of indigenous people (e.g. "InkaniNet");

— to collect and publicize existing codes of professional conduct and codes of ethics related to information technologies.

Roundtable 5: Cognitive Education

The participants suggested that:

— there is a need to take specific action in order to

ensure that the Information Society is for the benefit of all and our educational systems are meeting the challenges posed. This is particularly true because:

- commercial interests are primarily generating developments and not social considerations;
- technological tools are being used for the existing educational system rather than adjusting the educational system to take into consideration the availability of the new tools;
- existing educational systems have not evolved quickly enough to take the technological developments into consideration;
- one of the priority sectors of the population should be the children;
- although distance learning is an important tool for the future, the tools and methodologies have not fully matured yet. Further work is still needed.

- Specific actions should be taken in order to address the necessary changes in the educational system. The following actions are proposed:
  - promote the continuation of the dialogue initiated by this Conference on the issue of education in the cyberworld;
  - launch a series of studies on:
    a. how to ensure that teachers — particularly in the primary and secondary education system — be given the necessary skills to teach children in the 21st century;
    b. how can the current shortage of ICT skilled personnel best be handled and how to increase the level of graduates;

c. what are the implications on developing countries of the current phenomenon of the migration of the skilled work force in information and communication technologies towards the developed world;

d. what are the alternative mechanisms for evaluating student capabilities in the new context (e.g. increased importance of group working, capacity of memorizing facts or to analyze large volumes of data, etc.);

e. how to promote citizenship in the global context. How should this be reflected in school curricula;

f. how to forecast early enough the necessary skills that the future workforce will need in order to adjust the education system to address these needs.

— There is a need for a series of mechanisms and actions to be put in place.

These include:

- launching the series of studies outlined above;
- continue to develop an observatory of best practice examples in this field so experiences can be shared;
- continue the dialogue process which has been initiated by this Conference and complementing it by setting up various fora (physical and virtual) bringing together representatives of the developing and developed world, minority groups, indigenous people, private sector, educational experts, technology experts, international and regional organizations etc..

Roundtable 6: Social, Economic and Multicultural responsibilities

A number of issues provoked discussion during the session:

— The first one is the question of global governance. Its vision is predominately optimistic. The challenge is to prepare worldwide regulation for the era of individualization. There will have to be a re-examination of existing political structures to ensure a worldwide framework which is transparent and effective. At its heart, this issue calls for innovation and creativity from political leaders to bring about change which will respect fundamental individual and collective rights.

— Systems for filtering and self-regulation is another important question. Aware of the opportunities for a decentralized approach and of the possibilities for those who use the technology themselves to determine the rules by which it is used, participants considered that the systems of filtering should be non-intrusive and flexible.

— Existing standards of self-regulation through industry codes are low and most self-regulators have failed to deliver the standards they had set themselves. It is noted that key issues related to information technology — cultural and democratic pluralism, matters of cultural diversity and social justice — are absent from the codes of many of these agencies. Above all, the question of effective enforcement that can maintain public confidence remains unanswered. This is one area where the participants believe that there is a need for serious work on the part of

UNESCO to review the quality of existing self-regulatory structures and to press for more effective and inclusive codes of practice.

— Above all, participants are concerned about social exclusion and it is strongly felt that actions that combat exclusion should be given priority by UNESCO and other international agencies. This is an issue which is a problem in all countries as well as being traditionally a problem between countries which are rich in technical and economic resources and those in the process of development.

Social exclusion can be minimized by:

- programmes of training for information technology and computer literacy to be made available for all;
- provision of affordable access to new information technology to all groups in society from all areas of the world;
- expansion of the base of access through decentralized systems of administration, the provision of public information access points available to all groups in society and the availability of cheap, simple and robust technologies;
- expansion of the linguistic and cultural base of information technology resources to challenge the existing dominance of the English language and North American cultural products and values. (Special emphasis here is placed on the need of indigenous people.)

— Finally, the participants are united in the belief that the debate about the future in this critical field is much too narrow. It needs to be expanded to ensure that the key players—community leaders, information professionals, industry representatives as well as political leaders and regulators—are all brought to the same table. Without this level of inclusive debate serious progress towards addressing the societal challenges will not be made. UNESCO's role in facilitating the expansion of the debate is of critical importance.

Statement of the 2nd UNESCO INFO ethics Congress'98

UNESCO, since the adoption of the Universal Declaration of Human Rights fifty years ago, has emphasized constantly that:

— "everyone has the right to freedom of opinion and expression, this right includes freedom to hold opinions without interference and to seek, receive and impart information and ideas to any media and regardless of frontiers" (Article 19), and

— "no one shall be subjected to arbitrary interference with his privacy, family house or correspondence, nor to attacks upon his honour and reputation. Everyone has the right to the protection of law against such interference or attacks" (Article 12) .

While the new communication media provide new opportunities they also produce new threats to these principles.

We, the participants of the INFOethics'98 Congress, consider the promotion of the role of information in the public domain, of multilingualism, the protection of privacy, confidentiality and security are vital issues.

In the light of the conclusions of the Conference,

— we recognize that the new information and communication environment will influence our societal structure and value systems;

— we believe, however, that it is the people who shall shape the future;

— we recognize that the improvement of the new environment is within the mandate of the United Nations Educational, Scientific and Cultural Organization (UNESCO);

— we believe that the new electronic world should reflect and reinforce the world's cultural and linguistic diversity and encourage international co-operation;

— we consider knowledge a public good that needs to be made publicly available in accordance with the principles of the free flow of information and of fair use.

We consider that among the most urgent problems in this context are those of freedom of access and personal privacy.

Access to the resources of the Internet should reinforce democratic participation and is a contemporary realization of the universal principle of the freedom of expression.

Privacy is one of the most threatened values and needs special protection in the electronic world.

We recommend that UNESCO, in co-operation with UN and other international organizations, should:

1. promote and defend freedom of expression and privacy protection in cyberspace as well as in traditional media;
2. support all measures to overcome barriers between the information rich and the information poor;
3. promote and extend access to the public domain of information and communication;
4. promote education and training to achieve media competence for everyone;
5. contribute to a worldwide electronic forum on information ethics designed to support UNESCO's work in that field;
6. promote interdisciplinary debate on all ethical implications of new communication technologies;
7. support actions to prevent the criminal abuse of the Internet;
8. support cultural diversity and multilingualism in cyberspace and take measures which allow every individual, every culture and every language to contribute to and benefit from the new store of world knowledge.

Convention on Cybercrime

Council of Europe, Budapest, 23 November 2001

Preamble

The member States of the Council of Europe and the other States signatory hereto,

Considering that the aim of the Council of Europe is to achieve a greater unity between its members;

Recognising the value of fostering co-operation with the other States parties to this Convention;

Convinced of the need to pursue, as a matter of priority, a common criminal policy aimed at the protection of society against cybercrime, inter alia by adopting appropriate legislation and fostering international co-operation;

Conscious of the profound changes brought about by the digitalisation, convergence and continuing globalisation of computer networks;

Concerned at the risk that computer networks and electronic information may also be used for committing criminal offences and that evidence relating to such offences may be stored and transferred by these networks;

Recognising the need for co-operation between States and private industry in combating cybercrime and the need to protect legitimate interests in the use and development of information technologies;

Believing that an effective fight against cybercrime requires increased, rapid and well-functioning international co-operation in criminal matters;

Convinced that the present Convention is necessary to deter actions directed against the confidentiality, integrity and availability of computer systems, networks and computer data, as well as the misuse of such systems, networks and data, by providing for the criminalisation of such conduct, as described in this Convention, and the adoption of powers sufficient for effectively combating such criminal offences, by facilitating the detection, investigation and prosecution of such criminal offences at both the domestic and international level, and by providing arrangements for fast and reliable international co-operation;

Mindful of the need to ensure a proper balance between the interests of law enforcement and respect for fundamental human rights, as enshrined in the 1950 Council of Europe Convention for the Protection of Human Rights and Fundamental Freedoms, the 1966 United Nations International Covenant on Civil and Political Rights, as well as other applicable international human rights treaties, which reaffirm the right of everyone to hold opinions without interference, as well as the right to freedom of expression, including the freedom to seek, receive, and impart information and ideas of all kinds, regardless of frontiers, and the rights concerning the respect for privacy;

Mindful also of the protection of personal data, as conferred e.g. by the 1981 Council of Europe Convention for the Protection of Individuals with Regard to Automatic Processing of Personal Data;

Considering the 1989 United Nations Convention on the Rights of the Child and the 1999 International Labour Organization Worst Forms of Child Labour Convention;

Taking into account the existing Council of Europe conventions on co-operation in the penal field as well as similar treaties which exist between Council of Europe member States and other States and stressing that the present Convention is intended to supplement those conventions in order to make criminal investigations and proceedings concerning criminal offences related to computer systems and data more effective and to enable the collection of evidence in electronic form of a criminal offence;

Welcoming recent developments which further advance international understanding and co-operation in combating cybercrimes, including actions of the United Nations, the OECD, the European Union and the G8;

Recalling Recommendation N° R (85) 10 concerning the practical application of the European Convention on Mutual Assistance in Criminal Matters in respect of letters rogatory for the interception of telecommunications, Recommendation N° R (88) 2 on piracy in the field of copyright and neighbouring rights, Recommendation N° R (87) 15 regulating the use of personal data in the police sector, Recommendation N° R

(95) 4 on the protection of personal data in the area of telecommunication services, with particular reference to telephone services as well as Recommendation N° R (89) 9 on computer-related crime providing guidelines for national legislatures concerning the definition of certain computer crimes and Recommendation N° R (95) 13 concerning problems of criminal procedural law connected with Information Technology;

Having regard to Resolution No. 1 adopted by the European Ministers of Justice at their 21st Conference (Prague, June 1997), which recommended the Committee of Ministers to support the work carried out by the European Committee on Crime Problems (CDPC) on cybercrime in order to bring domestic criminal law provisions closer to each other and enable the use of effective means of investigation concerning such offences, as well as to Resolution N° 3, adopted at the 23rd Conference of the European Ministers of Justice (London, June 2000), which encouraged the negotiating parties to pursue their efforts with a view to finding appropriate solutions so as to enable the largest possible number of States to become parties to the Convention and acknowledged the need for a swift and efficient system of international co-operation, which duly takes into account the specific requirements of the fight against cybercrime;

Having also regard to the Action Plan adopted by the Heads of State and Government of the Council of Europe, on the occasion of their Second Summit (Strasbourg, 10 - 11 October 1997), to seek common responses to the development of the new information technologies, based on the standards and values of the Council of Europe;

Have agreed as follows:

Chapter I – Use of terms

Article 1 – Definitions

For the purposes of this Convention:

a. "computer system" means any device or a group of inter-connected or related devices, one or more of which, pursuant to a program, performs automatic processing of data;

b. "computer data" means any representation of facts, information or concepts in a form suitable for processing in a computer system, including a program suitable to cause a computer system to perform a function;

c. "service provider" means:

   i. any public or private entity that provides to users of its service the ability to communicate by means of a computer system, and

   ii. any other entity that processes or stores computer data on behalf of such communication service or users of such service.

d. "traffic data" means any computer data relating to a communication by means of a computer system, generated by a computer system that formed a part in the chain of communication, indicating the communication's origin, destination, route, time, date, size, duration, or type of underlying service.

Chapter II – Measures to be taken at the national level

Section 1 – Substantive criminal law

Title 1 – Offences against the confidentiality, integrity and availability of computer data and systems

Article 2 – Illegal access

Each Party shall adopt such legislative and other measures as may be necessary to establish as criminal offences under its domestic law, when committed intentionally, the access to the whole or any part of a computer system without right. A Party may require that the offence be committed by infringing security measures, with the intent of obtaining computer data or other dishonest intent, or in relation to a computer system that is connected to another computer system.

Article 3 – Illegal interception

Each Party shall adopt such legislative and other measures as may be necessary to establish as criminal offences under its domestic law, when committed intentionally, the interception without right, made by technical means, of non-public transmissions of computer data to, from or within a computer system, including electromagnetic emissions from a computer system carrying such computer data. A Party may require that the offence be committed with dishonest intent, or in relation to a computer system that is connected to another computer system.

Article 4 – Data interference

1. Each Party shall adopt such legislative and other measures as may be necessary to establish as criminal offences under its domestic law, when committed intentionally, the damaging, deletion, deterioration, alteration or suppression of computer data without right.
2. A Party may reserve the right to require that the conduct described in paragraph 1 result in serious harm.

Article 5 – System interference

Each Party shall adopt such legislative and other measures as may be necessary to establish as criminal offences under its domestic law, when committed intentionally, the serious hindering without right of the functioning of a computer system by inputting, transmitting, damaging, deleting, deteriorating, altering or suppressing computer data.

Article 6 – Misuse of devices

1. Each Party shall adopt such legislative and other measures as may be necessary to establish as criminal offences under its domestic law, when committed intentionally and without right:
    a. the production, sale, procurement for use, import, distribution or otherwise making available of:

i. a device, including a computer program, designed or adapted primarily for the purpose of committing any of the offences established in accordance with Article 2 – 5;

ii. a computer password, access code, or similar data by which the whole or any part of a computer system is capable of being accessedwith intent that it be used for the purpose of committing any of the offences established in Articles 2 - 5; and

b. the possession of an item referred to in paragraphs (a)(1) or (2) above, with intent that it be used for the purpose of committing any of the offences established in Articles 2 – 5. A Party may require by law that a number of such items be possessed before criminal liability attaches.

2. This article shall not be interpreted as imposing criminal liability where the production, sale, procurement for use, import, distribution or otherwise making available or possession referred to in paragraph 1 of this Article is not for the purpose of committing an offence established in accordance with articles 2 through 5 of this Convention, such as for the authorised testing or protection of a computer system.

3. Each Party may reserve the right not to apply paragraph 1 of this Article, provided that the reservation does not concern the sale, distribution or otherwise making available of the items referred to in paragraph 1 (a) (2).

Title 2 – Computer-related offences

Article 7 – Computer-related forgery

Each Party shall adopt such legislative and other measures as may be necessary to establish as criminal offences under its domestic law, when committed intentionally and without right, the input, alteration, deletion, or suppression of computer data, resulting in inauthentic data with the intent that it be considered or acted upon for legal purposes as if it were authentic, regardless whether or not the data is directly readable and intelligible. A Party may require an intent to defraud, or similar dishonest intent, before criminal liability attaches.

Article 8 – Computer-related fraud

Each Party shall adopt such legislative and other measures as may be necessary to establish as criminal offences under its domestic law, when committed intentionally and without right, the causing of a loss of property to another by:

a. any input, alteration, deletion or suppression of computer data,

b. any interference with the functioning of a computer system, with fraudulent or dishonest intent of procuring, without right, an economic benefit for oneself or for another.

Title 3 – Content-related offences

Article 9 – Offences related to child pornography

1. Each Party shall adopt such legislative and other measures as may be necessary to establish as criminal

offences under its domestic law, when committed intentionally and without right, the following conduct:

a. producing child pornography for the purpose of its distribution through a computer system;

b. offering or making available child pornography through a computer system;

c. distributing or transmitting child pornography through a computer system;

d. procuring child pornography through a computer system for oneself or for another;

e. possessing child pornography in a computer system or on a computer-data storage medium.

2. For the purpose of paragraph 1 above "child pornography" shall include pornographic material that visually depicts:

a. a minor engaged in sexually explicit conduct;

b. a person appearing to be a minor engaged in sexually explicit conduct;

c. realistic images representing a minor engaged in sexually explicit conduct.

3. For the purpose of paragraph 2 above, the term "minor" shall include all persons under 18 years of age. A Party may, however, require a lower age-limit, which shall be not less than 16 years.

4. Each Party may reserve the right not to apply, in whole or in part, paragraph 1(d) and 1(e), and 2(b) and 2(c).

Title 4 – Offences related to infringements of copyright and related rights

Article 10 – Offences related to infringements of copyright and related rights

1. Each Party shall adopt such legislative and other measures as may be necessary to establish as criminal offences under its domestic law the infringement of copyright, as defined under the law of that Party pursuant to the obligations it has undertaken under the Paris Act of 24 July 1971 of the Bern Convention for the Protection of Literary and Artistic Works, the Agreement on Trade-Related Aspects of Intellectual Property Rights and the WIPO Copyright Treaty, with the exception of any moral rights conferred by such Conventions, where such acts are committed wilfully, on a commercial scale and by means of a computer system.

2. Each Party shall adopt such legislative and other measures as may be necessary to establish as criminal offences under its domestic law the infringement of related rights, as defined under the law of that Party, pursuant to the obligations it has undertaken under the International Convention for the Protection of Performers, Producers of Phonograms and Broadcasting Organisations done in Rome (Rome Convention), the Agreement on Trade-Related Aspects of Intellectual Property Rights and the WIPO Performances and Phonograms Treaty, with the exception of any moral rights conferred by such Conventions, where such acts are committed wilfully, on a commercial scale and by means of a computer system.

3. A Party may reserve the right not to impose criminal liability under paragraphs 1 and 2 of this article in limited circumstances, provided that other effective remedies are available and that such reservation does not derogate from the Party's international obligations set forth in the international instruments referred to in paragraphs 1 and 2 of this article.

Title 5 – Ancillary liability and sanctions

Article 11 – Attempt and aiding or abetting

1. Each Party shall adopt such legislative and other measures as may be necessary to establish as criminal offences under its domestic law, when committed intentionally, aiding or abetting the commission of any of the offences established in accordance with Articles 2 – 10 of the present Convention with intent that such offence be committed.
2. Each Party shall adopt such legislative and other measures as may be necessary to establish as criminal offences under its domestic law, when committed intentionally, an attempt to commit any of the offences established in accordance with Articles 3 through 5, 7, 8, 9 (1) a and 9 (1) c of this Convention.
3. Each Party may reserve the right not to apply, in whole or in part, paragraph 2 of this article.

Article 12 – Corporate liability

1. Each Party shall adopt such legislative and other measures as may be necessary to ensure that a legal

person can be held liable for a criminal offence established in accordance with this Convention, committed for its benefit by any natural person, acting either individually or as part of an organ of the legal person, who has a leading position within the legal person, based on:

a. a power of representation of the legal person;

b. an authority to take decisions on behalf of the legal person;

c. an authority to exercise control within the legal person.

2. Apart from the cases already provided for in paragraph 1, each Party shall take the measures necessary to ensure that a legal person can be held liable where the lack of supervision or control by a natural person referred to in paragraph 1 has made possible the commission of a criminal offence established in accordance with this Convention for the benefit of that legal person by a natural person acting under its authority.

3. Subject to the legal principles of the Party, the liability of a legal person may be criminal, civil or administrative.

4. Such liability shall be without prejudice to the criminal liability of the natural persons who have committed the offence.

Article 13 – Sanctions and measures

1. Each Party shall adopt such legislative and other measures as may be necessary to ensure that the

criminal offences established in accordance with Articles 2 – 11 are punishable by effective, proportionate and dissuasive sanctions, which include deprivation of liberty.

2. Each Party shall ensure that legal persons held liable in accordance with Article 12 shall be subject to effective, proportionate and dissuasive criminal or non-criminal sanctions or measures, including monetary sanctions.

Section 2 – Procedural law

Title 1 – Common provisions

Article 14 – Scope of procedural provisions

1. Each Party shall adopt such legislative and other measures as may be necessary to establish the powers and procedures provided for in this Section for the purpose of specific criminal investigations or proceedings.

2. Except as specifically otherwise provided in Article 21, each Party shall apply the powers and procedures referred to in paragraph 1 to:

   a. the criminal offences established in accordance with articles 2-11 of this Convention;

   b. other criminal offences committed by means of a computer system; and

   c. the collection of evidence in electronic form of a criminal offence.

3. a. Each Party may reserve the right to apply the measures referred to in Article 20 only to offences or

categories of offences specified in the reservation, provided that the range of such offences or categories of offences is not more restricted than the range of offences to which it applies the measures referred to in Article 21. Each Party shall consider restricting such a reservation to enable the broadest application of the measure referred to in Article 20.

b. Where a Party, due to limitations in itslegislation in force at the time of the adoption of the present Convention, is not able to apply the measures referred to in Articles 20 and 21 to communications being transmitted within a computer system of a service provider, which system

   i. is being operated for the benefit of a closed group of users, and

   ii. does not employ public communications networks and is not connected with another computer system, whether public or private, that Party may reserve the right not to apply these measures to such communications. Each Party shall consider restricting such a reservation to enable the broadest application of the measures referred to in Articles 20 and 21.

Article 15 – Conditions and safeguards

1. Each Party shall ensure that the establishment, implementation and application of the powers and procedures provided for in this Section are subject to conditions and safeguards provided for under its domestic law, which shall provide for the adequate

protection of human rights and liberties, including rights arising pursuant to obligations it has undertaken under the 1950 Council of Europe Convention for the Protection of Human Rights and Fundamental Freedoms, the 1966 United Nations International Covenant on Civil and Political Rights, and other applicable international human rights instruments, and which shall incorporate the principle of proportionality.

2. Such conditions and safeguards shall, as appropriate in view of the nature of the power or procedure concerned, inter alia, include judicial or other independent supervision, grounds justifying application, and limitation on the scope and the duration of such power or procedure.

3. To the extent that it is consistent with the public interest, in particular the sound administration of justice, a Party shall consider the impact of the powers and procedures in this Section upon the rights, responsibilities and legitimate interests of third parties.

Title 2 - Expedited preservation of stored computer data

Article 16 – Expedited preservation of stored computer data

1. Each Party shall adopt such legislative and other measures as may be necessary to enable its competent authorities to order or similarly obtain the expeditious preservation of specified computer data, including traffic data, that has been stored by means of a computer system, in particular where there are

grounds to believe that the computer data is particularly vulnerable to loss or modification.

2. Where a Party gives effect to paragraph 1 above by means of an order to a person to preserve specified stored computer data in the person's possession or control, the Party shall adopt such legislative and other measures as may be necessary to oblige that person to preserve and maintain the integrity of that computer data for a period of time as long as necessary, up to a maximum of 90 days, to enable the competent authorities to seek its disclosure. A Party may provide for such an order to be subsequently renewed.

3. Each Party shall adopt such legislative or other measures as may be necessary to oblige the custodian or other person who is to preserve the computer data to keep confidential the undertaking of such procedures for the period of time provided for by its domestic law.

4. The powers and procedures referred to in this article shall be subject to Articles 14 and 15.

Article 17 – Expedited preservation and partial disclosure of traffic data

1. Each Party shall adopt, in respect of traffic data that is to be preserved under Article 16, such legislative and other measures as may be necessary to:

    a. ensure that such expeditious preservation of traffic data is available regardless of whether one or more service providers were involved in the transmission of that communication; and

b. ensure the expeditious disclosure to the Party's competent authority, or a person designated by that authority, of a sufficient amount of traffic data to enable the Party to identify the service providers and the path through which the communication was transmitted.

2. The powers and procedures referred to in this article shall be subject to Articles 14 and 15.

Title 3 – Production order

Article 18 – Production order

1. Each Party shall adopt such legislative and other measures as may be necessary to empower its competent authorities to order:

   a. a person in its territory to submit specified computer data in that person's possession or control, which is stored in a computer systemor a computer-data storage medium; and

   b. a service provider offering its services in the territory of the Party to submit subscriber information relating to such services in that service provider's possession or control;

2. The powers and procedures referred to in this article shall be subject to Articles 14 and 15.

3. For the purpose of this article, "subscriber information" means any information, contained in the form of computer data or any other form, that is held by a service provider, relating to subscribers of its services, other than traffic or content data, by which can be established:

a. the type of the communication service used, the technical provisions taken thereto and the period of service;

b. the subscriber's identity, postal or geographic address, telephone and other access number, billing and payment information, available on the basis of the service agreement or arrangement;

c. any other information on the site of the installation of communication equipment available on the basis of the service agreement or arrangement.

Title 4 – Search and seizure of stored computer data

Article 19 – Search and seizure of stored computer data

1. Each Party shall adopt such legislative and other measures as may be necessary to empower its competent authorities to search or similarly access:

   a. a computer system or part of it and computer data stored therein; and

   b. computer-data storage medium in which computer data may be stored in its territory.

2. Each Party shall adopt such legislative and other measures as may be necessary to ensure that where its authorities search or similarly access a specific computer system or part of it, pursuant to paragraph 1 (a), and have grounds to believe that the data sought is stored in another computer system or part of it in its territory, and such data is lawfully accessible from or available to the initial system, such authorities shall be able to expeditiously extend the search or similar accessing to the other system.

3. Each Party shall adopt such legislative and other measures as may be necessary to empower its competent authorities to seize or similarly secure computer data accessed according to paragraphs 1 or 2. These measures shall include the power to :
   a. seize or similarly secure a computer system or part of it or a computer-data storage medium;
   b. make and retain a copy of those computer data;
   c. maintain the integrity of the relevant stored computer data; and
   d. render inaccessible or remove those computer data in the accessed computer system.
4. Each Party shall adopt such legislative and other measures as may be necessary to empower its competent authorities to order any person who has knowledge about the functioning of the computer system or measures applied to protect the computer data therein to provide, as is reasonable, the necessary information, to enable the undertaking of the measures referred to in paragraphs 1 and 2.
5. The powers and procedures referred to in this article shall be subject to Articles 14 and 15.

Title 5 – Real-time collection of computer data

Article 20 – Real-time collection of traffic data

1. Each Party shall adopt such legislative and other measures as may be necessary to empower its competent authorities to:
   a. collect or record through application of technical means on the territory of that Party, and

b. compel a service provider, within its existing technical capability, to:

i. collect or record through application of technical means on the territory of that Party, or

ii. co-operate and assist the competent authorities in the collection or recording of, traffic data, in real-time, associated with specified communications in its territory transmitted by means of a computer system.

2. Where a Party, due to the established principles of its domestic legal system, cannot adopt the measures referred to in paragraph 1 (a), it may instead adopt legislative and other measures as may be necessary to ensure the real-time collection or recording of traffic data associated with specified communications in its territory through application of technical means on that territory.

3. Each Party shall adopt such legislative and other measures as may be necessary to oblige a service provider to keep confidential the fact of and any information about the execution of any power provided for in this Article.

4. The powers and procedures referred to in this article shall be subject to Articles 14 and 15.

Article 21 – Interception of content data

1. Each Party shall adopt such legislative and other measures as may be necessary, in relation to a range of serious offences to be determined by domestic law, to empower its competent authorities to:

   a. collect or record through application of technical means on the territory of that Party, and

b. compel a service provider, within its existing technical capability, to:

i. collect or record through application of technical means on the territory of that Party, or

ii. co-operate and assist the competent authorities in the collection or recording of, content data, in real-time, of specified communications in its territory transmitted by means of a computer system.

2. Where a Party, due to the established principles of its domestic legal system, cannot adopt the measures referred to in paragraph 1 (a), it may instead adopt legislative and other measures as may be necessary to ensure the real-time collection or recording of content data of specified communications in its territory through application of technical means on that territory.

3. Each Party shall adopt such legislative and other measures as may be necessary to oblige a service provider to keep confidential the fact of and any information about the execution of any power provided for in this Article.

4. The powers and procedures referred to in this article shall be subject to Articles 14 and 15.

Section 3 – Jurisdiction

Article 22 – Jurisdiction

1. Each Party shall adopt such legislative and other measures as may be necessary to establish jurisdiction over any offence established in

accordance with Articles 2 – 11 of this Convention, when the offence is committed :

a. in its territory; or

b. on board a ship flying the flag of that Party; or

c. on board an aircraft registered under the laws of that Party; or

d. by one of its nationals, if the offence is punishable under criminal law where it was committed or if the offence is committed outside the territorial jurisdiction of any State.

2. Each Party may reserve the right not to apply or to apply only in specific cases or conditions the jurisdiction rules laid down in paragraphs (1) b – (1) d of this article or any part thereof.

3. Each Party shall adopt such measures as may be necessary to establish jurisdiction over the offences referred to in Article 24, paragraph (1) of this Convention, in cases where an alleged offender is present in its territory and it does not extradite him/her to another Party, solely on the basis of his/her nationality, after a request for extradition.

4. This Convention does not exclude any criminal jurisdiction exercised in accordance with domestic law.

5. When more than one Party claims jurisdiction over an alleged offence established in accordance with this Convention, the Parties involved shall, where appropriate, consult with a view to determining the most appropriate jurisdiction for prosecution.

Chapter III – International co-operation

Section 1 – General principles

Title 1 – General principles relating to international co-operation

Article 23 – General principles relating to international co-operation

The Parties shall co-operate with each other, in accordance with the provisions of this chapter, and through application of relevant international instruments on international co-operation in criminal matters, arrangements agreed on the basis of uniform or reciprocal legislation, and domestic laws, to the widest extent possible for the purposes of investigations or proceedings concerning criminal offences related to computer systems and data, or for the collection of evidence in electronic form of a criminal offence.

Title 2 – Principles relating to extradition

Article 24 – Extradition

1. a. This article applies to extradition between Parties for the criminal offences established in accordance with Articles 2 – 11 of this Convention, provided that they are punishable under the laws of both Parties concerned by deprivation of liberty for a maximum period of at least one year, or by a more severe penalty.

   b. Where a different minimum penalty is to be applied under an arrangement agreed on the basis of uniform or reciprocal legislation or an extradition treaty, including the European Convention on Extradition, applicable between two or more parties, the minimum penalty provided for under such arrangement or treaty shall apply.

2. The criminal offences described in paragraph 1 of this Article shall be deemed to be included as extraditable offences in any extradition treaty existing between or among the Parties. The Parties undertake to include such offences as extraditable offences in any extradition treaty to be concluded between or among them.

3. If a Party that makes extradition conditional on the existence of a treaty receives a request for extradition from another Party with which it does not have an extradition treaty, it may consider this Convention as the legal basis for extradition with respect to any criminal offence referred to in paragraph 1 of this article.

4. Parties that do not make extradition conditional on the existence of a treaty shall recognise the criminal offences referred to in paragraph 1 of this article as extraditable offences between themselves.

5. Extradition shall be subject to the conditions provided for by the law of the requested Party or by applicable extradition treaties, including the grounds on which the requested Party may refuse extradition.

6. If extradition for a criminal offence referred to in paragraph 1 of this article is refused solely on the basis of the nationality of the person sought, or

because the requested Party deems that it has jurisdiction over the offence, the requested Party shall submit the case at the request of the requesting Party to its competent authorities for the purpose of prosecution and shall report the final outcome to the requesting Party in due course. Those authorities shall take their decision and conduct their investigations and proceedings in the same manner as in the case of any other offence of a comparable nature under the law of that Party.

7. a. Each Party shall, at the time of signature or when depositing its instrument of ratification, acceptance, approval or accession, communicate to the Secretary General of the Council of Europe the name and addresses of each authority responsible for the making to or receipt of a request for extradition or provisional arrest in the absence of a treaty.

   b. The Secretary General of the Council of Europe shall set up and keep updated a register of authorities so designated by the Parties. Each Party shall ensure that the details held on the register are correct at all times.

Title 3 – General principles relating to mutual assistance

Article 25 – General principles relating to mutual assistance

1. The Parties shall afford one another mutual assistance to the widest extent possible for the purpose of investigations or proceedings concerning criminal offences related to computer systems and data, or for the collection of evidence in electronic form of a criminal offence.

2. Each Party shall also adopt such legislative and other measures as may be necessary to carry out the obligations set forth in Articles 27 - 35.

3. Each Party may, in urgent circumstances, make requests for mutual assistance or communications related thereto by expedited means of communications, including fax or e-mail, to the extent that such means provide appropriate levels of security and authentication (including the use of encryption, where necessary), with formal confirmation to follow, where required by the requested Party. The requested Party shall accept and respond to the request by any such expedited means of communication.

4. Except as otherwise specifically provided in Articles in this Chapter, mutual assistance shall be subject to the conditions provided for by the law of the requested Party or by applicable mutual assistance treaties, including the grounds on which the requested Party may refuse co-operation. The requested Party shall not exercise the right to refuse mutual assistance in relation to the offences referred to in Articles 2 to 11 solely on the ground that the request concerns an offence which it considers a fiscal offence.

5. Where, in accordance with the provisions of this chapter, the requested Party is permitted to make mutual assistance conditional upon the existence of dual criminality, that condition shall be deemed fulfilled, irrespective of whether its laws place the offence within the same category of offence or denominates the offence by the same terminology as the requesting Party, if the conduct underlying the

offence for which assistance is sought is a criminal offence under its laws.

Article 26 – Spontaneous information

1. A Party may, within the limits of its domestic law, without prior request, forward to another Party information obtained within the framework of its own investigations when it considers that the disclosure of such information might assist the receiving Party in initiating or carrying out investigations or proceedings concerning criminal offences established in accordance with this Convention or might lead to a request for co-operation by that Party under this chapter.
2. Prior to providing such information, the providing Party may request that it be kept confidential or used subject to conditions. If the receiving Party cannot comply with such request, it shall notify the providing Party, which shall then determine whether the information should nevertheless be provided. If the receiving Party accepts the information subject to the conditions, it shall be bound by them.

Title 4 – Procedures pertaining to mutual assistance requests in the absence of applicable international agreements

Article 27 – Procedures pertaining to mutual assistance requests in the absence of applicable international agreements

1. Where there is no mutual assistance treaty or arrangement on the basis of uniform or reciprocal

legislation in force between the requesting and requested Parties, the provisions of paragraphs 2 through 9 of this article shall apply. The provisions of this article shall not apply where such treaty, arrangement or legislation is available, unless the Parties concerned agree to apply any or all of the remainder of this article in lieu thereof.

2. a. Each Party shall designate a central authority or authorities that shall be responsible for sending and answering requests for mutual assistance, the execution of such requests, or the transmission of them to the authorities competent for their execution.

   b. The central authorities shall communicate directly with each other.

   c. Each Party shall, at the time of signature or when depositing its instrument of ratification, acceptance, approval or accession, communicate to the Secretary General of the Council of Europe the names and addresses of the authorities designated in pursuance of this paragraph.

   d. The Secretary General of the Council of Europe shall set up and keep updated a register of central authorities so designated by the Parties. Each Party shall ensure that the details held on the register are correct at all times.

3. Mutual assistance requests under this Article shall be executed in accordance with the procedures specified by the requesting Party except where incompatible with the law of the requested Party.

4. The requested Party may, in addition to grounds for refusal available under Article 25, paragraph (4), refuse assistance if:

a. the request concerns an offence which the requested Party considers a political offence or an offence connected with a political offence; or

b. it considers that execution of the request is likely to prejudice its sovereignty, security, ordre public or other essential interests.

5. The requested Party may postpone action on a request if such action would prejudice criminal investigations or proceedings conducted by its authorities.

6. Before refusing or postponing assistance, the requested Party shall, where appropriate after having consulted with the requesting Party, consider whether the request may be granted partially or subject to such conditions as it deems necessary.

7. The requested Party shall promptly inform the requesting Party of the outcome of the execution of a request for assistance. If the request is refused or postponed, reasons shall be given for the refusal or postponement. The requested Party shall also inform the requesting Party of any reasons that render impossible the execution of the request or are likely to delay it significantly.

8. The requesting Party may request that the requested Party keep confidential the fact and substance of any request made under this Chapter except to the extent necessary to execute the request. If the requested Party cannot comply with the request for confidentiality, it shall promptly inform the requesting Party, which shall then determine whether the request should nevertheless be executed.

9. a. In the event of urgency, requests for mutual assistance or communications related thereto may be sent directly by judicial authorities of the requesting Party to such authorities of the requested Party. In any such cases a copy shall be sent at the same time to the central authority of the requested Party through the central authority of the requesting Party.

   b. Any request or communication under this paragraph may be made through the International Criminal Police Organisation (Interpol).

   c. Where a request is made pursuant to subparagraph (a) and the authority is not competent to deal with the request, it shall refer the request to the competent national authority and inform directly the requesting Party that it has done so.

   d. Requests or communications made under this paragraph that do not involve coercive action may be directly transmitted by the competent authorities of the requesting Party to the competent authorities of the requested Party.

   e. Each Party may, at the time of signature or when depositing its instrument of ratification, acceptance, approval or accession inform the Secretary General of the Council of Europe that, for reasons of efficiency, requests made under this paragraph are to be addressed to its central authority.

Article 28 – Confidentiality and limitation on use

1. When there is no mutual assistance treaty or arrangement on the basis of uniform or reciprocal

legislation in force between the requesting and the requested Parties, the provisions of this article shall apply. The provisions of this article shall not apply where such treaty, arrangement or legislation, is available unless the Parties concerned agree to apply any or all of the remainder of this article in lieu thereof.

2. The requested Party may make the furnishing of information or material in response to a request dependent on the condition that it is:
   a. kept confidential where the request for mutual legal assistance could not be complied with in the absence of such condition, or
   b. not used for investigations or proceedings other than those stated in the request.
3. If the requesting Party cannot comply with a condition referred to in paragraph 2, it shall promptly inform the other Party, which shall then determine whether the information is nevertheless provided. When the requesting Party accepts the condition, it shall be bound by it.
4. Any Party that furnishes information or material subject to a condition referred to in paragraph 2 may require the other Party to explain, in relation to that condition, the use made of such information or material.

Section 2 – Specific provisions

Title 1 – Mutual assistance regarding provisional measures

Article 29 – Expedited preservation of stored computer data

1. A Party may request another Party to order or otherwise obtain the expeditious preservation of data

stored by means of a computer system, which is located within the territory of that other Party and in respect of which the requesting Party intends to submit a request for mutual assistance for the search or similar access, seizure or similar securing, or disclosure of the data.

2. A request for preservation made under paragraph 1 shall specify:

a. the authority that is seeking the preservation;

b. the offence that is the subject of a criminal investigation or proceeding and a brief summary of related facts;

c. the stored computer data to be preserved and its relationship to the offence;

d. any available information to identify the custodian of the stored computer data or the location of the computer system;

e. the necessity of the preservation; and

f. that the Party intends to submit a request for mutual assistance for the search or similar access, seizure or similar securing, or disclosure of the stored computer data.

3. Upon receiving the request from another Party, the requested Party shall take all appropriate measures to preserve expeditiously the specified data in accordance with its domestic law. For the purposes of responding to a request, dual criminality shall not be required as a condition to providing such preservation.

4. A Party that requires dual criminality as a condition for responding to a request for mutual assistance for

the search or similar access, seizure or similar securing, or disclosure of the data may, in respect of offences other than those established in accordance with Articles 2 – 11 of this Convention, reserve the right to refuse the request for preservation under this article in cases where it has reason to believe that at the time of disclosure the condition of dual criminality cannot be fulfilled.

5. In addition, a request for preservation may only be refused if :

a. the request concerns an offence which the requested Party considers a political offence or an offence connected with a political offence; or

b. the requested Party considers that execution of the request is likely to prejudice its sovereignty, security, ordre public or other essential interests.

6. Where the requested Party believes that preservation will not ensure the future availability of the data or will threaten the confidentiality of, or otherwise prejudice the requesting Party's investigation, it shall promptly so inform the requesting Party, which shall then determine whether the request should nevertheless be executed.

7. Any preservation effected in response to the request referred to in paragraph 1 shall be for a period not less than 60 days in order to enable the requesting Party to submit a request for the search or similar access, seizure or similar securing, or disclosure of the data. Following the receipt of such request, the data shall continue to be preserved pending a decision on that request.

Article 30 – Expedited disclosure of preserved traffic data

1. Where, in the course of the execution of a request made under Article 29 to preserve traffic data concerning a specific communication, the requested Party discovers that a service provider in another State was involved in the transmission of the communication, the requested Party shall expeditiously disclose to the requesting Party a sufficient amount of traffic data in order to identify that service provider and the path through which the communication was transmitted.

2. Disclosure of traffic data under paragraph 1 may only be withheld if :

a. the request concerns an offence which the requested Party considers a political offence or an offence connected with a political offence; or

b. the requested Party considers that execution of the request is likely to prejudice its sovereignty, security, ordre public or other essential interests.

Title 2 – Mutual assistance regarding investigative powers

Article 31 – Mutual assistance regarding accessing of stored computer data

1. A Party may request another Party to search or similarly access, seize or similarly secure, and disclose data stored by means of a computer system located within the territory of the requested Party, including data that has been preserved pursuant to Article 29.

2. The requested Party shall respond to the request through application of international instruments, arrangements and laws referred to in Article 23, and in accordance with other relevant provisions of this Chapter.
3. The request shall be responded to on an expedited basis where:

a. there are grounds to believe that relevant data is particularly vulnerable to loss or modification; or

b. the instruments, arrangements and laws referred to in paragraph 2 otherwise provide for expedited co-operation.

Article 32 – Trans-border access to stored computer data with consent or where publicly available

A Party may, without obtaining the authorisation of another Party:

a. access publicly available (open source) stored computer data, regardless of where the data is located geographically; or

b. access or receive, through a computer system in its territory, stored computer data located in another Party, if the Party obtains the lawful and voluntary consent of the person who has the lawful authority to disclose the data to the Party through that computer system.

Article 33 – Mutual assistance regarding the real-time collection of traffic data

1. The Parties shall provide mutual assistance to each other with respect to the real-time collection of traffic

data associated with specified communications in its territory transmitted by means of a computer system. Subject to paragraph 2, assistance shall be governed by the conditions and procedures provided for under domestic law.

2. Each Party shall provide such assistance at least with respect to criminal offences for which real-time collection of traffic data would be available in a similar domestic case.

Article 34 – Mutual assistance regarding the interception of content data

The Parties shall provide mutual assistance to each other with respect to the real-time collection or recording of content data of specified communications transmitted by means of a computer system to the extent permitted by their applicable treaties and domestic laws.

Title 3 – 24/7 Network

Article 35 – 24/7 Network

1. Each Party shall designate a point of contact available on a 24 hour, 7 day per week basis in order to ensure the provision of immediate assistance for the purpose of investigations or proceedings concerning criminal offences related to computer systems and data, or for the collection of evidence in electronic form of a criminal offence. Such assistance shall include facilitating, or, if permitted by its domestic law and practice, directly carrying out:

a. provision of technical advice;

b. preservation of data pursuant to Articles 29 and 30; and

c. collection of evidence, giving of legal information, and locating of suspects.

2. a. A Party's point of contact shall have the capacity to carry out communications with the point of contact of another Party on an expedited basis.

b. If the point of contact designated by a Party is not part of that Party's authority or authorities responsible for international mutual assistance or extradition, the point of contact shall ensure that it is able to co-ordinate with such authority or authorities on an expedited basis.

3. Each Party shall ensure that trained and equipped personnel are available in order to facilitate the operation of the network.

Chapter IV – Final provisions

Article 36 – Signature and entry into force

1. This Convention shall be open for signature by the member States of the Council of Europe and by non-member States which have participated in its elaboration.

2. This Convention is subject to ratification, acceptance or approval. Instruments of ratification, acceptance or approval shall be deposited with the Secretary General of the Council of Europe.

3. This Convention shall enter into force on the first day of the month following the expiration of a period of

three months after the date on which five States, including at least three member States of the Council of Europe, have expressed their consent to be bound by the Convention in accordance with the provisions of paragraphs 1 and 2.

4. In respect of any signatory State which subsequently expresses its consent to be bound by it, the Convention shall enter into force on the first day of the month following the expiration of a period of three months after the date of the expression of its consent to be bound by the Convention in accordance with the provisions of paragraphs 1 and 2.

Article 37 – Accession to the Convention

1. After the entry into force of this Convention, the Committee of Ministers of the Council of Europe, after consulting with and obtaining the unanimous consent of the Contracting States to the Convention, may invite any State not a member of the Council and which has not participated in its elaboration to accede to this Convention. The decision shall be taken by the majority provided for in Article 20 (d) of the Statute of the Council of Europe and by the unanimous vote of the representatives of the Contracting States entitled to sit on the Committee of Ministers.

2. In respect of any State acceding to the Convention under paragraph 1 above, the Convention shall enter into force on the first day of the month following the expiration of a period of three months after the date of deposit of the instrument of accession with the Secretary General of the Council of Europe.

Article 38 – Territorial application

1. Any State may, at the time of signature or when depositing its instrument of ratification, acceptance, approval or accession, specify the territory or territories to which this Convention shall apply.
2. Any State may, at any later date, by a declaration addressed to the Secretary General of the Council of Europe, extend the application of this Convention to any other territory specified in the declaration. In respect of such territory the Convention shall enter into force on the first day of the month following the expiration of a period of three months after the date of receipt of the declaration by the Secretary General.
3. Any declaration made under the two preceding paragraphs may, in respect of any territory specified in such declaration, be withdrawn by a notification addressed to the Secretary General of the Council of Europe. The withdrawal shall become effective on the first day of the month following the expiration of a period of three months after the date of receipt of such notification by the Secretary General.

Article 39 – Effects of the Convention

1. The purpose of the present Convention is to supplement applicable multilateral or bilateral treaties or arrangements as between the Parties, including the provisions of:

- the European Convention on Extradition opened for signature in Paris on 13 December 1957;
- the European Convention on Mutual Assistance in Criminal Matters opened for signature in Strasbourg on 20 April 1959;

- the Additional Protocol to the European Convention on Mutual Assistance in Criminal Matters opened for signature in Strasbourg on 17 March 1978.

2. If two or more Parties have already concluded an agreement or treaty on the matters dealt with in this Convention or otherwise have established their relations on such matters, or should they in future do so, they shall also be entitled to apply that agreement or treaty or to regulate those relations accordingly. However, where Parties establish their relations in respect of the matters dealt with in the present convention other than as regulated therein, they shall do so in a manner that is not inconsistent with the Convention's objectives and principles.

3. Nothing in this Convention shall affect other rights, restrictions, obligations and responsibilities of a Party.

Article 40 – Declarations

By a written notification addressed to the Secretary General of the Council of Europe, any State may, at the time of signature or when depositing its instrument of ratification, acceptance, approval or accession, declare that it avails itself of the possibility of requiring additional elements as provided for under Article 2, Article 3, Article 6, paragraph 1 (b), Article 7, Article 9, paragraph 3 and Article 27, paragraph 9 (e).

Article 41 – Federal clause

1. A federal State may reserve the right to assume obligations under Chapter II of this Convention

consistent with its fundamental principles governing the relationship between its central government and constituent States or other similar territorial entities provided that it is still able to co-operate under Chapter III.

2. When making a reservation under paragraph 1, a federal State may not apply the terms of such reservation to exclude or substantially diminish its obligations to provide for measures set forth in Chapter II. Overall, it shall provide for a broad and effective law enforcement capability with respect to those measures.

3. With regard to the provisions of this Convention, the application of which comes under the jurisdiction of constituent States or other similar territorial entities, that are not obliged by the constitutional system of the federation to take legislative measures, the federal government shall inform the competent authorities of such States of the said provisions with its favourable opinion, encouraging them to take appropriate action to give them effect.

Article 42 – Reservations

By a written notification addressed to the Secretary General of the Council of Europe, any State may, at the time of signature or when depositing its instrument of ratification, acceptance, approval or accession, declare that it avails itself of the reservation(s) provided for in Article 4, paragraph 2, Article 6, paragraph 3, Article 9, paragraph 4, Article 10, paragraph 3, Article 11, paragraph 3, Article 14, paragraph 3, Article 22, paragraph 2, Article 29, paragraph 4, and Article 41, paragraph 1. No other reservation may be made.

Article 43 – Status and withdrawal of reservations

1. A Party that has made a reservation in accordance with Article 42 may wholly or partially withdraw it by means of a notification addressed to the Secretary General. Such withdrawal shall take effect on the date of receipt of such notification by the Secretary General. If the notification states that the withdrawal of a reservation is to take effect on a date specified therein, and such date is later than the date on which the notification is received by the Secretary General, the withdrawal shall take effect on such a later date.

2. A Party that has made a reservation as referred to in Article 42 shall withdraw such reservation, in whole or in part, as soon as circumstances so permit.

3. The Secretary General of the Council of Europe may periodically enquire with Parties that have made one or more reservations as referred to in Article 42 as to the prospects for withdrawing such reservation(s).

Article 44 – Amendments

1. Amendments to this Convention may be proposed by any Party, and shall be communicated by the Secretary General of the Council of Europe to the member States of the Council of Europe, to the non-member States which have participated in the elaboration of this Convention as well as to any State which has acceded to, or has been invited to accede to, this Convention in accordance with the provisions of Article 37.

2. Any amendment proposed by a Party shall be communicated to the European Committee on Crime

Problems (CDPC), which shall submit to the Committee of Ministers its opinion on that proposed amendment.

3. The Committee of Ministers shall consider the proposed amendment and the opinion submitted by the European Committee on Crime Problems (CDPC) and, following consultation with the non-member State Parties to this Convention, may adopt the amendment.

4. The text of any amendment adopted by the Committee of Ministers in accordance with paragraph 3 of this article shall be forwarded to the Parties for acceptance.

5. Any amendment adopted in accordance with paragraph 3 of this article shall come into force on the thirtieth day after all Parties have informed the Secretary General of their acceptance thereof.

Article 45 – Settlement of disputes

1. The European Committee on Crime Problems (CDPC) shall be kept informed regarding the interpretation and application of this Convention.

2. In case of a dispute between Parties as to the interpretation or application of this Convention, they shall seek a settlement of the dispute through negotiation or any other peaceful means of their choice, including submission of the dispute to the European Committee on Crime Problems (CDPC), to an arbitral tribunal whose decisions shall be binding upon the Parties, or to the International Court of Justice, as agreed upon by the Parties concerned.

Article 46 – Consultations of the Parties

1. The Parties shall, as appropriate, consult periodically with a view to facilitating:

a. the effective use and implementation of this Convention, including the identification of any problems thereof, as well as the effects of any declaration or reservation made under this Convention;

b. the exchange of information on significant legal, policy or technological developments pertaining to cybercrime and the collection of evidence in electronic form;

c. consideration of possible supplementation or amendment of the Convention.

2. The European Committee on Crime Problems (CDPC) shall be kept periodically informed regarding the result of consultations referred to in paragraph 1.

3. The European Committee on Crime Problems (CDPC) shall, as appropriate, facilitate the consultations referred to in paragraph 1 and take the measures necessary to assist the Parties in their efforts to supplement or amend the Convention. At the latest three years after the present Convention enters into force, the European Committee on Crime Problems (CDPC) shall, in co-operation with the Parties, conduct a review of all of the Convention's provisions and, if necessary, recommend any appropriate amendments.

4. Except where assumed by the Council of Europe, expenses incurred in carrying out the provisions of paragraph 1 shall be borne by the Parties in the manner to be determined by them.

5. The Parties shall be assisted by the Secretariat of the Council of Europe in carrying out their functions pursuant to this Article.

Article 47 – Denunciation

1. Any Party may, at any time, denounce this Convention by means of a notification addressed to the Secretary General of the Council of Europe.
2. Such denunciation shall become effective on the first day of the month following the expiration of a period of three months after the date of receipt of the notification by the Secretary General.

Article 48 – Notification

The Secretary General of the Council of Europe shall notify the member States of the Council of Europe, the non-member States which have participated in the elaboration of this Convention as well as any State which has acceded to, or has been invited to accede to, this Convention of:

a. any signature;

b. the deposit of any instrument of ratification, acceptance, approval or accession;

c. any date of entry into force of this Convention in accordance with Articles 36 and 37;

d. any declaration made under Article 40 or reservation made in accordance with Article 42;

e. any other act, notification or communication relating to this Convention.

In witness whereof the undersigned, being duly authorised thereto, have signed this Convention.

Done at Budapest, this 23rd day of November 2001, in English and in French, both texts being equally authentic, in a single copy which shall be deposited in the archives of the Council of Europe. The Secretary General of the Council of Europe shall transmit certified copies to each member State of the Council of Europe, to the non-member States which have participated in the elaboration of this Convention, and to any State invited to accede to it.

Bibliography

Bjorn-Anderson, N. and Numford, E. (eds)., *Information Society*, North-Holland, 1982.

Coates Joseph F., "The Future of Computer Data Security", *Vital Speeches of the Day*, February 15, 1982.

Danziger James N., *Computer and Politics: High Technology in American Local Government* Columbia University Press, New York, 1981.

David. I. Bainbridge, 'Software copyrights', Butterworths Publications, 1999.

Diane Rowland & Elizabeth Macdonald, 'Information technology law', Cavendish Publishing Ltd., London, 1997.

Edward Wilding, 'Computer evidence—A forensic investigation hand book', Sweet and Maxwell, London, 1997.

Exploratory Workshop on the Societal Impacts of Robotics Office of Technology Assessment, US Congress, Washington DC 1982.

Mc Grew-Hill Encyclopedia of Science & Technology—Vol.3, Sweet and Maxwell Ltd., 1999.

Michael Edenbough, 'Intellectual Property Law', Cavendish Publishing Ltd., Great Britain 1995.

Myo, Elton. *The Social Problems of an Industrial Civilisation*, Routledge and Kegan Paul, 1949.

'National legal instruments of intellectual property rights law', Vol.1, Department of Business Laws, National Law School of India University, Nagarbhavi, 1998.

Pamela Davis, Peter Francis, Victor Jupp (Editors of the work), 'Invisible Crimes, Their victims and their regulations', MacMillan Press Ltd., Great Britain, 1999.

Parag Diwan & Shammi Kapoor, 'Cyber & E-Commerce Laws, Bharat Publishing House, 2000.

Peter Carey, 'Media Law', Sweet & Maxwell Ltd., 1999.

Rahul Mathan, 'The law relating to computers and Internet', Butterworths India, 2000.

Smith & Hogan, Criminal Law, Butterworths, London, 1996.

Stewrt, V. *Change: The Challenge for Management*, McGraw-Hill, 1983.

The Spreading Danger of Computer Crime, *Business Week*, April 20, 1981.

The issue of "hackers"—people who break into computer systems for kicks—is discussed in *Newsweek*, September 5, 1983. A critical review of that article, "Moral Clarity in the Computer Age", appears in *Communications*, October 1983.

Whisler, Thomas, *The Impact of Computer on Organisation*, Praeger, 1970.

Index